# Animal Histories
OF THE
# Civil War Era

CONFLICTING WORLDS

*New Dimensions of the American Civil War*

T. Michael Parrish, Series Editor

# Animal Histories of the Civil War Era

Edited by
EARL J. HESS

LOUISIANA STATE UNIVERSITY PRESS
BATON ROUGE

Published with the assistance of the V. Ray Cardozier Fund

Published by Louisiana State University Press
lsupress.org



Manufactured in the United States of America
FIRST PRINTING

DESIGNER: Andrew Shurtz
TYPEFACE: Monotype Fournier
PRINTER AND BINDER: Sheridan Books

COVER IMAGE: A Union veteran and his dog, with US flag, pose for a photograph. Courtesy Library of Congress.

Library of Congress Cataloging-in-Publication Data are available at the Library of Congress.

ISBN 978-0-8071-7691-7 (cloth)
ISBN 978-0-8071-7714-3 (pdf)
ISBN 978-0-8071-7715-0 (epub)

# Contents

# Acknowledgments

This project came about because of a panel on the subject of animals and the Civil War era at the Southern Historical Association annual conference in November 2018. I had developed an interest in animal history prior to this meeting and was keen to attend as a member of the audience. I asked Joan Cashin, who had put the panel together, and Paula Tarankow, one of the speakers, to join me for an edited volume on the subject. Joan suggested other contributors, as did Peter Carmichael and Judkin Browning.

I wish to thank every contributor for their hard work, collegiality, and professionalism in helping put together this collection of essays. Everyone involved did a fine job, and I very much appreciate their contributions and their sharing of ideas, sources, and enthusiasm. I also thank Rand Dotson, editor in chief of Louisiana State University Press, who provided enthusiastic support for the book. The two anonymous reviewers of the manuscript for the press gave us valuable advice about how to improve the introduction and the essays, while Michael Parrish generously shared sources on the subject with me. Finally, I thank my wife, Pratibha Dabholkar, for her strong support and excellent advice on the project from its inception at the SHA panel to its conclusion with the publication of this book.

# Animal Histories OF THE Civil War Era

# Introduction

EARL J. HESS

THIS COLLECTION of essays is an effort to fulfill needs in two strings of academic studies that have much to offer each other. The history of animals and their role in human history is a burgeoning part of academic studies, but it has not yet paid attention to the American Civil War. While Civil War studies is older and has produced literally thousands of books and articles, it has paid little attention to the role of animals in the great internecine conflict. There is, in other words, a gaping hole in the Civil War literature concerning animals and a similar void in the work of animal historians where the Civil War ought to be.

These essays are the first effort to fill both gaps in these two literatures. The list of contributors includes three scholars in animal history with an interest in the Civil War and eight scholars in Civil War history with an interest in animal studies. The collection introduces animal studies to the Civil War community with a mixture of theory, research-laden case studies, and descriptive essays. It does so with an eye to the human-interest story as well as to the academic contextualization that is important in making something significant of our natural interest in nonhuman animals. In addition, it enables animal-history scholars to understand how the Civil War fits into their literature.

The most fundamental objective of this book is to raise the awareness of Civil War scholars to the presence of nonhuman animals in the story of the war, alerting them to the ways in which animals participated in the war experience and were affected by the massing and movement of armies. It also illuminates the ways in which many of those animals affected the men in uniform and the civilian population of both sides. Indeed, the Civil War is a prime example of concentrated interaction between animals and humans under extreme duress; the prospects for cross-disciplinary study are exciting.

## ANIMAL HISTORY

The roots of animal history arose nearly half a century ago in the animal-rights movement sparked by Peter Singer's *Animal Liberation* in 1975 and Tom Regan's *The Case for Animal Rights* in 1983. Out of the animal rights movement emerged the field of animal studies, which focuses on how humans interact with nonhuman animals today. It was natural to expand the concept of human-animal interaction to the historical past. As a result, studies of animal history began to appear during the past couple of decades. While there are important linkages between animal studies and animal history, the two are different streams of research and analysis.[1]

Both animal studies and animal history are interdisciplinary in nature, deriving great potency from the eclectic mix of methodologies, sources, and concepts to be found in history, science, environmentalism, psychology, philosophy, and many other disciplines. There are two traditions in the scholarship involved in both animal studies and animal history. One is to produce a human-centered look at how animals fit into peoples' institutions, personal lives, culture, and society. At times this portrays the animal as a mechanism, another cog in human history, but it at least illuminates how that cog works. The other tradition is to give the animal a center-stage role in the human past. This tradition tends to give full attention to animals as sentient creatures with motivations, needs, desires, and a degree of agency in their own right, with human interactions playing one of many roles in their lives. In fact, a major point of discussion in the second tradition of animal studies and animal history is agency and the extent to which animals that have a relationship with humans can exercise freedom of choice within that relationship. That discussion has involved many scholars who are far from a consensus as to how far we should see animals as agents of their own destiny.[2]

With its tendency to break down time periods and international boundaries, animal-history scholarship reminds us that interspecies contact is both timeless and universal. It also has a hefty potential to be challenging, provocative, and edgy, and one can see all these characteristics in the field. "When we grant that animals have subjectivity, including their own interests, wants, and desires," writes Margo DeMello, it becomes more difficult to assume that humans have a right to dominate the planet for their own needs. This is why Susan Nance has stated that animal history "is one of the hottest and most controversial subjects in academia and in trade publishing today."[3]

Animal history lies squarely within the fold of social and cultural history. Its scholars study visual representations, letters, diaries, memoirs, government reports, and other sources typically used by other historians too. The difference is they look through those sources for the animals in them, a subject usually overlooked by other historians with interests besides those of the interspecies relationships.[4]

Most animal historians tend to focus on social elites rather than common ranks of society, if for no other reason than that the vast majority of usable sources come from elites. To a degree, this privileges people with more education, more sensitivity, and more awareness of animals, their suffering, and their rights. The animal-history literature rarely dips into the lower ranks of society or into rural populations. Fine studies by Janet M. Davis on animal welfare in modern America and Katherine Grier on pet keeping in the late nineteenth century give preference to upper-middle-class and urban populations.[5]

Most animal historiography tends still to be a people-centered discussion of the animal, how it fits into human patterns of thought and action. There is nothing wrong with this approach; in fact, it is essential since most animals discussed are domesticated species whose lives are inevitably linked with humans and their institutions. But part of the historiography goes further toward featuring the animal as a character in itself. A series of such studies is being published by Reaktion Books in London, with each one covering a particular animal. Brett Mizelle's *Pig*, for example, covers the natural history of the hog, its role in human history, and especially its role as a source of meat for hungry people. So far, Reaktion has published nearly one hundred books on various animals, each offering an overview of all aspects associated with them and lavishly illustrated.[6]

Another fertile context for animal history is environmental history. Scholars may debate whether foregrounding animals as sentient creatures with agency properly belongs to environmental history, but there can be no doubt that the natural context is as important as the human context of animal history. In a sense, the concentrated study of animals takes environmental history one step further.[7]

## ANIMALS AND WAR

Despite a couple of decades of work, animal historians have yet to develop a full understanding of how animals are affected by war and how war affects animals. They were involved in armed conflict as surely as they were involved in urban life, human emotions, conceptions of social uplift, and in the human-centered food chain. But a scholarly literature of animal military history is, at best, only in the beginning stage.

This is unfortunate because the history of armies and of the wars they fought partakes of both environmental history and animal history. Wars involved the movement of large military formations across great expanses of territory, and with that movement came the destruction of natural resources and of animals, both domesticated and wild. Armies used animals extensively, especially horses and mules, to achieve mobility; the military systems that mobilized, harnessed, trained, and cared for those equines had an enormous effect on the animals' lives. A true understanding of animals in war requires an awareness of environmental and institutional factors in military history.

There are a handful of books and articles on animals in war, much of it of a popular and all too often superficial nature. Jilly Cooper pioneered this strain in *Animals in War,* published in London in 2000. Juliet Gardiner followed with *The Animals' War: Animals in Wartime from the First World War to the Present Day,* also in London, in 2006. Neither Cooper nor Gardiner link their work with the theories or constructs proposed by academic authors. They tell the story factually, with a minimum of research and a lot of easily digested information.[8]

There is, of course, a role played by books like these in popularizing the concept of human-animal relationships in wartime. But we will not fully benefit from a focus on animals and war until academic historians take up the call and investigate the topic. To date, few scholars have done so. One can read Gervase Phillips's contribution to the *Routledge Companion to Animal-Human History* to get an idea of how scholars can approach the involvement of animals in warfare. Phillips strongly asserts that animals have emotional lives of their own, especially when involved in military endeavors. They have at least a limited degree of agency even when weaponized by humans and need to be included to have a well-rounded understanding of the impact of war on human populations. Rather than machines, animals are active, emotional agents in the history of armed conflict.[9]

Animal-rights advocates have paid attention to warfare in order to decry the use of sentient creatures by the military establishment. One can hardly blame them. Scientists who work with the armed forces to train animals as weapons have written of their accomplishments as if the sentient creatures they manipulate are mere machines to be used in any way people desire.

Robert E. Lubow, a professor of experimental psychology at Tel Aviv University, created an institute to develop methods of training animals for war purposes in the 1970s. His book, designed to explain how he went about this work, delineates the use of animals for both humane and destructive purposes. While dogs were trained to find land mines or bombs, pigeons, dolphins, and sea lions were trained to take war to the enemy in various ways. These latter were examples of what scholars call "weaponized" animals. Lubow has cited examples from World War II to Vietnam and the effort to combat terrorism.[10]

The kind of work Lubow described has continued, and it draws bitter condemnation from animal-rights activists and peace activists alike. The volume *Animals and War: Confronting the Military-Animal Industrial Complex,* edited by Colin Salter, Anthony J. Nocella II, and Judy K. C. Bentley, brought together a number of philosophers, animal activists, and antiwar activists to present a thorough and pointed critique "of pro-war and negative peace narratives." The authors especially denounce the use of animals in military experiments while they target "the intersection of the military-industrial and animal-industrial complexes." The evidence they present and the perspective they espouse make of these essays a chilling exposé of the callous way animals have been used by the military systems of many nations in sometimes spurious and illogical projects.[11]

## TOWARD A CIVIL WAR ANIMAL HISTORY

What little has been done in starting a literature on animals in the Civil War reflects the early works on animals and war more generally. Thus far, the historiography has been largely produced by popular historians and focuses on heroic narratives of horses and dogs. Gene C. Armistead's *Horses and Mules in the Civil War: A Complete History with a Roster of More Than 700 War Horses,* 2013;

Charles G. Worman's *Civil War Animal Heroes: Mascots, Pets, and War Horses,* 2011; and Marilyn W. Seguin's *Dogs of War: And Stories of Other Beasts of Battle in the Civil War,* 1998, are among the few books to my knowledge.[12] All three authors chronicle the presence of animals in Civil War history but do not engage the animal-studies literature or use analysis of any kind about the significance of animals in war. The latest and so far best study of Civil War environmental history, authored by academic scholars Judkin Browning and Timothy Silver, devotes a chapter to animals. It is mostly descriptive and places animals within their environmental context.[13]

The potential number of topics within animal studies pertaining to the Civil War is surprisingly large. There has always been heated discussion among humanists and philosophers about whether people should be considered as part of or separate from the animal world. Scientists, however, place humans well within that world, and animal historians often refer to other living creatures as "nonhuman animals" to make an important point—that we share much more than just the planet and its resources with the creatures that we so often abuse and use for our own purposes.

The Civil War engulfed the world of animals as well as of humans, mobilizing thousands of equines, dogs, cattle, sheep, and hogs as agents of military operations or as food for hungry soldiers. Animals pulled artillery pieces and wagons, gave cavalrymen a mobile fighting platform, and served as pets for soldiers and mascots for regiments. Wildlife habitats were disrupted, destroyed, and altered by the movement of massive armies through the countryside. Insects bedeviled countless soldiers and severely affected their health in the field. Animals of all kinds populated the Civil War landscape, physically, visually, and aurally as well as metaphorically.

The Civil War is a prism through which to examine the role of animals of all kinds in an intense, deadly, and oftentimes brutal endeavor. Warfare concentrates emotion, fear, bravery, hope, and despair into compact historical events of the human experience, and it imposes similar strains on animals. Armed conflict spans days, months, or years of time rather than decades, and it compresses human and animal experience into tightly packed episodes. The experience of war may be relatively brief, but its effect can last a lifetime. Scholars must have a long vision combined with an appreciation of the intense, short-lived experience of war for both animals and humans in order to fully capture the importance of this new field of study.

For example, more people witnessed a far-more-concentrated use of animals during the war years than was normal during their peacetime lives. They saw not a handful of horses or mules at a time, but literally thousands gathered for coordinated tasks that spanned day after day of a long war. They witnessed ill treatment, disease, overwork, and battlefield killing and maiming of animals never imagined during peace. Did this experience have an influence on human attitudes toward animals after the war? We can never know unless someone searches the primary sources with a keen eye for this kind of detail.

In fact, the Civil War is a unique historic episode for animal history. About three million men served in the Union and Confederate armies at a time when literacy rates were much higher than for any previous conflict. In addition, there was as yet no army censorship of soldier letters. As a result the conflict produced hundreds of thousands of letters, diaries, and memoirs by common soldiers that are filled with references to animals of all kinds. In addition to ample documentation in official reports, which lay out the administrative side of animal use, voluminous personal accounts represent a large database offering scholars an opportunity to gauge popular perceptions of animals that do not so readily exist for society in peacetime.

Understanding popular attitudes can be significant in illuminating many aspects of animal history. Whether most common members of society were aware of animals as sentient creatures, believed they deserved better treatment, or supported natural conservation of the environment and the animals that lived in it has not been a topic of study thus far. It would open up a new area of the field.

For example, the Civil War took place at the dawn of the animal-rights movement in the United States. Such a movement had started in England during the early decades of the nineteenth century with the founding of the Royal Society for the Prevention of Cruelty to Animals in 1824. American Henry Bergh met the president of the Royal Society in 1865 while returning from diplomatic service in Russia and founded the American Society for the Prevention of Cruelty to Animals in New York on April 10, 1866. By 1879, thirty-three of the thirty-eight states had passed anticruelty laws, and the movement continued to grow during the latter decades of the century.[14]

The animal-protection movement had its origin in the great social-reform wave of the early nineteenth century and was allied with abolitionism, women's rights, and vegetarianism. But, according to Janet Davis, the Civil War "helped catalyze the formation of an organized secular movement" to promote awareness of animal welfare. She believes that photographs of the soldier dead on Civil War battlefields, which included dead horses, and the observation of cruelty to draft animals such as mules in the army, helped increase awareness among the postwar population. In her view, the war served as a platform upon which cruelty to animals was vividly demonstrated and had a life-long effect on many soldiers and civilians who took the lesson seriously.[15]

Davis offers no evidence to clinch her case that the Civil War was more than coincidently connected with a key moment in the development of an animal--welfare cause. A handful of other scholars are far more cautious about linking the war with the developing animal-awareness movement. Diane L. Beers covers the history of animal-rights activism from 1865 to the present but does not discuss any influence of the Civil War. Katherine Grier points out that, by the 1860s, "the domestic ethic of kindness to animals was widely accepted by American families who embraced Victorian culture's ideals of gentility, liberal evangelical theology, and domesticity, and their attendant beliefs in social progress and moral uplift. Gentle treatment of animals was regarded as an important attribute of good character." She also notes that the real boom into something like a modern sensibility occurred during the 1870s, but she does not see the Civil War as playing any role in this development.[16]

Was it just by happenstance that Bergh created the ASPCA a year after Appomattox? Was animal welfare bound to happen anyway, even without the horrible suffering of the Civil War? Or did veterans North and South actually play a role in raising awareness of animal welfare for the rest of their lives after witnessing how military systems had mobilized and then destroyed thousands of animals? These are important questions waiting to be answered by students of Civil War history.

## THE ESSAYS IN RELATION TO EXISTING SCHOLARSHIP

The collection opens with a look at the most divisive issue ever to afflict the United States, the existence and perpetuation of human slavery. Michael E. Woods adds yet another element to the varied ways that issue has been dealt with by historians. When the US Army began to import and experiment with camels for transportation purposes in the Desert Southwest, it sparked a camel craze that took on far more significance than army logistics. Men and women dedicated to expanding slavery in the Southwest became involved as the camels also became an object of agricultural improvement in the Southeast. Members of the Slave Power, which Woods convincingly argues was a real if somewhat amorphous collection of people who pursued the expansion of the institution, "integrated a variety of camel capers into their hemispheric proslavery project." That such an innocent species as the camel could be wrapped up in these major themes of antebellum history speaks volumes for the importance of animal history in understanding the Civil War era.

Three of the thirteen essays deal with horses. This is justified by the fact that horses and mules were the most numerous and visible animals encountered in the war, and they have drawn more attention from animal historians outside the Civil War field as well. Horses tend to be the privileged species in animal history generally, with dogs running a close second place.

Scholarship on horses in war well illustrates the two traditions mentioned earlier as characterizing animal history. Studies that view equines as part of a large military system that mobilized, used, and cared for them while employing them as weapons of war or as elements in a logistical chain exist alongside studies that look at the emotional connections between horses and their human handlers. Richard Di Nardo wrote a groundbreaking book on the German army's use of equines during the Second World War that was published in 1991. He points out the extent to which the Germans employed horses as draft animals despite their army's reputation as the pioneer of mechanized warfare.[17]

Another example of the horse as a weapon of war, viewed within the context of the military system that used it, is Louis A. Dimarco's *War Horse: A History of the Military Horse and Rider*, 2008. In it, equines are treated as another element in the list of military assets. Dimarco produced a mechanistic view of the animal that fails to convey the sense of a sentient creature. Also, these weaponized animals had at least some degree of agency even within what often is seen as a rigid military system.[18]

The emotional bond between horses and people is a growing part of the literature. Andrew McEwen posits an important therapeutic benefit for the soldiers and their animals alike. "Human-animal bonding was a key coping mechanism for Canadian soldiers in the Great War," he writes. It allowed them to "briefly escape the horrors of war by caring for vulnerable animals equally in search of comfort in a bewildering environment."[19]

Riitta-Marja Leinonen has studied not only the military system that mobilized horses for war but also the reaction of civilian horse owners and their animals.

The Finnish government requisitioned thousands of farm horses for military purposes during World War II and was careful to return as many of the survivors to their owners as possible after the conflict. She found that while the owners loved their animals and rejoiced when they came back, even many horses remembered their lives on the farm and demonstrated unmistakable joy at returning to their owners after service in the army.[20]

In this collection, the three essays on horses cover many aspects of the equine--human experience. David J. Gerleman's essay details the military system that mobilized and used horses and mules, took care of them, and disposed of them when no longer needed at the end of the war. Administrative history is important in setting the context within which horses and mules lived, worked, suffered, and died. Gerleman's essay well illustrates the immensity and complexity of the system that mobilized equines in the Civil War, especially that of the Federal government, which dwarfed Confederate governmental efforts.

As my own contribution to this section points out, the horses mobilized for service with Civil War field artillery were selected (when possible) for particular physical attributes, their duty being the toughest for any equines in the war. The cannons and caissons they pulled were unusually heavy, requiring special training, special harness, and acclimation to dangerous combat environments. The artillery horse was, in effect, an animal warrior, and most of them adjusted pretty well to their unusual role. The essay also stresses the emotional bonds that developed between artillery horses and their drivers. For many equines and soldiers, those bonds were deep and lasting. As pointed out in this contribution, similar training accorded to show animals, especially race horses, provides an apt comparison for horses serving a military function in wartime.

Abraham Gibson's essay reminds us of the importance of horses to the efforts of both sides in the Civil War. He reveals that agricultural history and environmental history clearly conspire with military history to provide multiple contexts for understanding the horse and its influence on the Civil War. The relative disparity of horses available to the North compared to the South played an important role in shaping the contours of the conflict and determining its outcome. Horse mobility underwrote military operations, enabling the Federals and disabling the Confederates. In short, horse power constituted an important component of war making.

Wild animals rarely appear in studies of animal history. The strong tendency is for scholars to examine domesticated animals, especially pets and work animals, rather than creatures that live separately from humans and only sporadically interact with them. When wildlife do appear in animal-history literature, it usually is to gauge how human audiences judge and evaluate them as symbols of their own values. Wolves become demons, for example, and wild, exotic creatures in zoos and menageries become spectacles of entertainment. These animals rarely take center stage but are examined within the human context. No study, to my knowledge, looks intently at wildlife in connection with war.[21]

Yet, Richard van Emden, in *Tommy's Ark: Soldiers and Their Animals in the Great War*, 2010, found that British soldiers encountered many wild animals while stationed in the trenches of the western front. They noticed birds, insects, and mammals. The static nature of World War I military operations and the necessity of living in holes in the ground created the most animal-intensive war in history. Birds twittered within hearing of soldiers, insects and rodents lived closely with them, bees populated inactive sectors of no-man's land where wildflowers grew. Cats and dogs abandoned by civilians roamed the combat zone as well, becoming feral in a remarkably short time.[22]

Animals played an important therapeutic role for British soldiers. The presence of birds relieved stress and worry. They were "angels in disguise," thought one man. "Without the birds I dare not think how I should have got through the war at all," concluded Philip Gosse. Indeed, for many, merely being outdoors brought home a deeper awareness of the natural environment. "I was often conscious of the great contrast between the man-made ugliness and horrors of the war-torn countryside, and the fresh, unchanging harmony and beauty of nature," wrote Fred Hodges.[23]

Animals also saved many lives. Thousands of canaries and mice were used as alarm bells in the extensive and often deep galleries and shafts constructed by military miners on the western front. They were sensitive to gases released by underground digging and served as a warning for the miners to wear gas masks or to evacuate the galleries before it was too late.[24]

My contribution in this section takes a similar tack on the topic of wildlife by looking at Civil War soldiers, how aware they were of wildlife, and the type of contact they had with many wild creatures, from birds to alligators and insects. A wide variety of attitudes and interactions can be charted by surveying soldier letters, diaries, and memoirs. Moreover, the essay deals with the impact of combat on wildlife populations caught on the battlefield and the outcome of fishing and hunting by soldiers on those populations. It also discusses a possible connection between wartime exposure to wild animals, on the one hand, and the burgeoning natural-conservation movement of the Civil War era, on the other.

Insects are a major component of wildlife, but they have hardly been noticed by scholars engaged in studies of animals in war. The possibilities are wide and varied but, as of yet, hardly touched upon. One can read Lisa Jean Moore and Mary Kosut, for example, who write of apiary bioterrorism when they discuss the "militarization of bees in wartime." While that seems a bit extreme, at least if applied to the Civil War era, the important role of bees in wartime activity is slowly receiving its due.[25]

For this book, Mark Smith contributes to that progress with his examination of the importance of bees in Civil War–era society and the role these insects played in the experience of soldiering. In addition to an important contribution to animal history, Smith's essay is part of a significant historiographical trend that explores the past through the senses of contemporaries. In a cultural sense, bees became metaphors for wartime activity and for aspects of the combat experience. Their impact on the human experience has been more important than we think.

The fate of domesticated animals caught in war has hardly been broached in the animal-history literature, but it is a wide-open area waiting for more study. One example is a fine article by Martin S. Alexander that documents the experiences of farm animals as well as pets in the wake of widespread refugee flight from the German invasion of France in the spring of 1940.[26]

My essay on wildlife mentioned above briefly posits a relationship between domestic animals and wildlife in the Civil War. The ready accessibility soldiers enjoyed to farm animals (when they foraged for food to supplement or replace their army rations) led to less fishing and hunting of wildlife, sparing those wild populations from even more destruction during the conflict.

In his essay, Jason Phillips reminds us that hogs were vitally important in the meat-oriented diet of most Americans in the Civil War era. The raising of them and the processing of their carcasses on a large scale brought hogs into the realm of human institutions, culture, and society on a more intimate level than that of wildlife. The environmental context of hog production also is vital in understanding their significance. Phillips concentrates on the southern hog, at times in comparison with its northern counterpart. "The relationship between southern pigs and Confederate independence reveals how nineteenth-century agriculture, capitalism, and ecology entangled and oppressed animals and humans," he asserts.

The animal as a consumable for humans and the converse, vegetarianism, certainly have their role in animal history. The relatively few studies on animals as consumables for humans tend to focus on the often inhumane nature of the industrial system that raises and slaughters animals for human consumption. Histories of vegetarianism have so far ignored warfare as an element of the story.[27] Armies, however, are good case studies of both meat eating and vegetarianism because they exist on a planned, mandated diet that brings in institutional history, cultural trends in food ways, and the eating habits of large populations of young men.

My essay on meat eating and the vegetarian perspective during the Civil War asserts that carnism, the culture surrounding meat eating, was strong during the era and in many ways harmful to the health of soldiers North and South. Carnism influenced the army ration, which was heavy on meat and short on plant-based foods. The military system expended a great deal of effort and money providing meat to soldiers, even though many of them had trouble digesting it. While many soldiers preferred meat, an equal number hungered for more fruits and vegetables. The imbalanced diet led to widespread scurvy and night blindness, but neither mainstream American society nor the army learned these lessons concerning the need for a larger intake of fruits and vegetables.

Carnism is a selective food culture, identifying certain species as legitimate consumables and others as forbidden. Horses and dogs both are included in the legitimate category in some countries and forbidden in others, becoming pets or work animals instead of food.

In the West dogs have been elevated to a special position as "man's best friend." The relationship between dogs and war is therefore a topic that has achieved a higher-than-usual profile. A useful international survey of the subject can be found in David Karunanithy's 2008 publication *Dogs of War: Canine Use in Warfare from Ancient Egypt to the 19th Century Seminole Wars.* Chris Pearson has explored the emotional bonds that sustained humans when interacting with their dogs in the French army during World War I. The American army maintained a corps of six thousand working military dogs during the Vietnam era. The ethical treatment of canines by the military system from World War II to the War on Terror (it has gone up and down during this time) has been surveyed by Janet M. Alger and Steven F. Alger. They found that the army treated military dogs in a mixed way during World War II, very badly in Vietnam, but better in subsequent wars.[28]

On the other hand, Hilda Kean has described the tragic fate of pets in Britain at the outset of World War II. Frightened by predictions of air raids and worried about taking care of cats and dogs with impending food rationing, many people voluntarily had their pets euthanized. It is estimated that 400,000 were killed during the first week of the war, representing the equivalent of more than a quarter of the pets in London. This was over six times the number of people who died as a direct result of German air raids during the entire war.[29]

A follow-up study by Kean and Philip Howell looked at dogs during the Blitz. Using the content of interviews conducted by the government with pet owners, they assert that dogs and cats exhibited emotional reactions to the bombing that deserve attention by animal historians as well as by social, cultural, and military historians. "We have reframed emotion as a shared bodily capacity communicable across species boundaries," the authors conclude. Kean further argues that more work should be done "on the re-interpreting of historical moments, such as warfare or industrialisation, through an animal lens."[30]

In this collection, Joan Cashin does just that by viewing the history of dogs in America through the lens of the Civil War. She surveys the role they played in American life before 1861 and employs theories concerning agency and the nature of canine-human relationships. She agrees that it was a "flexible but nonetheless profoundly inequitable" relationship before the war, becoming even more so under the stress of conflict. Not only were dogs weaponized by both sides but the war also led to a "starkly utilitarian" extreme in that relationship, giving rise to increased animal cruelty. The war also intensified long-held concerns about sheep-killing dogs now that the conflict placed an increased burden on farmers to produce food for the troops. Many states, North and South, debated increased measures of dog control. The most extreme of these was a Virginia proposal to kill all dogs in the state and use their carcasses to produce material supportive of the war effort.

Lorien Foote's essay also discusses issues surrounding dog control, using South Carolina as a case study and spreading her attention from the prewar period through the conflict and into Reconstruction. She discusses dogs as weapons used to maintain white supremacy and to sustain conscription in the Confederacy. She also explains how dogs marked race and social class in South Carolina and how emancipation and resistance to reconstruction affected the canine population of the state. Agricultural reformers wanted to eliminate dog keeping among Black people, but advocates for the freed people and lower-class whites successfully fought against state control over dogs during Reconstruction because they supported subsistence hunting. It is astonishing how readily dogs, in one way or another, became entwined with an array of human interests, such as hunting, property protection, sheep killing, race relations, the Civil War, and Reconstruction. Cashin and Foote exemplify the concept that the canine-human relationship is flexible and subject to change in periods of great stress.

Many historians prefer to emphasize the positive side of the animal-human relationship by focusing on the affective bonds linking pets of all kinds with their human hosts. Van Emden did this in *Tommy's Ark*. Although restricted to the British Army, he found numerous examples of soldiers who kept pets and units that kept mascots. This seems to have been a universal theme in military history no matter what the period or nationality, lending support to the concept of considering animals not only as participants in war but also as veterans of war after the fighting ended.

In fact, animals have been treated as survivors of, if not veterans of, war for nearly a century. The War Dog Memorial of Hartsdale, New York, opened in 1923. More recently, a War Dog Memorial was created in Guam in 1994, the same year that the Marine Australian War Dog Memorial came into being. The Japanese Dog, Horse, and Pigeon Military Memorial appeared in stages between 1958 and 1992. Another memorial is the Military Working Dog Teams National Monument at Lackland Air Force Base, San Antonio, Texas. Most of these memorials extol the level of sacrifice by the animals (and are oriented mostly toward dogs). They also provide a heroic narrative, raising the image of service animals to the status of soldiers.[31]

But a handful of memorials to animals in war provide a less celebratory and more somber narrative. The World War I Animal War Memorial at Pozieres, France, which was dedicated in 2017, has an inscription that reads, "They Held No Malice, They Served All Nations." No memorial is more bittersweet than the Animals in War Memorial dedicated near Hyde Park in London in 2004. Consisting of a semicircular wall with statues of two pack mules on one side, heading for an opening in the wall, and statues of a horse and a dog on the other, it bears the provocative inscription, "They Had No Choice." This perspective renders it atypical of glowing war memorials created for humans and animals, with some exceptions like the Vietnam Memorial in Washington, DC, which is somber and reflective.[32]

In this book Brian Matthew Jordan explores these themes in the Civil War. We learn that animals are not only regimental mascots but veterans too. Jordan argues they belonged to a "regimental community" that embraced many different human actors. Those animals that survived the war became its "living relics" after Appomattox. Including animals as "historical actors" can shed light on "the culture of a Civil War regiment and the character of Civil War memory." After a survey of mascots generally, Jordan focuses on the most famous mascot-turned--veteran, Old Abe the Battle Eagle of the 8th Wisconsin Infantry, as a case study illustrating all these themes.

Continuing the discussion of animals past the Civil War, the collection takes us well past Appomattox to end with two essays that reflect changing levels of national reunion. The first of these notes continued tension while the second discusses reconciliation.

When Congress began to debate a proposal to create a national zoo in 1888, it revealed not only divided opinion on the role of the US government but also brought into the open previously muted sectional divisions. In his essay Daniel Vandersommers examines the language of that debate. "Animals were used by Congressmen to conjure sectional ideologies" and became part of the heated discussion in surprising ways. Vandersommers notes the persistent laughter that erupted in these debates, when normally unspoken subjects such as the Civil War and the names of various animals were uttered within chambers where one did not hear such things. He ponders the significance of this laughter and the role of animals, familiar and exotic alike, in contested political discourse nearly thirty years after Appomattox.

Vandersommers is a contributor to a small but growing literature on the history and cultural significance of zoos. Studies of zoos that touch on war experiences, such as John M. Kinder's essay on zoo animals in World War II Germany, are relatively rare.[33]

When sectional reconciliation became mainstream culture by the 1880s and 1890s, it brought with it a complicated set of dynamics that worked both toward and away from healing. In her essay Paula Tarankow brings to this discussion the role of animals. She sees in the career of Beautiful Jim Key, a show horse that drew audiences numbering in the tens of thousands, and his owner and handler, a former slave, a potent opportunity to study "the challenges and possibilities of fostering connectivity across race and species lines." She deals with race relations, the rise of sensitivity toward animal welfare, and animal-human interaction in a commercialized show setting. Tarankow explains that animal-human relations played out differently in the North compared to the South, influenced by competing views on the legacy of pre–Civil War slavery. The time frame of this essay, 1898 to 1906, takes the tensions of the Civil War into the next century—but animals were still along for the ride.

In fact, as all the contributions in this collection demonstrate, animals have always been along for the ride—we just did not realize it. This is a timely point, because the study of animals in the Civil War era is on the verge of blossoming. If the essays in this compendium can play a role in that fluorescence, they will have served their purpose.

## NOTES

1. Margo DeMello, *Animals and Society: An Introduction to Human-Animal Studies* (New York: Columbia University Press, 2012), 4–5, 7. See Peter Singer, *Animal Liberation: A New Ethic for Our Treatment of Animals* (New York: Avon, 1975); and Tom Regan, *The Case for Animal Rights* (Berkeley: University of California Press, 1983).

2. Jason C. Hribal, "Animals, Agency, and Class: Writing the History of Animals from Below," *Human Ecology Review* 14, no. 1 (2007): 101–12; Sarah E. McFarland and Ryan Hediger, eds., *Animals and Agency: An Interdisciplinary Exploration* (Leiden, The Netherlands: Brill, 2009).

3. DeMello, *Animals and Society*, 6; Susan Nance, "Animal History: The Final Frontier?," *American Historian* 6 (November 2015): 28.

4. See, for example, Linda Kalof, *Looking at Animals in Human History* (London: Reaktion Books, 2007).

5. Janet M. Davis, *The Gospel of Kindness: Animal Welfare and the Making of Modern America* (New York: Oxford University Press, 2016), 4; Scott A. Miltenberger, "Viewing the Anthrozootic City: Humans, Domesticated Animals, and the Making of Early Nineteenth-Century New York," in *The Historical Animal*, ed. Susan Nance (Syracuse, NY: Syracuse University Press, 2015), 263; Katherine C. Grier, *Pets in America: A History* (Chapel Hill: University of North Carolina Press, 2006), 182.

6. Brett Mizelle, *Pig* (London: Reaktion Books 2012).

7. Judkin Browning and Timothy Silver, *An Environmental History of the Civil War* (Chapel Hill: University of North Carolina Press, 2020), 102–32.

8. Jilly Cooper, *Animals in War* (London: William Heinemann, 2000); Juliet Gardiner, *The Animals' War: Animals in Wartime from the First World War to the Present Day* (London: Piatkus Books, 2006).

9. Gervase Phillips, "Animals in and at War," in *The Routledge Companion to Animal-Human History*, Hilda Kean and Philip Howell, eds. (London: Routledge, 2019), 422–23, 429–36, 438.

10. Robert E. Lubow, *The War Animals* (Garden City, NY: Doubleday, 1977), 1, 35, 117, 123, 127–52, 192–202, 216–25.

11. Colin Salter, Anthony J. Nocella II, and Judy K. C. Bentley, eds., *Animals and War: Confronting the Military-Animal Industrial Complex* (Lanham, MD: Lexington Books, 2014), 2, 6, 13.

12. Gene C. Armistead, *Horses and Mules in the Civil War: A Complete History with a Roster of More Than 700 War Horses* (Jefferson, NC: McFarland, 2013); Charles G. Worman, *Civil War Animal Heroes: Mascots, Pets, and War Horses* (Lynchburg, VA: Schroeder, 2011); Marilyn W. Seguin, *Dogs of War: And Stories of Other Beasts of Battle in the Civil War* (Boston: Brandon, 1998).

13. Browning and Silver, *Environmental History of the Civil War,* 102–32.

14. DeMello, *Animals and Society,* 402–3; Davis, *Gospel of Kindness,* 8–9, 12.

15. Davis, *Gospel of Kindness,* 14.

16. Diane L. Beers, *For the Prevention of Cruelty: The History and Legacy of Animal Rights Activism in the United States* (Athens: Ohio University Press, 2006), 40–44; Grier, *Pets in America,* 182. See also Brian M. Lowe, "Wars of Images and Representations: Contested Meanings and Narratives Surrounding Animal Advocacy," in *Animals and War: Studies of Europe and North America,* ed. Ryan Hediger (Leiden, The Netherlands: Brill, 2013), 211–35. Lowe sees a more aggressive attitude in favor of animal rights by the late nineteenth century.

17. R. L. Di Nardo, *Mechanized Juggernaut or Military Anachronism?: Horses and the German Army of World War II* (Westport, CT: Greenwood, 1991).

18. Louis A. Dimarco, *War Horse: A History of the Military Horse and Rider* (Yardley, PA: Westholme, 2008).

19. Andrew McEwen, "'He Took Care of Me': The Human-Animal Bond in Canada's Great War," in Nance, *Historical Animal,* 273–76, 283, 287.

20. Riitta-Marja Leinonen, "Finnish Narratives of the Horse in World War II," in Hediger, *Animals and War,* 123–50.

21. Harriet Ritvo, *The Animal Estate: The English and Other Creatures in the Victorian Age* (Cambridge, MA: Harvard University Press, 1987), 4–5.

22. Richard van Emden, *Tommy's Ark: Soldiers and Their Animals in the Great War* (London: Bloomsbury, 2010), 2–3, 5–6, 91–92, 127, 141, 156, 210.

23. Ibid., 204, 275–76, 308.

24. *The Work of the Royal Engineers in the European War, 1914–19: Military Mining* (Chatham, UK: W. and J. Mackay, 1922), 67–71.

25. Lisa Jean Moore and Mary Kosut, "Bees, Border, and Bombs: A Social Account of Theorizing and Weaponizing Bees," in Hediger, *Animals and War,* 29–43; Gary L. Miller, "Historical Natural History: Insects and the Civil War," *American Entomologist* 43, no. 4 (Winter 1997): 227–45.

26. Martin S. Alexander, "War and Its Bestiality: Animals and Their Fate during the Fighting in France, 1940," *Rural History* 25, no. 1 (2014): 105–6, 108.

27. Chris Otter, “Eating Animals,” in Kean and Howell, *Routledge Companion to Animal-Human History*, 474, 476; James Gregory, *Of Victorians and Vegetarians: The Vegetarian Movement in Nineteenth-Century Britain* (London: Tauris Academic Studies, 2007); Karen Iacobbo and Michael Iacobbo, *Vegetarian America: A History* (Westport, CT: Praeger, 2010).

28. David Karunanithy, *Dogs of War: Canine Use in Warfare from Ancient Egypt to the 19th Century Seminole Wars* (London: Yarak, 2008); Chris Pearson, “‘Four-Legged *Poilus*’: French Army Dogs, Emotional Practices, and the Creation of Militarized Human-Dog Bonds, 1871–1918,” *Journal of Social History* 52, no. 3 (Spring 2019): 741–42; Mary Kathleen Murray, “The Contributions of the American Military Working Dog in Vietnam” (MA thesis, US Army Command and General Staff College, 1998), 1–2; Janet M. Alger and Steven F. Alger, “Canine Soldiers, Mascots, and Stray Dogs in U.S. Wars: Ethical Considerations,” in Hediger, *Animals and War*, 77–104.

29. Hilda Kean, “The Dog and Cat Massacre of September 1939 and the People's War,” *European Review of History* 22, no. 5 (2015): 741–42, 745–46.

30. Philip Howell and Hilda Kean, “The Dogs That Didn't Bark in the Blitz: Transpecies and Transpersonal Emotional Geographies on the British Home Front,” *Journal of Historical Geography* 61 (2018): 46–47, 51–52.

31. Information on various memorials to animals in war can readily be found on the internet. For more discussion of animals-in-war commemoration, see Hilda Kean, “Animals and War Memorials: Different Approaches to Commemorating the Human-Animal-Relationship,” in Hediger, *Animals and War*, 237–62; and Salter, Nocella, and Bentley, *Animals and War*, 30–32.

32. Judith Tydor Baumel-Schwartz, “Beloved Beasts: Reflections on the History and Impact of the British ‘Animals in War’ Memorial,” *History & Memory* 29, pt. 1 (Spring/Summer 2017): 104, 106, 110, 119, 122.

33. John M. Kinder, “Zoo Animals and Modern War: Captive Casualties, Patriotic Citizens, and Good Soldiers,” in Hediger, *Animals and War*, 45–75.

# I

# Animals in the Antebellum Era

# Antebellum Camel Capers and the Global Slave Power

MICHAEL E. WOODS

RESIDENTS OF Indianola, Texas, had watched many shipments pass through their busy port, but nothing prepared them for the "outlandish brutes" that disembarked in April 1856.[1] Locals' varied responses to the arrival of thirty-four camels, imported from the eastern Mediterranean by the US Army, reflected their social context. Amelia Lewis was a carefree child when the camels, bedecked with red blankets, paraded past and remembered chasing them, despite the fear they provoked in many of her neighbors. But Jack Green could only glance at the beasts before resuming his toil on the wharf. "I was a slave," he recalled, "and I don't have no bizness out thar with dem camels." Later, when the exotic herd paused at the plantation home of Pauline Shirkey, a resourceful handler built a temporary corral out of the most plentiful material at hand: cotton bales.[2] Whether they inspired delight, dread, or repressed curiosity, the camels had made landfall in a slaveholding, staple-crop-producing society.

From Indianola, the camels marched deep into the Texas interior, across parched southwestern expanses to the Pacific Ocean, and thence into the annals of western lore and Civil War trivia. Traces of their fanciful journeys linger at historic sites such as Camp Verde, Texas, ground zero for the army's camel experiment, and Quartzsite, Arizona, where a metal camel perches atop the tomb of

Hadji Ali—better known stateside as Hi Jolly—who served as one of the camel drivers. Inevitably, Hollywood picked up the story, first in a 1954 film entitled *Southwest Passage* and later in an irreverent 1976 comedy called *Hawmps!* Enterprising authors regularly return to the camel caper in trivia books, local histories, and even a memoir penned from an ungulate perspective.[3]

But the antebellum camel experiment had a dark underbelly. Neither an isolated incident nor an innocent diversion from the sectional conflict, the army's test program was one part of a larger camel fad that was covered with the fingerprints of proslavery partisans. Studying antebellum Americans' fascination with camels underscores proslavery advocates' bold vision for western expansion, demonstrates the breadth of southern agricultural reform, and suggests a new way to think about the Slave Power. By following the movements of dozens of living camels across both the South and the Southwest, as well as their even gaudier parade through American print culture, the Slave Power becomes visible as a loose but formidable network of public and private agents—including politicians, military officers, agricultural reformers, slave traders, cotton planters, and journalists—that reached the shores of West Africa, the waters of the Caribbean, and the deserts of the American Southwest. From this angle, it appears less as a colossal government conspiracy or a figment of paranoid imaginations and more as a sinister constellation of intriguers who imagined a bright future for slavery and integrated a variety of camel capers into their hemispheric proslavery project.

The figure most enduringly associated with antebellum camel exploits is Jefferson Davis. Before becoming the Confederacy's only president, Davis, a Mississippi cotton planter, served in the US Senate and as President Franklin Pierce's secretary of war (1853–57). As a veteran of miserable army excursions across the southern Great Plains and of the Monterrey–Buena Vista Campaign during the US–Mexican War (1846–48), he was also keenly aware of the logistical difficulty of moving soldiers and supplies across arid and often rugged western terrain.[4] The American conquest of California, New Mexico, and Utah in 1848 raised the stakes in the search for reliable western transport. On the one hand, the land grab exacerbated the problem of military mobility; on the other hand, it tantalized Davis and fellow southern expansionists who, as Kevin Waite argues, "articulated a sweeping proslavery vision of empire in the West."[5] It was in this context that Davis studied how other armies had tackled similar challenges—and camels caught his eye. He read and translated a French account of their military use in North Africa and later spoke with observers who had seen them in action during the Crimean War (1853–56).[6] As early as March 1851, Senator Davis offered an amendment to a military spending bill that would earmark $30,000 to import fifty camels for army testing in the Southwest. The response was bitterly disappointing: his amendment was not only rejected but also derided with laughter.[7] The Mississippian would have to wait several years to advance his ostensibly outlandish project.

Davis's early failure, like his later success, was highly visible, but his idea was not unique. Indeed, throughout the late 1840s and 1850s, camels lumbered across the American imagination thanks to a steady stream of publications by scientists, explorers, diplomats, and soldiers who speculated that the animals could provide transportation in the nation's burgeoning western empire. Some of these texts were highly fanciful, such as Joseph Warren Fabens's 1851 novel, *The Camel Hunt,* which spins a romantic tale about an expedition to carry camels from Algeria to California.[8] Others were more practical, such as the narratives of western explorers like Gwinn Harris Heap and John Russell Bartlett, who surmised that camels could outperform horses or mules on arduous western treks.[9] Some authors had seen camels in person, including George Perkins Marsh, former US minister to the Ottoman Empire, who extolled their potential in a series of lectures at the Smithsonian Institution before writing a hefty book in which he predicted that camels would prove indispensable in arid regions worldwide, from South Africa and Australia to the American Southwest.[10] Similar enthusiasm had echoed in military circles since 1836, when George H. Crossman, who had witnessed the difficulties of campaigning in Florida during the Second Seminole War (1835–42), proposed establishing a camel corps.[11]

Not all of these writers were committed to promoting slavery, but some early camel proposals bore the imprint of proslavery politics. Most insidious was George R. Gliddon's alleged role in nurturing Davis's support for federally funded camel research. Born in England and raised in Alexandria, Egypt, where his father was an American consul, Gliddon moved to the United States and lectured widely on Egyptology. He also embraced the theory of polygenesis—the notion that people of different races were descended from separately created original pairs and thus were members of different species—and its pseudoscientific proslavery implications. In 1854 Gliddon and Mobile physician Josiah Nott published *Types of Mankind,* a proslavery polygenist text proclaiming that Africans had been created for servitude. They bolstered their anatomical arguments with Gliddon's historical research, from which he concluded that ancient Egypt's

FIG. 1.1. Camels Come to America. *Harper's New Monthly Magazine* featured the camel on the front page of its October 1857 issue (page 577). The illustration, and the seventeen-page article that followed, helped ignite a camel craze in the pre–Civil War South that ultimately connected with deadly issues, such as spreading slavery, and less contentious issues, such as improving southern agricultural practices. The image of the "Ship of the Desert" also captured readers' attention by portraying the camel as an exotic animal from a faraway continent, even as many Americans speculated about their usefulness throughout North America.

white ruling class had owned black slaves.[12] In a sequel, *Indigenous Races of the Earth* (1857), Gliddon claimed credit for the entire US Army camel project, from rousing Davis's curiosity about the animals to their introduction into Texas in 1856.[13] It is unclear whether this notorious self-promoter, who knew far more about marketing than he did about Egypt, was telling the truth, but his involvement was ominous. Davis the western expansionist and Gliddon the scientific racist put a proslavery stamp on the impetus for camel research.

The widely heralded successes of the army's program multiplied the connections between camels and proslavery activity. Certainly, the military was not alone in such endeavors. In the early 1850s, entrepreneurs launched a number of private camel-importing firms, including the American Camel Company, chartered in New York and capitalized at $100,000.[14] But the army's project received the most newspaper coverage, inspired the most devious proslavery spinoffs, and triggered a chain of unintended consequences that blurred the lines not only between public research and private enterprise but also between national defense and slavery's aggrandizement.

Although not a lone visionary, Davis was uniquely well positioned to advance the camel project after he joined Pierce's cabinet as secretary of war. In early 1855 he persuaded Congress to appropriate $30,000 for research and duly dispatched Maj. Henry C. Wayne, another longtime camel enthusiast, to purchase an assortment of the animals. After stops at Tunis, Constantinople, Cairo, and Smyrna, Wayne returned with thirty-four camels and five Arab and Turkish handlers, reaching Indianola on April 29, 1856. The following January, a second federal expedition brought back forty-one additional beasts.[15]

The camels created a stir in Indianola, where they not only impressed onlookers with their strength but also enraged property owners by frightening horses and eating rows of cacti used as fences. After resting the animals, Wayne marched them inland, passing through Victoria and San Antonio before reaching their first long-term post at Camp Verde. By year's end, Wayne had tested the camels on several excursions and reported encouraging results. He hoped to commence a breeding program to increase the numbers available for military service.

When James Buchanan replaced Franklin Pierce as president in early 1857, the project continued, although not according to Wayne's wishes. The new secretary of war, John B. Floyd, rejected the camel-breeding proposal and focused instead on field testing the existing stock. In the summer of 1857, Floyd sent a camel detachment with Edward F. Beale to survey the route for a road across

New Mexico Territory to the Colorado River. Beale reported that the expedition was a success, and by early 1858, he had taken some of the camels on to Los Angeles. But this was the high point of the experiment. Between 1858 and 1861, the army dabbled with a few more camel ventures, using the animals to haul mail between outposts in southern California and to explore the Big Bend region of southwestern Texas. When the Civil War began in 1861, some of the animals were captured by Confederate forces, while others remained in Union hands, but none played a major role in the conflict. After the war, the army concluded that the iron horse had supplanted the ships of the desert and, by March 1866, auctioned off its entire herd. Some animals wound up in circuses, including five that were sold to the Ringling Brothers, while mining companies purchased many others. Some were simply turned loose in the desert. It was an inglorious end to an ambitious program.

But there was more to the camel experiment than a colorful frontier tale. Shifting the focus from the south*west* to the south*east* begins to illuminate the project's connections to proslavery activity. Early signs of these unexpected links appeared in newspaper coverage of the camel project, which captivated southern journalists and readers. Because the animals made landfall in East Texas—the western frontier of the cotton kingdom—initial demonstrations of their incredible strength dramatized their potential usefulness on cotton plantations. In the spring of 1857, for instance, an Indianola correspondent reported to a North Carolina paper that one camel could carry two five-hundred-pound bales of cotton "with as much ease as a mule would with a sack of corn" and speculated that it probably could have borne another bale without trouble.[16] Similar accounts reached Virginia, Georgia, and elsewhere as southern journalists gauged camels' might in terms of their section's iconic staple.[17] Among those who witnessed feats of cotton-lifting power was army officer Robert E. Lee, who was stationed in Texas in the mid-1850s.[18]

These tantalizing reports reached the cotton kingdom at a moment when many planters were eagerly seeking new ways to maximize productivity. As cotton prices rose and soils became depleted in the 1850s, southern agricultural innovators studied a variety of scientific, technological, and managerial improvements. Some urged stricter methods of financial recordkeeping and time management; others welcomed the railroad and the steam-powered cotton gin as harbingers of mechanical progress; some, like Edmund Ruffin, hailed fertilizers and other advances in scientific agriculture as saviors of the plantation economy;

and others doubled down on brutality to extract more labor from enslaved people. Whether they sought to strengthen the South within the Union or to prepare it for independence, these visionaries believed that, with the right knowledge, tools, and practices, they could forge a more rational—and profitable—system of staple-crop production.[19] It was in this context that camel promoters found a receptive southern audience.

The army experiment's leading spokesman was Major Wayne, Davis's point man in the Mediterranean and in Texas. After the US–Mexican War, Wayne had served in the Quartermaster Corps in Washington, DC, where he learned about camels from George H. Crossman. After commencing the project, Wayne, a Savannah native, reckoned that camels could do invaluable labor on southeastern plantations as well as western forts and trails, and he published this intriguing idea in a letter to Washington's *National Intelligencer*. Self-identifying as "a Southern man, from a cotton, corn, and rice growing section," Wayne announced that "we" of the South "might use camels with advantage in our agricultural labors," particularly for short-range transportation within plantations or from plantations to market. Camels could carry half a ton across limited distances and were cheaper to care for than mules or horses. They could easily be imported into Gulf Coast ports like Mobile and Pensacola and, if shipped efficiently, need not cost more than a good mule. Hardier than horses or mules, they were widely used for both urban and plantation labor in Egypt and could thrive in the Deep South's warm climate. Addressing the peculiar concerns of American planters, he added that "no animal [is] better suited" to management by "the negro." Camels could benefit the entire country, the major concluded, but most especially his native section.[20]

Writing as a loyal southerner, firsthand observer, and scientific expert, Wayne inserted the camel into a larger conversation about agricultural improvement. The animals had initially captured attention as exotic marvels, but he suggested adopting them as a regular feature of southern plantations. The idea caught fire: in late 1858 and early 1859 as his letter was reprinted in newspapers from Maryland to Louisiana and drew particular attention from editors in the lower Mississippi valley, the heart of the cotton kingdom.[21] It was also republished in the January 1859 issue of *Southern Cultivator*, an Augusta-based monthly that shared the spirit of optimism and progress that permeated most southern agricultural journals. Dedicated to "improv[ing] both the soil and the mind," the *Southern Cultivator* sought to "introduce a more enlightened system of agriculture" in the South and ran articles on fertilizers, crop diversification, slave management, and sundry hints for boosting productivity.[22] In an age of exuberant experimentation, camels found vocal supporters among the agricultural avant-garde.

Some southerners scoffed at these notions, but even direct criticism helped publicize the prospect of bringing camels down to Dixie. Mark R. Cockrill, a renowned Tennessee cotton planter and stock breeder, threw down the gauntlet to camel aficionados in late 1858, offering to wager two thousand dollars on several trials of endurance and strength that would pit horses and mules against camels. His challenge sparked a series of responses extolling the camels' performance in Texas. Like Wayne's letter, Cockrill's attack and the resulting rebuttals circulated widely in the southern press.[23]

Interest in camels spread quickly among progressive agriculturists. Within two months of the appearance of Wayne's letter, a Georgia subscriber to *Southern Cultivator* had written to the editor, asking, "Who's Got a Camel for Sale?"[24] A similar enquiry from Louisiana appeared the following year, just as advertisements began offering animals for sale in Selma, Alabama, and New Orleans.[25] The journal also kept readers apprised of the southwestern expeditions led by Beale.[26] And proponents of progressive agriculture added camels to their broader vision for technological innovation. After extolling the efficiency of steam-powered wheat threshing, the *Savannah Republican* reaffirmed its support for camels, among other instruments of progress: "We go in for steam engines and camels for the plantations of the South."[27]

But probably no one did more to promote the use of camels in the cotton states than Dallas County, Alabama, cotton planter Benjamin M. Woolsey. Born in Georgia in 1823, Woolsey studied at Emory College and practiced law in Mobile before moving to Dallas County, the heart of Alabama's Black Belt, in 1847. A local leader in Whig Party politics, he served several terms in the state legislature, though devoting most of his time to cotton planting and business ventures in nearby Selma. Woolsey's career fit the mold of the agricultural reformer and local booster: exuding a Whiggish ethos of uplift and development, he championed railroad construction, led the Selma Fire Department, and, during the Civil War, helped oversee the distribution of salt to needy civilians. After the war, he directed a railroad company and dabbled in efforts to import Chinese laborers. Open to innovation and keen to lead by example, Woolsey was a natural pioneer in plantation-based camel research.[28]

In May 1859 Woolsey purchased several camels, which he put to very public use hauling corn from his plantation to a mill in Selma. The animals carried astonishingly immense loads; one camel, though not yet fully grown, could haul over one thousand pounds, thus doing the work of a mule team and wagon. Later that month Woolsey wrote a letter to the *Savannah Republican* proclaiming his experiment a success. The camels had arrived weak and undernourished, but they quickly recovered and "have proved equal to all the demands made upon them," including hauling massive burdens and pulling plows. He cautiously predicted that camels might supplant mules, thanks to their superior strength, ability to subsist on almost any food, capacity to reproduce, and low cost of upkeep. Like other such correspondence, Woolsey's letter spread quickly and ignited a brief camel craze that burned hottest in Alabama.[29] By year's end, a demonstration had drawn admiring crowds at the Alabama state fair, and a contest between a camel and a mule, held in Montgomery, ended with a victory for the former.[30] Although Woolsey later decided that mules performed better on slippery or muddy soil, he continued to maintain that camels could fill an important niche on many cotton plantations.[31]

Wayne and Woolsey's enthusiasm produced an unexpected outcome for the army's camel experiment: what had begun as an effort to improve military transportation in the Southwest now promised to boost plantation productivity in the Southeast. Their evolving project looked quite different from more infamous Slave Power schemes, including overturning restrictions on slavery's geographic spread. But the camel project had given well-positioned southerners a chance to promote both southwestern expansion and southeastern productivity in ways that surpassed Davis and Wayne's initial hopes. Beyond deriving civilian benefits from military research, however, there was a still more sinister facet to the camel project. Almost immediately, the growth of a private market for the animals became entwined with the Atlantic slave trade.

For almost as long as Americans imagined importing camels, they anticipated some connection to international slave trading. The protagonists in Joseph Warren Fabens's *The Camel Hunt,* for instance, are detained by a British naval patrol on suspicion of being slavers due to their oversized water casks and the abundance of ropes for carrying the camels.[32] More brutal was the abrupt leap made in March 1859 by a *Southern Cultivator* subscriber, who announced that the cotton states needed "more laborers and cheaper ones" as well as "more and cheaper draught animals." He urged importing both without delay: "Let 'Cuffy' come and his appropriate co-laborers the Camel. However people may differ about the negro, nobody can be offended by the importation and breeding of the camel, so let us have the Camels right off, and then defy the world to prevent our getting as many of the wool bearing bipids as we may need."[33]

This defiant proclamation alluded to the divisive question of resuming the Atlantic slave trade. Since 1808, the importation of enslaved people from abroad and Americans' participation in international slave trading had been prohibited. But illicit trading persisted, and as planters craved more labor to meet the booming demand of the 1850s, interest intensified in purchasing enslaved Africans. Some southern politicians demanded that the slave-trade prohibition be repealed outright, creating a rallying point for extremists in the late 1850s, although it failed to gain widespread traction.[34] What did take off was the smuggling of captives into the United States in violation of the law. An early historian estimated that 30,000–60,000 Africans were imported each year in the late 1850s. While that figure has been challenged, it is evident that illicit trading did increase near the decade's end—just as the camel craze intensified. A series of high-profile cases, in which slave ships were intercepted and the misery of their captive passengers revealed, kept the issue in the press. Many slave ships were owned by shadowy traders, often of Portuguese or Brazilian origin, who operated from New York City offices and conducted both legal commerce and human trafficking.[35]

Fatefully, slavers gravitated toward the same shoreline that beckoned to Major Wayne and provided the proving ground for camels' cotton-hauling abilities: the Gulf Coast of Texas. The state's intricate coastline allowed savvy smugglers to evade detection. Since the early nineteenth century, human traffickers had brought captives from Africa or Cuba to coastal hiding places and then sold them to Louisiana purchasers.[36] By 1850, Texas itself offered a thriving market for enslaved laborers. That state's rapidly multiplying plantations yielded 58,000 bales of cotton in 1850; by 1860, that figure reached 431,000.[37] Zealous for continued growth, Texas planters clamored for bound laborers. With domestic slave prices rocketing past fifteen hundred dollars, newly enslaved Africans, who might sell for three hundred dollars, were a relative bargain.[38] Predictably, white Texans were among the loudest proponents of repealing the ban on international slave trading. As one Galveston editor put it: "If you agree to slavery, you must agree to the trade. . . . Those who deny slavery and the slave-trade are enemies of the South."[39] Other proponents of repeal included Edward Riordan, a Galveston slave dealer, and Lieutenant Governor Francis Lubbock. Both were leading members of the Texas Stock Importing Company and hoped to add human cargoes to their shipments of blooded livestock.[40] Although the ban remained in place, Texans openly bought and sold smuggled captives. In June 1859 a Richmond, Texas, newspaper advised that four hundred Africans, "lately landed upon the coast of Texas," would soon be auctioned off.[41]

As the epicenter of American camel testing and the leading edge of slavery's westward expansion, Texas provided a likely setting for camel capers to intertwine with illicit slave trading. Slave traders, moreover, had several incentives and ample opportunity to add camels to their cargoes. They already had business contacts in West Africa who could provide the animals, after all, and they needed camouflage for their nefarious commerce. As Fabens noted in his novel, clues like large water casks, suspicious quantities of foodstuffs, and foul odors could blow slavers' cover. To maintain plausible deniability, they sometimes pretended to be whalers or palm-oil merchants to explain away their large tanks, with some even hunting a few whales or carrying some legitimate cargoes to bolster their alibis. Indeed, unwary sailors could blunder into joining slaving voyages, thinking that they had signed on for a whaling expedition. Smugglers also secreted food supplies between decks and used chloride of lime to mask the stench from below that could alert British naval patrols to their wretched human cargoes.[42]

Amid this ceaseless struggle between enforcers and violators of the law, camels could provide crucial protection for the latter. They were available in familiar West African ports and could be sold through typical Texas channels. The animals required considerable sustenance and produced abundant waste. They appealed to American buyers who often sympathized with slave trading itself. As the focal point for both federal camel imports and slave smuggling, Texas promised to be a convenient destination for slavers operating under the cover of camels.

This situation's horrific possibilities were realized in an 1858 incident that revealed how deeply proslavery activity had become entwined with the camel craze. That October, the schooner *Thomas Watson* and a smaller ship named *Lucerne* arrived in Galveston carrying a glamorous passenger named Mrs. Watson and her herd of eighty-nine camels. A British consular officer suspected that the *Thomas Watson* was a slaver and refused to clear the ship to depart for Liverpool while he pressed American authorities to investigate. Meanwhile, Watson, along with the ship's owner, John A. Machado of New York, demanded that the State Department shut down the nosy British meddler. During the stalemate, the camels roamed through Galveston, devouring shrubbery and biting overcurious onlookers.[43]

The episode ended quietly when the *Thomas Watson* sailed out of port, but it reveals tantalizing interconnections between camel exploits and a range of proslavery plots. As for the camels, some were slaughtered and barbecued by hungry Galvestonians, but most survived. Many found refuge on Lubbock's ranch, living out their days on land owned by a proponent of the African slave trade and a staunch supporter of proslavery filibustering expeditions into Latin America. The remaining animals traveled on with Mrs. Watson to New Orleans and into the cotton kingdom. She answered Cockrill's challenge, showcased her camels at the 1859 Alabama State Fair, and sold several of them to Woolsey, whose test specimens came from this herd.[44] Even the vessel used to ferry Watson's camels from Galveston to New Orleans had a shady history: the *Fashion* was owned by the Mobile and Nicaragua Steamship Company and had carried William Walker and his fellow filibusters from New Orleans to Nicaragua, which they attempted to conquer and transform into a slave state; federal officials had tracked the ship closely in a vain attempt to prevent new recruits from reaching Walker.[45] Proslavery Texans looked simultaneously westward and southward in the search for fresh conquests, and many also relished the intertwined importation of camels and enslaved captives.

In the small world of proslavery politics, camel capers enlisted the support of agents with ties to a variety of schemes, from filibusters to secession. The leading figures in the Galveston episode were also deeply enmeshed in illicit slave trading. Machado, the *Thomas Watson*'s owner, was a notorious Portuguese American merchant who had had numerous brushes with the law. From his Wall Street office, Machado conducted legal and illegal commerce, mostly between Sierra Leone and the Americas, dealing in legitimate products like palm oil as well as enslaved captives. He had dispatched the *Thomas Watson*, disguised as a whaler, on several previous slaving voyages and had complained to the State Department when the ship was apprehended by a British patrol the previous year. Machado would continue his brutal business until he was indicted in 1863—then vanished.[46]

Equally mysterious was Mrs. Watson. Variously identified as a British lady and the widow of a sea captain, Mary Jane Watson may have been Machado's lover and was certainly one of his most trusted collaborators. She regularly commanded the *Thomas Watson* and would buy the ship in 1860. On the Galveston voyage, she had probably carried both camels and captives, unloading the latter somewhere on the Texas coast before arriving in port with nothing but camels in the hold. Later, multiple Texans claimed to have bought enslaved Africans who had arrived alongside camels, and one even boasted of buying a slave from Mrs. Watson herself. After leaving Galveston, she made a splash in Louisiana and Alabama, charming journalists who loved writing about the "pretty widow" and her marvelous camels. Watson sold several camels in Alabama, including one to the nephew of a former governor, but her luck ran out in 1862, when she evidently drank herself to death in Madrid.[47]

Watson's career sputtered out quickly, but the Galveston episode illuminates a remarkable web of proslavery actors with ties to everything from filibustering and westward expansion to illicit slave trading and secession. When viewed in the larger context of the antebellum camel craze, it helps us reinterpret the vital concept of the Slave Power.

Antebellum critics of slavery typically used the term "Slave Power" to cast southern slaveholders as members of an aristocracy that wielded disproportionate federal clout. Through the extra representation granted by the three-fifths compromise and their concomitant influence over all three branches of the federal government, the argument went, slaveholders could advance their own interests at the expense of humbler American voters. Critics pointed to laws like the Fugitive Slave Act of 1850 and measures like the 1845 annexation of Texas to demonstrate the Slave Power in action. Some took the concept to a conspiratorial extreme, such as a Maine Republican who lamented that "every branch of the national Government" was "as fully under the control of these few extreme men of the South, as are the slaves on their plantations."[48] But whether they defined it as the product of a conspiracy or the structural advantage enjoyed by proslavery southern elites, antislavery activists used the term to nurture a political coalition that triumphed in 1860. White northerners who cared nothing about enslaved people's suffering did respond to charges that slaveholders' stranglehold on federal policy harmed free people nationwide.[49]

Historians generally recognize the Slave Power concept's historical *significance*, but they have disagreed over its historical *accuracy*. Some critics rank it alongside the paranoid delusions of anti-Masons, anti-Catholics, and other antebellum conspiracy mongers.[50] Others point out that southern politicians did not march in lockstep and argue that the bitter disputes that fractured southern elites along geographic, partisan, and ideological lines disprove the theory that they conspired to rule the country.[51] Recent scholarship, however, suggests that antebellum Republicans and their precursors were largely correct in maintaining that slaveholders held outsized political influence.[52]

Historians might refine our understanding of proslavery political strength by revisiting the Slave Power in light of the camel capers that multiplied on the eve of the Civil War. Camel-related projects, ranging from army trials and plantation experiments to slaving voyages, do not expose the Slave Power as a tight-knit aristocracy that kept the federal government entirely under its sway, but neither do they prove that it was a figment of feverish abolitionist imaginations. Rather, they suggest that the Slave Power was a network of officeholders, soldiers, and civilians who all envisioned slavery as a dynamic, flourishing institution poised for continued growth throughout the Western Hemisphere. The fact that the same names appeared in a variety of proslavery adventures is striking. Davis went from well-positioned camel promoter to Confederate president. Lubbock, the camel-rescuing Texas executive, had backed filibusters and slave traders and would go on to serve in the Confederate army, not surrendering until he was captured along with Davis following the fall of Richmond. Watson sold enslaved people to Texas planters and camels to Alabama planters, covering an ugly crime with her beautiful face.

No single conspiracy connected these disparate people, but they all shared a stake in slavery's profitability and persistence. United by an interest in slavery's vitality, they developed a series of opportunistically intertwined camel experiments intended to secure land, technology, and labor for a powerful and growing slaveholding society. Seen from this perspective, the Slave Power appears less monolithic, though perhaps more sinister, than antebellum critics or previous historical studies have assumed. Sometimes they used federal might, as Davis did to commence the army experiments; other times they flouted federal law, as Watson did for a living. With one foot planted in Washington and the other in a shady private underworld, the Slave Power network operated to keep the "peculiar institution" firmly entrenched in all aspects of nineteenth-century life. Perhaps antebellum critics exaggerated the tightness of the Slave Power's grip, even as they underestimated the extent of its reach. Even so, hostility to its real and imagined clout steeled northern Republican voters and politicians for the momentous election of 1860 and, when the crisis came in 1861, nerved northerners for war.

## NOTES

1. "The Ship of the Desert," *Harper's New Monthly Magazine* 15 (October 1857), 578. Some elements of this essay appeared in Michael E. Woods, *Arguing until Doomsday:*

*Stephen Douglas, Jefferson Davis, and the Struggle for American Democracy* (Chapel Hill: University of North Carolina Press, 2020), 122–25.

2. Chris Emmett, *Texas Camel Tales: Incidents Growing up around an Attempt by the War Department of the United States to Foster an Uninterrupted Flow of Commerce through Texas by the Use of Camels* (San Antonio: Naylor Printing, 1932), 18, 20–22, 55–57 (quotation, 22).

3. Gary Fuller, *The Trivia Lover's Guide to the World: Geography for the Lost and Found* (Lanham, MD: Rowman & Littlefield, 2012), 100; Mike Cox, *West Texas Tales* (Charleston, SC: History Press, 2011), 85–87; Kathleen Karr, *Exiled: Memoirs of a Camel* (Tarrytown, NY: Marshall Cavendish, 2004).

4. William J. Cooper Jr., *Jefferson Davis, American* (New York: Alfred A. Knopf, 2000), 55–59, 129–56.

5. Kevin Waite, "Jefferson Davis and Proslavery Visions of Empire in the Far West," *Journal of the Civil War Era* 6, no. 4 (December 2016): 536–65 (quotation, 536). Proslavery southerners' ambitions for territorial expansion into Latin America and the Caribbean have attracted more attention than their Far West designs. On the latter, see Kevin Waite, "The Slave South in the Far West: California, the Pacific, and Proslavery Visions of Empire" (PhD diss., University of Pennsylvania, 2016); Daniel Lynch, "Southern California Chivalry: Southerners, Californios, and the Forging of an Unlikely Alliance," *California History* 91 (Fall 2014): 60–62; Stacey L. Smith, *Freedom's Frontier: California and the Struggle over Unfree Labor, Emancipation, and Reconstruction* (Chapel Hill: University of North Carolina Press, 2013); Michael A. Morrison, *Slavery and the American West: The Eclipse of Manifest Destiny and the Coming of the Civil War* (Chapel Hill: University of North Carolina Press, 1997); Donald S. Frazier, *Blood & Treasure: Confederate Empire in the Southwest* (College Station: Texas A&M University Press, 1995); and John C. Parish, "A Project for a California Slave Colony in 1851," *Huntington Library Bulletin* 8 (October 1935): 171–75.

6. [Varina Howell Davis], *Jefferson Davis, Ex-President of the Confederate States of America, a Memoir*, 2 vols. (New York: Belford, 1890), 1:526, 558.

7. Cong. Globe, 31st Cong., 2nd Sess., 826–27 (March 3, 1851).

8. Joseph W. Fabens, *The Camel Hunt: A Narrative of Personal Adventure* (Boston: James Munroe, 1851). Fabens remained interested in camels long after most of his contemporaries had abandoned the idea. In 1865 he presented a paper to the American Geographical and Statistical Society calling for further experimentation with camels in the West. It was later published as a pamphlet: Joseph Warren Fabens, *The Uses of the Camel: Considered with a View to His Introduction into Our Western States and Territories* (New York: Carleton, 1865).

9. Gwinn Harris Heap, *Central Route to the Pacific, from the Valley of the Mississippi to California* . . . (Philadelphia: Lippincott, Grambo, 1854), 128–31; John Russell Bartlett, *Personal Narrative of Explorations and Incidents in Texas, New Mexico, California, Sonora, and Chihuahua* . . . , 2 vols. (New York: D. Appleton, 1854), 2:576–84.

10. George P. Marsh, *The Camel: His Organization, Habits, and Uses Considered with Reference to His Introduction into the United States* (Boston: Gould and Lincoln, 1856).

11. Frank Bishop Lammons, "Operation Camel: An Experiment in Animal Transportation in Texas, 1857–1860," *Southwestern Historical Quarterly* 61, no. 1 (July 1957): 24.

12. J. C. Nott and Geo. R. Gliddon, *Types of Mankind* . . . (Philadelphia: Lippincott,

Grambo, 1854). On Gliddon's background, see William Stanton, *The Leopard's Spots: Scientific Attitudes toward Race in America, 1815–59* (Chicago: University of Chicago Press, 1960), 45–53.

13. J. C. Nott and Geo. R. Gliddon, *Indigenous Races of the Earth; or, New Chapters in Ethnological Inquiry* (Philadelphia: J. B. Lippincott, 1857), 545–46n413.

14. *Charter of the American Camel Company, Granted by the State of New York; with the Natural History of the Camel; Showing That the Camel Is the Animal of All Others the Best Adapted for the Business of Transportation over the Deserts Lying between the Mississippi and the Pacific Ocean* (New York: Published at the Office of the Company, 1854); Odie B. Faulk, *The U.S. Camel Corps: An Army Experiment* (New York: Oxford University Press, 1976), 33–34; A. A. Gray, Francis P. Farquhar, and William S. Lewis, *Camels in Western America* (San Francisco: California Historical Society, 1930); J. M. Guinn, "Camel Caravans of the American Deserts," *Annual Publication of the Historical Society of Southern California and Public Register, Los Angeles* 5, no. 2 (1901): 146–51; K. Allen Stewart, "Camels over Yuma," *American Mercury* (January 1954): 24–26.

15. This overview of the army experiment relies on Faulk, *U.S. Camel Corps,* which provides the richest detail and soundest analysis. The literature on the experiment is vast and varied in quality. Other useful sources include Charles C. Carroll, *The Government's Importation of Camels: A Historical Sketch* (Washington, DC: Government Printing Office, 1904); Walter L. Fleming, "Jefferson Davis's Camel Experiment," *University Bulletin Louisiana State University,* ser. 7, no. 1, pt. 2 (April 1909): 141–54; Lewis B. Lesley, "The Purchase and Importation of Camels by the United States Government, 1855–1857," *Southwestern Historical Quarterly* 33, no. 1 (July 1929): 18–33; and Lammons, "Operation Camel."

16. "Frosts and Famine in Texas," *Weekly North Carolina Standard* (Raleigh), April 29, 1857.

17. "Camels and Dromedaries," *Richmond Daily Dispatch,* May 19, 1857; "The Strength of the Camel," *Macon (GA) Weekly Telegraph,* May 26, 1857.

18. Carl Coke Rister, *Robert E. Lee in Texas* (Norman: University of Oklahoma Press, 1946), 80.

19. Avery O. Craven, "The Agricultural Reformers of the Ante-Bellum South," *American Historical Review* 33, no. 2 (January 1928): 302–14; Weymouth T. Jordan, "The Peruvian Guano Gospel in the Old South," *Agricultural History* 24, no. 4 (October 1950): 211–21; Sarah T. Phillips, "Antebellum Agricultural Reform, Republican Ideology, and Sectional Tension," *Agricultural History* 74, no. 4 (Autumn 2000): 799–822; Steven G. Collins, "System, Organization, and Agricultural Reform in the Antebellum South, 1840–1860," *Agricultural History* 75, no. 1 (Winter 2001): 1–27; David F. Allmendinger Jr., *Ruffin: Family and Reform in the Old South* (New York: Oxford University Press, 1990); John F. Kvach, *De Bow's Review: The Antebellum Vision of a New South* (Lexington: University Press of Kentucky, 2013); Walter Johnson, *River of Dark Dreams: Slavery and Empire in the Cotton Kingdom* (Cambridge, MA: Belknap Press of Harvard University Press, 2013).

20. Henry C. Wayne to the Editors of the *National Intelligencer* (Washington, DC), November 29, 1858, reprinted as "The Camel—His Nature, Habits, and Uses," *Southern Cultivator* 17 (January 1859): 29.

21. See, for instance, "The Camel," *Daily Exchange* (Baltimore), December 18, 1858; "The Camel," *Daily Southern Reveille* (Port Gibson, MS), January 7, 1859; "The Camel," *Memphis Daily Appeal*, January 9, 1859; "The Camel," *Yazoo Democrat* (Yazoo City, MS), January 22, 1859; "The Camel," *Western Democrat* (Charlotte, NC), January 25, 1859; *Shreveport South-Western*, January 26, 1859; and "The Camel—His Nature, Habits and Uses," *Opelousas (LA) Courier*, February 12, 1859.

22. "The Camel—His Nature, Habits, and Uses," *Southern Cultivator* 17 (January 1859): 29. On the *Southern Cultivator*, see William J. Cooper Jr., "The Cotton Crisis in the Antebellum South: Another Look," in *Approaching Civil War and Southern History* (Baton Rouge: Louisiana State University Press, 2019), 28–30; and George B. Ellenberg, *Mule South to Tractor South: Mules, Machines, Agriculture, and the Transformation of the Cotton South* (Tuscaloosa: University of Alabama Press, 2007), 14–16. For other examples of camel curiosity in agricultural reform literature, see "Editor's Table," *American Cotton Planter and Soil of the South* 1, no. 10 (October 1857): 320; and "Lime and the Peeler Plow," *American Cotton Planter and Soil of the South* 4, no. 1 (January 1860): 49.

23. "Novel Challenge," *Richmond Dispatch*, reprinted in *Wilmington Journal*, January 28, 1859; "The Camels," *Galveston News*, December 30, 1858, reprinted in *Nashville Patriot*, January 18, 1859; "Camels vs. Mules," *Washington (DC) Evening Star*, January 24, 1859. On Cockrill's career as an innovative agriculturist and breeder, see Donald L. Winters, *Tennessee Farming, Tennessee Farmers: Antebellum Agriculture in the Upper South* (Knoxville: University of Tennessee Press, 1994), 67, 176.

24. "Who's Got a Camel for Sale?" *Southern Cultivator* 17 (March 1859): 81.

25. "Camels—Are They 'Coming'?" *Southern Cultivator* 18 (March 1860): 90; "Camels for the South," *Southern Cultivator* 18 (August 1860): 248.

26. "The Camel on the Plains," *Southern Cultivator* 18 (March 1860): 79.

27. "New Wheat—Improvement," *Savannah Republican*, reprinted in *Charleston (SC) Mercury*, June 2, 1859.

28. On Woolsey's background and career, see W. Brewer, *Alabama: Her History, Resources, War Record, and Public Men, from 1540 to 1872* (Montgomery: Barrett & Brown, 1872), 224; John Hardy, *Selma: Her Institutions and Her Men* (Selma, AL: Times Book and Job Office, 1879), 189; William Garrett, *Reminiscences of Public Men in Alabama, for Thirty Years. With an Appendix* (Atlanta: Plantation Publishing, 1872), 576; Thomas McAdory Owen, *History of Alabama and Dictionary of Alabama Biography*, 4 vols. (Chicago: S. J. Clarke, 1821), 4:1807; "The Coolie Movement," *Charleston (SC) Daily News*, July 5, 1869; *Memphis Daily Appeal*, May 17, 1873.

29. For background and context on Woolsey's experiment, see Linda Derry, "Camels in Cahawba," *Alabama Heritage* 112 (Spring 2014): 28–35. His letter was widely reprinted under the title "Use of the Camel in the South": for examples, see *Nashville Patriot*, June 1, 1859; and *Edgefield (SC) Advertiser*, June 15, 1859. Other editors simply summarized Woolsey's exuberant findings: see "Camels in Dallas County," *Selma (AL) Sentinel*, reprinted in *Yazoo Democrat* (Yazoo City, MS), May 28, 1859; "Camels in Alabama," *Memphis Daily Appeal*, May 28, 1859; and "Camels on an Alabama Plantation," *Glasgow (MO) Weekly Times*, June 16, 1859.

30. Derry, "Camels in Cahawba," 32; *Daily Intelligencer* (Wheeling, VA), November 23, 1859; *Ripley (MS) Advertiser,* January 18, 1860.

31. "The Camel," *Edgefield (SC) Advertiser,* July 20, 1859.

32. Fabens, *Camel Hunt,* 141.

33. R.G.J., "The Camel and 'Cuffy,'" *Southern Cultivator* 17 (March 1859): 81.

34. Ronald T. Takaki, *A Pro-Slavery Crusade: The Agitation to Reopen the African Slave Trade* (New York: Free Press, 1971); Manisha Sinha, *The Counterrevolution of Slavery: Politics and Ideology in Antebellum South Carolina* (Chapel Hill: University of North Carolina Press, 2000), 125–52.

35. W. E. B. Du Bois, *The Suppression of the African Slave-Trade to the United States of America, 1638–1870* (1896; reprint, New York: Dover, 1970), esp. 179; Leonardo Marques, *The United States and the Transatlantic Slave Trade to the Americas, 1776–1867* (New Haven, CT: Yale University Press, 2016), esp. 11; Ernest Obadele-Starks, *Freebooters and Smugglers: The Foreign Slave Trade in the United States after 1808* (Fayetteville: University of Arkansas Press, 2007); Warren S. Howard, *American Slavers and the Federal Law, 1837–1862* (Berkeley: University of California Press, 1963); Harvey Wish, "The Revival of the African Slave Trade in the United States, 1856–1860," *Mississippi Valley Historical Review* 27, no. 4 (March 1941): 569–88.

36. Du Bois, *Suppression of the African Slave-Trade,* 112–13, 165–66; Obadele-Starks, *Freebooters and Smugglers,* 115–19; Eugene C. Barker, "The African Slave Trade in Texas," *Quarterly of the Texas State Historical Association* 6, no. 2 (October 1902): 145–58; Sean Kelley, "Blackbirders and *Bozales:* African-Born Slaves on the Lower Brazos River of Texas in the Nineteenth Century," *Civil War History* 54, no. 4 (December 2008): 406–23; Fred Lee McGhee, "The Black Crop: Slavery and Slave Trading in Nineteenth Century Texas" (PhD diss., University of Texas, 2000).

37. Andrew J. Torget, *Seeds of Empire: Cotton, Slavery, and the Transformation of the Texas Borderlands, 1800–1850* (Chapel Hill: University of North Carolina Press, 2015), 264; Earl Wesley Fornell, *The Galveston Era: The Texas Crescent on the Eve of Secession* (Austin: University of Texas Press, 1961), 23.

38. Fornell, *Galveston Era,* viii–ix.

39. *Galveston Weekly News,* March 3, 1857, quoted in Takaki, *Pro-Slavery Crusade,* 79.

40. Fornell, *Galveston Era,* 258–59.

41. Obadele-Starks, *Freebooters and Smugglers,* 168.

42. Edward Manning, *Six Months on a Slaver: A True Narrative* (New York: Harper & Brothers, 1879), 21–24, 40, 125–26; Howard, *American Slavers and the Federal Law,* 2–3; Marques, *United States and the Transatlantic Slave Trade,* 196–97; Sylviane A. Diouf, *Dreams of Africa in Alabama: The Slave Ship* Clotilda *and the Story of the Last Africans Brought to America* (New York: Oxford University Press, 2007), 31, 42, 51.

43. My account of this infamous episode and its aftermath relies primarily on three excellent studies: Fornell, *Galveston Era,* 251–63; McGhee, "Black Crop," 223–31; and Derry, "Camels in Cahawba."

44. M. J. Watson, "Camels—Mr. Cockrill's Challenge," *Galveston News,* December 30, 1858, reprinted in *Nashville Union and American,* January 23, 1859; "The Camels," *Galveston*

*News,* December 30, 1858, reprinted in *Shroudsburg (PA) Jeffersonian,* January 27, 1859; *National Era,* May 19, 1859; *Alexandria (VA) Gazette,* June 1, 1859; *New Orleans Daily Crescent,* June 17, 1859; *New York Herald,* December 18, 1859; Derry, "Camels in Cahawba."

45. Obadele-Starks, *Freebooters and Smugglers,* 147; Fornell, *Galveston Era,* 202, 211–12.

46. On Machado's background and his legal and illegal business activities, see "The Slave Trade," *New York Herald,* December 25, 1854; "The Case of the Schooner *George H. Townsend,*" *New York Herald,* January 6, 1855; *Alexandria (VA) Gazette,* February 19, 1858; "The Slaver *Mary Frances,*" *New York Herald,* October 24, 1861; "The Slave-Trade in New York; Rearrest of John A. Machado," *New York Times,* September 21, 1862; Howard, *American Slavers and the Federal Law,* 50–51, 178, 252, 261; Obadele-Starks, *Freebooters and Smugglers,* 168; and Marques, *United States and the Transatlantic Slave Trade,* 194, 196–97, 215, 222–23, 243–53, 298n17.

47. *New York Herald,* November 18, 1859; "Curious Enterprise of a Pretty Widow," *Yazoo Democrat* (Yazoo City, MS), November 19, 1858; "The Slave-Trade in New York; Rearrest of John A. Machado," *New York Times,* September 21, 1862; "The African Slave-Trade," *New York Times,* November 16, 1862; Howard, *American Slavers and the Federal Law,* 252; Obadele-Starks, *Freebooters and Smugglers,* 137, 180.

48. Quoted in Eric Foner, *Free Soil, Free Labor, Free Men: The Ideology of the Republican Party before the Civil War* (1970; reprint, New York: Oxford University Press, 1995), 88.

49. On the historical importance of the Slave Power concept, see especially Larry Gara, "Slavery and the Slave Power: A Crucial Distinction," *Civil War History* 15, no. 1 (March 1969): 5–18; Foner, *Free Soil,* 73–102; William E. Gienapp, "The Republican Party and the Slave Power," in *New Perspectives on Race and Slavery in America: Essays in Honor of Kenneth M. Stampp,* ed. Robert H. Abzug and Stephen E. Maizlish (Lexington: University Press of Kentucky, 1986), 51–78; Leonard L. Richards, *The Slave Power: The Free North and Southern Domination, 1780–1860* (Baton Rouge: Louisiana State University Press, 2000); and Corey M. Brooks, *Liberty Power: Antislavery Third Parties and the Transformation of American Politics* (Chicago: University of Chicago Press, 2016).

50. David Brion Davis, *The Slave Power Conspiracy and the Paranoid Style* (Baton Rouge: Louisiana State University Press, 1969).

51. Chauncey S. Boucher, "*In Re* That Aggressive Slavocracy," *Mississippi Valley Historical Review* 8, no. 1–2 (June–September 1921): 13–79.

52. Richards, *Slave Power,* suggests that the theory was compelling because it was at least partially correct.

# II

# Mobilizing Equines IN THE Civil War

# As Much a Military Supply as a Barrel of Gunpowder

*Horses and Mules as Nineteenth Century Engines of War*

DAVID J. GERLEMAN

THE CONNECTION of animals to history as a broader part of the humanities is an important theme that has gradually progressed from the fringes of historical inquiry toward its center and allowed the profession to branch out in new directions. Animal studies as part of the historical record is especially interesting because of its uniquely interdisciplinary nature, intertwining ethology, ecology, zoology, veterinary medicine, animal science, and even agronomy and meteorology. Such study is all the more important as a century-long reliance on internal combustion engines may tempt modern readers to view horses and mules as machine-like, able to be used when needed, parked when not, and always ready to immediately resume activity without any consideration for the care meted out in between. Exploring horse and mule participation in the Civil War therefore adds to a better and more complete understanding of the entire conflict.

Since domestication, equines have served as mankind's most vital civilization-building helpmate and preeminent military tool, whose importance lasted into the Second World War. Yet unlike men, equines did not consciously choose to go to war, and while soldiers could vent their sufferings by "either in crying, praying or cursing," animals could only mutely endure. Union officer John Beatty best summed up the often unhappy fate of animals sent to war across the centuries.

While on a march, he spotted a disabled horse rolled off the road and pinned on its back against a tree, trembling with fright, "his great eyes looking anxiously, imploringly for help," but there was "no help, no relief, no hope."[1]

In peace or war mid-nineteenth-century views of "dumb animals" remained heavily influenced by biblical rationales relegating them to "the lower order of beings" destined to benefit humans. Civil War horses and mules were collectively viewed as motive engines to be employed at mankind's command, meriting little consideration as sentient beings, even assigned unthinking patriotic roles in the conflict. "The horse is to share in the labors of converting the legions of [Confederate president Jefferson] Davis and [General P. G. T.] Beauregard to loyalty," trumpeted one northern magazine in 1861, while southern publications hailed them as "no insignificant actors in this great struggle for Southern liberty." The wartime newspaper accounts chronicling army horses suffering an "undue proportion of the horrors of war" may even have had the beneficial ramification of increasing postwar humanitarian attitudes and the creation of organizations like the American Society for the Prevention of Cruelty to Animals in 1866. Even as the conflict raged, appeals for more humane care of army stock had reached all the way to the White House, with cavalry trooper Alonzo Still reminding President Abraham Lincoln that "the horse is of all animals the most useful and at the same time the most abused of any."[2]

The ability of the Union and the Confederacy to horse its armies represented a key military factor that weighed heavily in deciding battlefield defeat or victory. Unlike other great powers, however, neither combatant had a standing system that could quickly mobilize the nation's livestock resources. The United States did fortuitously possess the largest share of the global horse population in 1861, tallying some 6,250,000 head, nearly double that of its closest rival, Russia.[3] While the loyal states held approximately 4,288,067 horses, the Confederacy possessed 1,743,697 head, with a significant portion located in the Trans-Mississippi beyond reach of most rebel quartermasters.[4]

Compelling financial and tactical considerations made both Union and Confederate leaders initially reluctant to draw heavily on their horse populations by authorizing large cavalry forces. Conventional beliefs held that the war would be brief, and each full-strength cavalry regiment required 1,280 horses and cost well over $300,000 in initial outlays plus nearly equal amounts per annum in upkeep expenses.[5] Precedence was therefore given to organizing field-artillery batteries, which needed 6-horse teams for each gun limber and caisson, totaling

FIG. 2.1. Cavalry Horse. An unidentified Union cavalryman poses with his horse in the field in this outstanding photograph of an animal outfitted for war service. This steed was one of more than 650,000 horses that served as engines of mobility and motive power in the Federal army, a small specimen of a mighty system that procured, trained, and used animals to secure Union victory during the Civil War. Liljenquist Family Collection of Civil War Photographs, Library of Congress, LC-DIG-ppmsca-67685.

approximately 100 horses per battery. Also required immediately were ambulance, supply, and baggage trains, with each vehicle drawn by 2-, 4-, or 6-horse or mule teams. Army transport needs only increased as the war went on so that, by 1864, Union forces alone possessed some 17,478 wagons and 1,400 ambulances.

Horses for Federal armies (and Confederate forces to a lesser degree) were obtained, with few exceptions, by publicly solicited bids from interested parties. The lowest reasonable bid was accepted, with the winner providing signed sureties for faithful execution, but the contract system had both benefits and serious flaws. Horse and mule contracts soon became synonymous with fraud as speculators and elected officials used them to "heal old political sores and cure bitter political feuds."[6] Many Union mounted regiments initially supplied their own horses through state, local, or personal auspices, but that option was phased out in 1862. The Confederacy, however, maintained that same policy throughout the conflict. While southern leaders belatedly would term requiring men to supply their own horses "radically wrong" and a hindrance to discipline and efficiency, yet they developed no alternative system before the war ended.[7]

Although complaints about bad horses were frequent, many Union units received fine animals thanks to knowledgeable regimental officers, with some of the mule teams purchased in 1861 remaining in service until war's end. The Union's horse-purchase system was continually reformed so that, by 1864, unsatisfactory stock could be traced back to exact inspectors and contractors, leading to firings, fines, or imprisonment.[8] The Confederate army relied heavily upon individual purchases mixed with state- and national- government acquisition; confiscation was only used in desperate cases. Reoccurring horse and mule shortages and a shrinking animal population plagued southern authorities, who had to balance civilian requirements "so as not to weaken agricultural force nor dissatisfy the people" with military necessity. By 1864, General Robert E. Lee was desperate enough to ask if horses could somehow be brought in from Texas or filtered through Union lines from other parts of the South. No viable remedy was found, and by the war's closing months, southern citizens openly resisted selling livestock to the Confederacy unless paid immediately in either gold or US money.[9]

The financial cost of horsing Civil War armies was prodigious. By conservative estimates, the Federal government alone spent over $150 million (in 1860 dollars) buying 650,000 horses and 450,000 mules for use during the war, with prices spiraling upward throughout the conflict. Southern horse and mule prices had been on par with the North, but animals that appraised at $125 in 1861 were valued in 1863 at $600 and fetched over $2,000 by 1865. In the North, maximum government prices were initially set at $119 for horses and $133 for mules, which meant contractors offered farmers $50 to $85 dollars per head, too low to reliably command the best stock. Insatiable military demand and competition from a growing economy repeatedly forced Washington to pay more so that, by March 1865, contract prices stood at $185 for cavalry horses, $190 for artillery horses, and mules at $195 each.[10]

Far more than their human counterparts, equine recruits had to meet strict physical guidelines before being accepted into military service. Federal specifications decreed animals were to have sound and balanced conformation. Legs had to be straight, the line of the back even and firm, the chest deep, and a strong skeletal structure supported by a well-muscled exterior. Eyes and ears should be alert, skin flexible with a glossy coat, and the animal's movement displaying a springy gait unimpeded by deformed hooves or flaws like spavin or ringbone.

Animals were then classed by weight and height: cavalry horses had to be at least 950 pounds and capable of bearing rider and equipment over rough terrain, with height ranging from 15 hands to 16.5 hands high; taller mounts were not sought since they could not be swiftly saddled or harnessed by men of average size. Artillery and wagon horses were to be "strong, quick, active," and slightly larger—at least 15.5 hands high and weighing 1,050–1,200 pounds—with large hooves and well broken to harness.[11]

Equine age requirements fluctuated throughout the war, with more-mature animals preferred. In 1861, cavalry horses between four and nine years old and artillery and wagon horses aged five to seven years were accepted. Officer complaints soon compelled the minimal age to be raised to five and then six years, with extensions made for animals aged nine to ten if "still vigorous, sprightly and healthy." Horses were to be of dark colors—black, bay, brown, or sorrel—with geldings overwhelmingly preferred, as the army had numerous reasons for declining to accept mares or stallions. Despite official prohibition, fully excluding mares from among the 170,000 horses in Federal wartime service was not possible, and the Confederacy never attempted such restrictions.[12]

Although the horse was the main engine of war, not far behind was his "less noble kindred the mule." As hybrid offspring of horses and donkeys (commonly male donkeys and female horses), the mule possessed many admirable traits, although sterile and unable to self-reproduce. In the prewar South, mules had increasingly supplanted oxen for heavy draught work, and by 1860, the region possessed 822,047 head, double the number ten years earlier. The border states contained 208,404 mules, while the northern states trailed with 311,986, but these numbers were deceptive. Many of the mules laboring on southern plantations and a large percentage of annual replacement stock were not locally supplied but came from the farms of Ohio, Kentucky, and Missouri.[13]

Union and Confederate armies depended upon mules for mobility, with six mules replacing four-horse teams. These beasts so efficiently traversed rough ground and could subsist on brush if necessary that, by January 1863, nearly all of the Army of the Potomac's 6,000 wagons were mule drawn. The following year some 130,000 mules toiled with Union forces, with acceptance specifications decreeing they be over fourteen hands high; three to nine years old; strong, stout, well developed; weigh at least 710 pounds; and have shed their four front colt's teeth. Iron-gray mules were prized as supposedly possessing the hardiest qualities, while light- or dappled-colored animals were viewed as lacking stamina. In order to ensure only sound mules were purchased, Union quartermaster regulations eventually mandated that all government stock be branded on the near shoulder "US" and on the neck with their purchasing officer's initials.[14]

Commanders of both armies throughout the war issued orders and circulars entreating better care for army horses for practical military reasons, if not stemming from humane sentimentality. Yet if horses were sometimes mistreated, then mules suffered even more. The common belief of the time was that abuse was necessary to handle mules as they were temperamental and "unpleasant to the unwary." Even their reputation for sturdiness and ability to endure less care than horses usually ensured that exact treatment from the hands of army teamsters. Famous for their profanity and whip-cracking skills, these men were initially hired as civilian employees from among urban hack and stage drivers, later augmented by contraband laborers. Usually uneducated and not subject to formal military discipline, teamsters tended to be overly harsh in their methods and often less than diligent in caring for their long-eared charges.[15]

Whether horse or mule, the animals destined for army service—like the vast majority of human recruits—were taken from isolated farms and villages and herded together into increasingly large contingents to be funneled to the front. Fear, curiosity, excitement, and apprehension were basic sentient emotions shared by both species as they entered an unaccustomed and periodically terrifying new world. For man and beast, one of the first terrors to be faced was riding on steam trains, just gaining prominence as a military-transport asset. Shipping livestock long distances in large numbers was new, untested, and a logistical nightmare; a single regiment, such as the Ninth Illinois Cavalry, required 130 railroad cars to move its men, equipment, and horses.[16]

Standardized army policies for animal shipment—like so many other Civil War practices—had to be improvised and improved through painful trial and error. When an administrative blunder supposedly left a trainload of horses sitting unattended for two days, Union quartermaster general Montgomery C. Meigs was so incensed he scarcely could be mollified even after the report was proven false. Shipment even under ideal circumstances inevitably took a heavy toll on animals through travel stress, injury, and dehydration, packed onto primitive uncovered railroad cars and shipped in all weathers without food, water, or coverings onboard. In the Confederacy a limited rail system and scarcity of rolling stock compelled rebel mounted units to physically march rather than mechanically ride to the front. In 1862 Richmond authorities officially forbade any horses being shipped by railroad unless specially ordered. Even men bringing badly needed remounts back to the army had rail transportation denied.[17]

Shipping horses by water was also fraught with difficulties because animals often had to remain confined for longer periods. Just getting them onboard was hazardous. The reverberation of steamboat whistles, clang of bells, and shouting of humans often caused the live cargo to balk when traversing the gangplank, resulting in some falling into the water.[18] Depending on vessel size, animals were usually placed in deck pens near the vessel's boilers, where the heat from both the machinery and crowded animals raised temperatures to uncomfortable levels. For ocean transport, horses were to be individually stalled, hitched short, and allowed only minimal freedom to prevent them suffering injuries. Insufficient preparation could have tragic results, exemplified by a New Orleans–bound transport that had to dump overboard sixty-eight horse carcasses after the unfortunate animals were strangled by their halters or trampled to death after their flimsy stalls collapsed during a storm at sea. One appalled newspaper accused those responsible for putting the poor beasts "to death by torture."[19]

On sea or land, hunger was a mutual battle fought by soldiers and animals daily. But while hungry men might find sustenance by local foraging, army equines were entirely dependent on human-provided provender. The forage needs of nineteenth-century armies were immense, and lack of hay and grain (respectively called long and short forage) could paralyze military movements, as underfed animals quickly fell off in weight, strength, and ability to labor. What might happen if any army was cut off from its supply of forage was demonstrated several times during war, most notably at the Siege of Vicksburg, where horses and mules were purposely driven out of Confederate lines so that their meager grain rations might be diverted to human use. Likewise, the sufferings of Union animals going for days without forage in encircled Chattanooga in the autumn of 1863 was painful to witness, the sight of them gnawing the bark off trees conveying "more plainly than words how intensely they were suffering for something to sustain life."[20]

Union and Confederate forces adopted nearly identical daily ration allotments for their army animals: ten pounds of hay and fourteen pounds of grain for horses, with mules receiving a few pounds less of each. These were ample if of good quality. But when hay ran short, men tried to compensate by feeding their animals increased grain, which could cause laminitis. Confederate quartermasters sometimes issued "offal" (grains too small for use as flour or bran and wheat husks discarded during milling) if no oats or corn were available. Straw or fodder (cornstalks) were substituted if hay was unobtainable, as roughage was necessary to keep horse and mule digestive tracts functioning. Uninterrupted forage shipments were therefore considered “a business of great magnitude and much difficulty.”[21]

Antebellum agricultural advances and the growth of horse-drawn farm mechanization significantly benefited the northern war effort by actually increasing grain and hay production during the conflict despite several bad growing seasons. In contrast, the prewar preference for cash crops like cotton restricted southern grain-production capacity, making supplying wartime Confederate armies with forage difficult. Unlike in the North, few public advertisements soliciting forage contracts appeared in southern newspapers. Limited rail transport meant Confederate forces were especially dependent on local pasturage to subsist their animals, with farmers paid ten cents per animal per day. Grain shortages required reductions for rebel artillery batteries in 1863. By the next summer, Lee’s army only received 2,000 of its 3,200-bushel-per-day grain requirements. The winter of 1864 was even worse, as little forage arrived and hard frosts killed off any pasturage remaining near army camps.[22]

Access to water, both in summer and winter, is an often overlooked consideration when understanding the functioning of nineteenth-century armies; it was dehydration, not the cold, that killed off the bulk of Napoleon’s horses during the retreat from Russia in 1812. A working horse consumed daily nearly fifteen gallons of water, depending on physical demands or weather conditions, although regulations held four gallons per horse sufficient under normal camp circumstances. As with access to food, army animals were dependent on human action to be able to drink, with military manuals specifying twice-daily watering in manageable groups to avoid overcrowding and fouling nearby streams. Animal dehydration on long, hot marches could severely cripple a military movement. Harnessed animals were the most restricted, often only able to snatch a few sips when crossing at river fords despite the preceding moving columns having so churned the water with silt and mud that it resembled “the color of chocolate.”[23]

Weather played a large role in the tribulations of a moving army. Conditions too dry and too hot meant chocking clouds of dust and animals disabled by dehydration and sunstroke; too wet, and marching columns and iron-rimmed wheeled vehicles quickly transformed dirt roads into nearly bottomless quagmires. The infamous “Mud March” of January 1863 best encapsulates how swiftly bad weather could wreck a military movement and ruin army livestock. Forty-eight hours of rain, sleet, and snow pelted the Army of the Potomac just as it launched a winter offensive. Frozen roads melted, and wheeled vehicles sank to their axles as their horse and mule teams floundered up to their bellies in mire; animals that fell and could not be extricated were shot and abandoned. Bedraggled artillery units soon returned to recently vacated camps piecemeal, with lone field pieces requiring thirty-two horses to move while accompanying battery wagons each needed twenty-four.[24]

Equine care varied widely throughout the army, despite promulgation of regulations intended to promote animal welfare, since enforcement depended upon regimental commanders. Professional soldiers like Col. John P. Hatch diligently attended to feeding and grooming while prohibiting "careless or cruel treatment" such as "kicking, striking, and jerking by the bits with the use [of] loud and angry language." Civilians-turned-officers were often less knowledgeable of animal care and less willing to force former friends and neighbors to perform onerous tasks like stable call. Charles Francis Adams blasted his colonel as "a nuisance" whose ignorance was "only surpassed by his conceit and vanity and love of display" while also being "the most cruel man on horses I ever saw in my life." Such complaints were not uncommon early in the war, before the most unfit officers were weeded out. On both sides of the lines, a mere glance at a unit's horses usually revealed whether its commander was a trained professional or a former civilian.[25]

Commanders on both sides repeatedly called for greater care and attention for army livestock, yet as Adams pointed out, brutal choices had to be made. "How it would astonish and terrify you," he wrote home, "to see the weak, gaunt, rough animals, with each rib visible and the hip-bones starting through the flesh" on which "dashing" cavalry movements were made. Adams did his best for his horses and was sorry for them, but war was cruel, and "it is my business to bring every man I can into the presence of the enemy, and so make war short." When a horse began to fail, there were two choices: "send them to the reserve camps at the rear and so strip yourself of your command," or force them on until they dropped. Adams had one rule: "a horse must go until he can't be spurred any further . . . [and] he lays down in sheer suffering under the saddle."[26]

Such cruelties began long before any equines reached the battlefronts. Training saddle horses or breaking mules to harness required time, patience, and basic animal understanding. Urgent wartime demands, however, resulted in constant evasion of official requirements that horses and mules already be broken to saddle and harness before purchase. As a result, green men and green horses were thrown together with unpleasant results, often made worse by the harsh curb bit used. Mules were broken to halter by dragging them behind army wagons, and a plethora of other taming approaches were tried. Some cavalry units compelled their wildest horses to repeatedly run up steep hills, propelled by "the wholesome discipline of sharp spurs, until the evil was sweated out of them."[27]

One elemental equine trait, perhaps not fully grasped by many Civil War soldiers, was that mounts identified as herd animals, and all their actions and reactions were predicated on that instinct. Whether domesticated or in the wild, they had herd pecking orders, which Benjamin Crowninshield unintentionally identified when noting that "there was always one 'boss' horse, who was never interfered with, on each picket rope." Horses that exasperated or enraged their riders by shying or becoming fractious at drill or parade may actually have been trying to avoid crowding a hierarchically superior animal. Some commanders who understood this behavior even directed the animals be stabled in exact drill order so as to limit hierarchical squabbling.[28]

Once conditioned as part of the regimental "herd," horses rarely wandered away from their picket ropes, and some did not like to be separated from that group. Stanton P. Allen discovered this when his new mount refused to stay quiet on sentry duty to such a degree that he was instructed to bash its head to quiet him before the enemy was alerted. Other horse traits were more welcome, and men soon learned to appreciate their mount's keen sense of smell and hearing, attesting that the horse was "a good sentinel; and by watching his ears closely one will never be deceived by an unexpected approach." Wartime incidents abound of men being thankfully amazed at their mount's abilities to help them avoid hidden dangers, find their way in dark and fog, or prevent capture by lurking guerrillas.[29]

Wartime experiences of camp and combat created camaraderie, not only among soldiers but also between men and horses. Sidney Davis was amused that his horse affectionately rubbed his head against him and regularly lay down beside him. Other troopers delighted in teaching their mounts clever tricks like drinking from a spigot or a canteen. While increasingly hardened to human death, some soldiers wept over losing a favored horse. When William Meyer encountered his wounded mount Billy during a hasty battlefield retreat, he stopped for a last caress before shooting him dead rather than let him suffer. Meyer then "cried as if I had lost a brother; he had been my most faithful, playful friend, my good reliable carrier and companion for many months." Even supposedly callous teamsters could be affected. When a lead mule pair slipped and plunged off a narrow bridge into the gorge below, they looked up at their driver "with an expression in their eyes as if pleading for help" as he stood weeping and repeating "my poor pets, my poor pets" until the wagon master ended their misery with his pistol.[30]

When armies moved, whether for long or short distances, army animals had to supply the motive power for this ordinary but demanding task. The first marches of a new spring campaign were always the hardest, as the recommended gradual conditioning to harden and strengthen the animals' muscles to brace them for long treks was generally lacking. Usually, the cavalry were active first, which meant veteran troopers began to discard all superfluous possessions and even remove stirrup covers to lighten the average 255-pound load each animal carried. Skilled officers ordered frequent halts to readjust saddle blankets and required mounts to be led up and down hills.[31]

Cavalry units were restricted to a walk when not in combat, but even a pace of four miles per hour was described as "killing to horses," and forced marches could have dreadful results. Isaac Gause surveyed the toll on his horse after one such event: "Her limbs were trembling, and every muscle quivered as the saddle was removed from where it had been since the last Sunday morning." When he took off the decayed saddle blanket, the animal's skin came with it, leaving its ribs bare; "I dared not look at the poor thing."[32]

Marches could be harder for the harnessed animals of the artillery, supply, and ambulance trains, as their routes were generally longer than the cavalry and they also had to traverse bad roads and rough terrain as a unit. Draft animals were expected to pull up to six hundred pounds, and if one span member broke down, greater labor was disproportionably thrown on the rest of the team. Unlike the cavalry, artillery horses and other harnessed animals on the march could not be unburdened by dismounting or grazed during halts, although cannoneers were ordered to lessen the draught weight by walking alongside the gun carriages and only riding on the limbers for thirty-minute intervals if not going uphill. For the artillery, sixteen miles in ten hours in ordinary country was normal speed, but battery commanders and wagon masters always had to be on the lookout for loose or cast horseshoes, which could quickly render barefoot animals wholly unfit for service in a few hours if traveling on rocky or macadamized roads.[33]

Combat often proved deadlier for horses then men, as "in battle the horse is a larger mark than the man, and hence is more frequently hit." The wounds were usually in the head or upper torso, although it sometimes took more than one hit to bring an animal down. One trooper left a vivid impression of how cavalry horses reacted to combat:

> In battle he partakes of the hopes and fears incidental to the occasion. On the skirmish line he will mope back and forth, with his head hanging down and ears lopped, as if very tired. At the sound of the trumpet he will move rapidly to the front or rear at the will of the trooper. When heavy battles are raging, if standing in line, he becomes nervous with the suspense, and will tremble and sweat and grow apprehensive. At any sound that indicates a move, the rider can feel him working the bit with his tongue. As he moves out he seeks to go faster and when restrained shows his disapproval by feigning to bolt. He will grasp the bit afresh, and dash ahead as if to brave the worst and have it over as quickly as possible.[34]

Men became experts identifying the peculiar sound bullets made when striking a horse. If the missile hit a fleshy area, it made a dull thud "much as a pebble does when thrown into the mud." But when it struck one of the legs, it made a hollow, snapping sound and knocked the animal off its feet and into a writhing heap. A horse's reactions when hit depended on the nature of the wound:

> If shot through the lungs, he will cough one hard choking cough, the blood flowing out of his mouth and nostrils. He will mope away for a short distance and stand with head down. If the wound is a painful one, such as a broken leg, he will utter one piercing shriek or hysterical scream that resembles the cry of the wild panther, and that causes a shudder to run through the frame of the bravest soldier. If a ball passes through his heart, he will make ten or twelve leaps with even more vigor than at any time during health, and then fall heavily, being dead before falling. If shot through the brain all support is gone, and he falls a dead weight, and straightens out without another move.[35]

Artillery units faced their own type of battlefield hazards, for if too many horses were killed or disabled, it would render an immobilized battery ripe for capture. Thus, enemy cannon and sharpshooters invariably targeted the clustered limber and caisson teams gathered to the rear of the firing line. Posting or withdrawing a battery under fire could be an incredibly dangerous maneuver. J.

Albert Monroe watched his battery go into action at Antietam only to see the horses "melt like wax before a fire" as they made the turn to bring the limber to the trail of the gun. Before a disabled animal could be cut from the traces, others fell and Monroe's own mount took six bullets, forcing the men to withdraw their cannon by hand.[36]

Veterans later recounted that the worst sights and sounds of a battlefield were often the badly wounded animals, as every major battle featured riderless horses, many trailing viscera, wandering aimlessly about. One sympathetic officer at Chancellorsville tried to end a blood-spouting animal's misery with pistol shots, but appalled observers watched the victim struggle to regain its feet as soon as he rode away.[37] Fannie Beers was horrified when passing a cavalry battlefield to hear "the plaintive cries and awful struggles" of the stricken mounts, "shot in every conceivable manner, showing shattered heads, broken and bleeding limbs, and protruding entrails . . . uttering cries of pain, while their distorted eyes seemed to reveal their suffering and implore relief. I saw a soldier shoot one of these poor animals, and felt truly glad to know that his agony was at an end." John Beatty expressed similar sentiments after observing a mule missing a leg remain standing for several days on the same spot where first wounded "patiently suffering, it knew not why nor for what."[38]

During roughly the war's first two years, Union forces followed a policy that if an animal broke down on the march, it was either abandoned or swapped for local stock, with redemptive receipts given. Many of these "US" branded animals later reappeared in rebel ranks, however, and by 1863, Union soldiers began to confiscate southern horses whether they were needed. Such a "hard war" policy was strongly advocated by Quartermaster General Meigs, who judged horses and mules "as much contraband of war as a barrel of gunpowder" and opined that rebels should never be "allowed to capture ours alive"; any Federal unit surrendering to the enemy should kill its animals first.[39]

Nothing so epitomized the war's growing waste and destruction as the killing of broken-down horses as a matter of official military policy. Charles Adams noted what was common from mid-1863 onward: "The air of Virginia is literally burdened today with the stench of dead horses, federal and confederate. You pass them on every road and find them in every field, while from their carrions you can follow the march of every army that moves." Animals that became exhausted or lame, needing only a few days rest and proper feed to be perfectly serviceable, were now to be shot to deny them to the enemy. "So terrible," wrote Surgeon

Elias Beck, "to see every time a poor horse would give out by sheer exhaustion—out with a pistol & shoot him—break up the saddle & walk on."[40]

Confederate armies could not implement such a drastic policy, as they operated almost exclusively on home territory and every animal, whether exhausted, sick, or diseased, was a possible resource. Yet when attacking Union supply trains, they too eventually decided that if captured teams could not be taken south, then they should be killed. Just one raid in October 1863 left 1,500 dead Federal mules lining the road of the Sequatchie Valley outside Chattanooga. Less than a year later, Union forces responded in kind at Fayetteville, Georgia, slaughtering 1,600 Confederate mules by running them through with sabers, as ammunition could not be spared. In a similarly gruesome event, Union cavalry near Ogeechee Shoals was forced to knock 400 horses in the head with axes to deny them to pursuing rebels.[41]

Just like any other valuable piece of military equipment, both sides recognized the benefits of rehabilitating and returning to service broken-down or sick horses and mules. If they were irretrievably injured or too severely diseased, then their disposal was also an issue to grapple with. At war's outset neither army had any formal system to care for sick or wounded animals, which stemmed, in part, from the antebellum Congress repeatedly refusing to establish a professional veterinary service, leaving the US Army "the only one in the civilized world without educated veterinarians."[42]

Pleas for veterinary hospitals were sent to the White House early in the conflict, but improvements in animal medical care were slow in coming. Although the Washington quartermaster depot was expanded to include a hospital stable accommodating 4,000 head, it still was not enough. In one sixteen-week period in late 1862, the Army of the Potomac alone turned in over 11,800 unserviceable horses, of which 24 percent either died or had to be shot to prevent contagion. Such rates of destruction did not escape notice, and newspapers increasingly demanded action, noting that "when a horse breaks down . . . little or no effort—certainly no organized effort—is made to bring him into serviceable condition. . . . It is high time that somebody should do something for them."[43]

Quartermaster General Meigs, to whom all veterinary-related inquiries were forwarded, recognized the importance of veterinarians, but no law permitted their military appointment; they could only serve as civilian employees for limited remuneration. Denial of commissioned-officer status coupled with low wages effectively kept the small pool of trained American veterinarians out of the Union army. In March 1863 Congress allowed one veterinary surgeon per cavalry regiment at the rank of sergeant-major, paid $75 per month, but the act changed little and did not extend to the artillery or to the wagon trains. Lack of skilled veterinarians forced many men to look after their horses themselves with home remedies, some officers resorting to keeping in their tents books such as Edward Mayhew's *The Illustrated Horse Doctor* in order to diagnose their unit's horse-health problems.[44]

In July 1863 the US Cavalry Bureau was formed to specifically attend to the needs of the mounted service, the only branch-specific agency created during the war. Under the bureau's auspices, a series of cavalry-remount depots were built, with the largest erected at Giesboro Point across the Anacostia River from Washington. Costing $1,225,000 to construct, Giesboro burgeoned into a massive complex, covering 625 acres with stables, forage houses, storehouses, blacksmith shops, barracks, mess halls, and stockyards able to hold 30,000 animals. A similar facility, with auxiliary outlet establishments in Missouri and Illinois, was built in Saint Louis to address the needs of western armies. In one year over 45,000 horses passed through the Missouri establishment alone, and Meigs estimated 50 percent of all broken-down horses that reached either major depot were eventually returned to military service.[45]

Lack of men, money, and material meant that the Confederacy dealt with its unserviceable animals in a far more haphazard and decentralized manner. Moreover, the shortage of veterinarians was even more pronounced in southern ranks, despite warnings from army leaders that unless "the best veterinary skill be secured as soon as possible," Confederate forces "may suffer incalculable mischief." It was usually left up to brigade or regimental commanders to establish remount camps where animals might be sent to recuperate. Rebel cavalrymen were also given "horse furloughs" to seek fresh animals or to take ailing ones home. Eventually, the Confederate quartermaster established several hinterland "horse infirmaries," one in Lynchburg, Virginia, and another near Oconee, Georgia.[46] Located in Laurens County on several hundred acres of pastureland, the Oconee infirmary began operation in the summer of 1863. Similar to the Lynchburg depot, it accommodated nearly 3,000 head and was operated by enslaved labor and a selection of invalid Confederate soldiers, though supervised by only two veterinarians.[47]

Each army wrestled with what to do with animals killed on the battlefield or euthanized behind the lines. Much depended on where the combat took place. In more populated locales like Gettysburg, horse and mule carcasses were buried or burned, whereas in more remote areas such as Chickamauga, they were largely left to rot. Animals that died in army corrals or were shot to prevent contagion presented a different challenge. Easy remedies, such as dumping carcasses in the Potomac or the Mississippi Rivers in hopes of their drifting out to sea, failed as the corpses quickly bloated, floated, and gravitated toward the riverbanks, thereby spreading pollution, stench, and maggots.[48]

Outside Washington, a forty-man animal-burial crew was kept busy near the Arlington and Ball's Crossroads corrals, but the mounting expenses concerned quartermaster officials. The hit- upon solution was to sell off to interested private concerns both the animal carcasses and the manure generated within the corrals. While an unpleasant business, the profits were not insignificant. A $2 per carcass investment, when skinned and rendered into hide, tallow, bones, hooves, and tail, could realize a $6 return. The dead-horse contracts of 1864 were predicted to yield an amazing $100,000 in profits. Even in death, horses and mules continued to serve the nation and the economy.[49]

The war's end in the spring of 1865 and the demobilizing of Union and Confederate armies raised additional horse and mule questions. As southern forces melted away, men took with them the best animals, leaving behind only the worst beasts as rebel government property. Lee's surrender caused the New York horse market to drop by 25 percent, with prices sagging all though the summer as the army rushed to sell off 207,000 horses and mules at public auction. Suggestions that horses be sold at reduced prices to discharged veterans or on credit to southern farmers were rejected as unnecessary since prices averaged $94 per head for mules, while horses (depending on location of sale) ranged from $26 to $97, with bids gradually ticking upward after August 1865.[50]

But the war's conclusion and the sale of excess stock did not end the US government's horse problems. Questions remained regarding army animals that had been captured by the rebels or abandoned by Union columns. Initially, the army attempted to reclaim "all animals which have once belonged to the United States branded U.S.," whether captured and sold by the enemy, unless they bore the mark "IC" or "S" under the mane. Lieutenant General Ulysses S. Grant's surrender terms allowing Lee's men to keep the animals claimed as private property further muddied the waters, preventing the army from fully implementing a sweeping reclamation policy. Yet ripples from the surrender of rebel armies would linger, as both Union soldiers and southern civilians for decades sought compensation for animals lost or confiscated during the war, reaching even into the twentieth century.[51]

The Civil War clearly impacted the nation's horse and mule populations in both numbers and distribution. Many northeastern states possessed fewer horses in 1865 than in 1860, but the percentage of loss was moderate, with New York, Pennsylvania, and Ohio the most significantly affected. Meanwhile, northwestern states like Iowa, Minnesota, and Wisconsin all gained in numbers due to expansion of settlement, farm mechanization, and city growth. Overall national mule stock declined by 20,000 head, with losses in Kentucky and Missouri the most evident. The 1870 census clearly reflected southern war devastation; all former Confederate states except Texas remained far below their antebellum horse populations, with Virginia mustering a little over half of its prewar numbers. Five years after Appomattox, the South had 254,208 fewer horses than in 1860, while the North had gained 1,205,422.[52]

The contribution of horses and mules to the Civil War may have been best summed up by Union officer Frank A. Haskell, who lavishly praised his mount Dick for enabling him "to do twice times as much as I could have done on foot" at Gettysburg and well deserved a horse monument. Certainly the war could not have been fought and won without them. Other old soldiers also paid tribute, remembering how quickly horses learned the bugle calls and how readily riderless horses resumed their places in line or column after a battle when the recall sounded, not wishing to be left behind. Marshall Thatcher recalled shedding "manly tears" when forced to abandon his dying horse by the roadside, thinking he had "died for his country," even while others of his equine species were doing the same thing "perhaps alone, but more probably upon the battlefield, with thousands of human beings to mingle their blood with his."[53] The memory of those human deaths and the invention of the internal-combustion engine likely explain why horse and mule participation in the war has largely been obscured or taken for granted. It is a significant gap in Civil War history that is long overdue to be filled.

## NOTES

1. John Beatty, *Memoirs of a Volunteer, 1861–1863,* ed. Harvey S. Ford (New York: Norton, 1946), 267.

2. "The Cavalry Horse," *Wilkes' Spirit of the Times,* December 28, 1861, 266; "The Noble Horse," *Daily Richmond Examiner,* June 18, 1864, 1; "Inspection of Army Horses,"

in *The Rebellion Record: A Diary of American Events,* ed. Frank Moore, vol. 6 (New York: D. Van Nostrand, 1866), 275–76; "Henry Bergh," *Daily State Journal* (Richmond), March 13, 1872, 1; "Society for the Prevention of Cruelty to Animals," *New York Herald,* February 12, 1866, 2; Still to Lincoln, October 1863, Entry (hereafter E) 225, Record Group (hereafter RG) 92, National Archives and Records Administration, Washington, DC (hereafter NARA).

3. "World Horse Population," *Southern Cultivator,* March 18, 1860, 104.

4. Philip M. Cole, *Civil War Artillery at Gettysburg* (Cambridge, MA: Da Capo, 2002), 110; Meigs to Stanton, November 3, 1864, *The War of the Rebellion: A Compilation of the Official Records of the Union and Confederate Armies,* 70 vols. in 128 parts (Washington, DC: Government Printing Office, 1880–1901), ser. 3, 4:880, 888–90 (hereafter *OR*); Department of the Interior, *Eighth Census of the United States* (Washington, DC: Government Printing Office, 1864), cix–cxi; "The Army Consumption of Horses," *National Intelligencer* (Washington, DC), December 19, 1864, 2.

5. Ekin to Meigs, January 31, 1866, E1261, RG 92, NARA; Ekin to Meigs, February 1, 1866, ibid.; Benjamin W. Crowninshield, *A History of the First Regiment of Massachusetts Cavalry Volunteers* (New York: Houghton, Mifflin, 1891), 6; "The Southern Cavalry," *Army and Navy Journal,* November 21, 1863, 196; Historical Committee, *History of the Ninth Regiment Illinois Cavalry Volunteers* (Chicago: Donohue & Henneberry, 1888), 365–66; S. H. Hastings, "The Cavalry Service and Recollections of the Late War," *Magazine of Western History* 11 (1890): 260; F. Colburn Adams, *The Story of a Trooper* (New York: Dick & Fitzgerald, 1865), 30.

6. Anonymous to Cameron, [September 1861], E301, RG 92, NARA; Drake to Cameron, September 3, 1861, ibid.; Shannon to Cameron, September 12, 1861, ibid.; Cong. Globe, 37th Cong., 2nd Sess., 298 (January 13, 1862); "The Army Horse," *Philadelphia Inquirer,* January 2, 1863, 2; "Army Horse Depot, at Washington," *Frank Leslie's Illustrated Newspaper,* February 1, 1862, 167.

7. Confederate War Department, *A Digest of the Military and Naval Laws of the C.S.A.,* (Columbia, SC: Evans and Cogswell, 1864), 45; Seddon to Davis, November 3, 1864, *OR,* ser. 4, 3:763; "An act to promote the efficiency of the cavalry," June 7, 1864, ibid., 499; Fitzgerald Ross, *Cities and Camps of the Confederate States,* ed. Richard B. Harwell (Urbana: University of Illinois Press, 1958), 81; "Proceedings of the Second Confederate Congress," *Southern Historical Society Papers* 52 (January 1865): 77, 23334.

8. Regimental Association, *History of the First Regiment Pennsylvania Reserve Cavalry* (Philadelphia: King & Baird, Printers, 1864), 11; J. H. Kidd, *Personal Recollections of a Cavalryman with Custer's Michigan Cavalry Brigade in the Civil War* (Ionia, MI: Sentinel, 1908), 48; Harvey Riley, *The Mule: A Treatise on the Breeding, Training, and Uses to Which He May Be Put* (Philadelphia: Clanton, Remsen, & Haffelfinger, 1869), 70–71; Meigs to Rosecrans, April 24, 1863, *OR,* ser. 1, 23(2):272–73; Wilson to Baker, February 24, 1864, E69, RG 108, NARA; Wilson to Meigs, March 6, 1864, ibid.; "Swindling the Government," *National Intelligencer* (Washington, DC), October 29, 1863, 3; Wilson to Ekin, September 7, 1864, E1270, RG 92, NARA; Circular, February 5, 1864, ibid.; Court-Martial of John Spicer (MM-1426), May 5, 1864, E15A, RG 153, ibid.; Holt to Lincoln (NN-1720), June 30, 1864, ibid.

9. Pendleton to Lee, February 17, 1864, *OR*, ser. 1, 33:1183–84; "Pressing Horses for Lee's Army," *New York Herald*, August 6, 1863, 2; General Orders No. 41, April 6, 1864, *OR*, ser. 4, 3:55–56, 273–74; Lee to Randolph, November 10, 1862, *OR*, ser. 1, 19(2):703; Lee to Stuart, November 7, 1862, ibid., 709; Randolph to Lee, November 14, 1862, ibid., 716; Douglas Southall Freeman, ed., *Lee's Dispatches: Unpublished Letters of General Robert E. Lee, C.S.A., to Jefferson Davis and the War Department of the Confederate States of America, 1862–1865* (New York: G. P. Putnam's Sons, 1915), 274–75; "Raiding," *Daily Richmond Examiner*, January 8, 1864, 2; Cole to Lawton, February 1, 1865, *OR*, ser. 1, 46(2):1190; Cole to Corley, February 20, 1865, *ibid.*, 1242.

10. Ekin to Meigs, January 31, February 1, 1866, E1261, RG 92, NARA; Meigs to Ekin, August 7, 1865, E225, ibid.; Williams to Cameron, September 5, 1861, E301, ibid.; Tucker to Bates, September 9, 1861, ibid.; Bain to Cameron, September 13, 1861, ibid.; "Miscellaneous," *Vermont Chronicle* (Bellows Falls), January 9, 1864, 6; "The Horse Market," *National Intelligencer* (Washington, DC), April 12, 1865, 3; "Muster Roll of John P. Brock, 1861," Special Collections, Virginia Tech University, Blacksburg; "Muster Roll of Horse and Equipments," E62, RG 109, NARA; Ekin to Meigs, October 17, 1865, *OR*, ser. 3, 5:256.

11. William H. Dean, "Conditioning Horses," *Cavalry Journal* 40 (January–April 1931): 11; "Proposals for Horses and Mules," *Washington (DC) Evening Star*, March 24, 1865, 4; *Instruction for Field Artillery*, 46, UD45, RG 156, NARA.

12. Circular, September 1864, E225, RG 92, NARA; Meigs to Ekin and Rucker to Meigs, April 23–24, 1863, E9, vol. 68, ibid.; Second Massachusetts Cavalry, Orders and Letters Books, E112, RG 94, ibid.; "Management of Horses," *Country Gentleman*, January 31, 1861, 77; "Cavalry Horses," *Wilkes' Spirit of the Times*, July 13, 1861; "Cavalry," *National Intelligencer* (Washington, DC), December 19, 1863, 3; "Things in General," *New Hampshire Statesman* (Concord), November 2, 1861, 2; "Proposals for Horses and Mules," *Washington (DC) Evening Star*, March 24, 1865, 4; "Horses in the United States as Connected with the War," *Prairie Farmer*, November 19, 1864, 323; Gerald E. Griffin, "Conformation of the Horse," *Journal of the United States Cavalry Association* 23 (September 1912): 20717; Kidd, *Personal Recollections of a Cavalryman*, 48; Regimental History Committee, *History of the Third Pennsylvania*, 22; Ralph Hass, *Dear Esther: The Civil War Letters of Private Aungier Dobbs*, ed. Philip Ensley (Apollo, PA: Closson, 1991), 4.

13. "The Noble Horse," *Daily Richmond Examiner*, June 18, 1864, 1; US House, , *Report of the Commissioner of Agriculture*, 38th Cong., 1st sess., 186364, H. Exec. Doc. 91, 183; "Mules vs Horses," *Country Gentleman*, May 18,1865, 316; Crosby to Meigs, September 2, 1861, E225, RG 92, NARA; George B. Ellenberg, *Mule South to Tractor South: Mules, Machines, and the Transformation of the Cotton South* (Tuscaloosa: University of Alabama Press, 2007), 12.

14. "Horses and Means of Transportation," *Daily Morning News* (Savannah, GA), February 21, 1862, 1; "Our Army Horses," *New York Herald*, June 2, 1863, 2; "Speech of Gen. Wallace," *Daily Evansville (IN) Journal*, August 14, 1862, 2; Contract of Dale and Criswell, June 10, 1861, E225, RG 92, NARA; General Order No. 19, September 29, 1863, E195, ibid.; General Order No. 43, September 23, 1864, E9, vol. 80, ibid.; Kautz to Lowell,

March 16, 1864, E69, RG 108, NARA; Van Vliet to Meigs, April 28, 1862, *OR*, ser. 1, 11(1):161; Meigs to Halleck, January 20, 1863, ibid., 21:983–84; Riley, *The Mule*, 23.

15. "The Government Horse Corral," *Boston Daily Advertiser*, October 22, 1862, 2; "All the Horses in the Army of the Potomac," *Boston Daily Advertiser*, September 7, 1863, 1; "The Supplies and General Arrangements," *New York Herald*, October 29, 1861, 3; "About Army Mules," *American Stock Journal*, November 1861, 322–23; John D. Billings, *Hardtack and Coffee* (1887; reprint, ed. Richard Harwell, Chicago: R. R. Donnelley & Sons, 1960), 311–17; Riley, *The Mule*, 4, 8–9, 13, 19; John D. Imboden, "Incidents of the First Bull Run," in *Battles and Leaders of the Civil War*, ed. Robert U. Johnson and Clarence C. Buel, 4 vols. (New York: Century, 1887), 1:238.

16. Historical Committee, *History of the Ninth Regiment Illinois Cavalry*, 365–66.

17. Meigs to Halleck, October 21, 1862, *OR*, ser. 1, 19(1):19; Hastings, "Cavalry Service," 260; "Misrepresentations Exposed," *North American and United States Gazette* (Philadelphia), January 28, 1862, 1; "Army Horses," *Prairie Farmer*, January 2, 1864, 5; Confederate General Order No. 57, August 14, 1862, *OR*, ser. 4, 2:51; Confederate War Department, *Regulations for the Army of the Confederate States Quartermaster Department* (Richmond: Ritchie & Dunnavant, 1862), 147–48; Eleanor D. McSwain, ed., *Crumbling Defenses or Reminiscences of John Logan Black* (Macon, GA: privately published, 1960), 72.

18. Marshall P. Thatcher, *A Hundred Battles in the West, St. Louis to Atlanta, 1861–65* (Detroit: privately published, 1884), 71; W. R. Carter, *History of the First Regiment of Tennessee Volunteer Cavalry in the Great War of the Rebellion* (Knoxville: Gaut-Ogden, 1902), 63.

19. War Department, *U.S. Army Regulations of 1861*, 123; "Shipping Horses," *Harper's Weekly*, November 2, 1861, 696–97; "Army Horses," *Lowell (MA) Daily Citizen*, January 24, 1862, 2; "The Indifferent State of the Cavalry," *North American and United States Gazette* (Philadelphia), February 11, 1862, 1.

20. Pemberton to Cooper, August 25, 1863, *OR*, ser. 1, 24(1):275; "Sunday Night's Dispatches," *Wisconsin State Journal* (Madison), June 1, 1863, 1; "Horses in the Cumberland Army," *Daily Evening Bulletin* (San Francisco), November 27, 1863, 1; Joseph F. Fullerton, "The Army of the Cumberland at Chattanooga," in Johnson and Buel, *Battles and Leaders*, 3:719–26.

21. General Order No. 42, November 5, 1863, *OR*, ser. 1, 29(2):423; Special Order No. 44, June 28, 1864, ibid., 40(1):41–42; *Regulations for the Army of the Confederate States* (Richmond: J. W. Randolph, 1863), 116; "The Horses of the War," *Wilkes' Spirit of the Times*, October 19, 1861, 101; "Proposals for Forage," *Washington (DC) Evening Star*, March 24, 1865, 4; James L. Paxton Requisition, November 1864, RG 109, NARA, M347, microfilm.

22. "Agriculture of the United States in 1860," Dept. of the Interior, *Eighth Census*, lxiv–lxvi, xlviii–xlix, 186; "Low Price of Southern Lands," *Southern Cultivator*, November 1859, 350; "Grasses in the South," ibid., July 1860, 215; Meigs to Stanton, November 3, 1864, *OR*, ser. 3, 4:880, 888–90; "Army Correspondence," *Savannah Republican*, June 18, 1863, 4; "Interesting Statement," *Natchez Courier*, 1; Lee to Longstreet, July 19, 1863, *OR*, ser. 1, 27(3):1025; Freeman, *Lee's Dispatches*, 246–47; William N. McDonald and Bushrod C.

Washington, eds. *A History of the Laurel Brigade* (N.p.: privately published, 1907), 331; William H. Runge, ed., *Four Years in the Confederate Artillery: The Diary of Private Henry Robinson Berkeley* (Chapel Hill: University of North Carolina Press, 1961), 116.

23. George Libaire, ed., *With Napoleon in Russia: The Memoirs of General Armand de Caulaincourt* (New York: William Morrow, 1935), 161, 212, 236; Charles D. Rhodes, "The Federal Cavalry, Its Organization and Equipment," in *The Photographic History of the Civil War*, 10 vols. (New York: Review of Reviews, 1911), 4:59; Clarence Lininger, "Care of Horses in the Field," *Cavalry Journal* 37 (April 1928): 230; Confederate War Department, *The Quartermaster's Guide* (Richmond: West & Johnson, 1862), 1089; C. Worthington Ford, ed., *A Cycle of Adams Letters, 18611865*, 2 vols. (Boston: Houghton Mifflin, 1920), 2:4; Imboden, "Incidents of the First Bull Run," 238.

24. "Causes of the Abandonment of the Late Projected Movement," *Weekly Perrysburg (OH) Journal*, February 4, 1863, 1; "The Mud Embargo," *National Intelligencer* (Washington, DC), February 26, 1863, 4; "Northern Dates," *Abingdon Virginian*, February 6, 1863, 1.

25. First Vermont Cavalry Orders and Letters Books, 1861–65, E112, RG 94, NARA; War Department, *Field Artillery Tactics*, 94; George B. McClellan, *Regulations and Instructions for the Field Service of the U. S. Cavalry in Time of War* (Philadelphia: J. B. Lippincott, 1861), 153; Ford, *Cycle of Adams Letters*, 1:206; "Regular and Volunteer Officers," *Atlantic Monthly* (September 1864): 349.

26. "Impressions of a Visit to the Army of the Potomac," *Vermont Chronicle* (Bellows Falls), April 2, 1864, 2; Ford, *Cycle of Adams Letters*, 2:3–5.

27. *Instruction for Field Artillery*, 48–49, UD45, RG 156, NARA; Sidney M. Davis, *Common Soldier Uncommon War: Life as a Cavalryman in the Civil War*, ed. Charles F. Cooney (Baltimore: Port City, 1994), 51; James K. Ewer, *The Third Massachusetts Cavalry in the War for the Union* (Maplewood, MA: Wm. G. J. Perry Press, 1903), 79; Riley, *The Mule*, 45; Willard Glazier, *Three Years with the Federal Cavalry* (New York: R. H. Ferguson, 1872), 35–36.

28. Crowninshield, *History of the First Regiment of Massachusetts Cavalry*, 292; Third New York Cavalry Orders and Letter Books, 1861–65, RG 94, NARA.

29. Stanton P. Allen, *Down in Dixie: Life in a Cavalry Regiment in the War Days* (Boston: D. Lothrop, 1893), 249; McClellan, *Regulations and Instructions*, 59; Charles H. Kirk, ed., *History of the Fifteenth Pennsylvania Volunteer Cavalry* (Philadelphia: n.p., 1906), 444; Isaac Gause, *Four Years with Five Armies* (New York: Neale, 1908), 383; N. D. Preston, *History of the Tenth Regiment of Cavalry New York State Volunteers* (New York: D. Appleton, 1892), 63; Edward P. Tobie, *History of the First Maine Cavalry, 18611865* (Boston: First Maine Cavalry Association, 1887), 114; Davis, *Common Soldier Uncommon War*, 178, 207, 236, 303.

30. Davis, *Common Soldier Uncommon War*, 55, 179, 410; James H. Stevenson, *Boots and Saddles: A History of the First Volunteer Cavalry Known as the First New York (Lincoln) Cavalry* (Harrisburg, PA: Patriot, 1879). 143; W. W. Blackford, *War Years with Jeb Stuart* (New York: Charles Scribner's Sons, 1946), 22–23; William E. Meyer, *The Sailor on Horseback: Personal Narratives of Events in the War of the Rebellion* (Providence: Rhode Island Soldiers

and Sailors Historical Society, 1912), 34, 38; William Douglas Hamilton, *Recollections of a Cavalryman after Fifty Years, 1861–1865* (Columbus, OH: F. J. Heer Printing, 1915), 62.

31. Circular No. 44, June 9, 1864, 10–11, E1270, RG 92, NARA; Garrard to Kelton, January 22, 1864, E69, RG 108, ibid.; Davis, *Common Soldier Uncommon War*, 98; Dean, "Conditioning Horses," 10–11; John A. B. D. Williams, *Leaves from a Trooper's Diary* (Philadelphia: privately published, 1869), 2324; Allen, *Down in Dixie*, 94–95.

32. Second Massachusetts Cavalry, Special Order, May 14, 1863, E112, RG 94, NARA; Ford, *Cycle of Adams Letters*, 2:3; Henry R. Pyne, *Ride to War: The History of the First New Jersey Cavalry*, ed. Earl Schenck Miers (New Brunswick, NJ: Rutgers University Press, 1961), 26; Gause, *Four Years with Five Armies*, 164–65.

33. *Instruction for Field Artillery*, 47–48, UD45, RG 156, NARA; General Order No. 115, October 1, 1862, *OR*, ser. 1, 19(2):446–47; General Order No. 164, ibid., 643–44; Sibley to Stoneman, October 8, 1862, E9, vol. 63, RG 92, NARA; Thomas T. Munford, "Reminiscences of Cavalry Operations," *Southern Historical Society Papers* 12 (January–December 1884): 346; Robert J. Trout, ed., *Memoirs of the Stuart Horse Artillery Battalion*, vol. 2 (Knoxville: University of Tennessee Press, 2010), 91.

34. Gause, *Four Years with Five Armies*, 383–84; Glazier, *Three Years in the Saddle*, 338; Robert W. Frost and Nancy D. Frost, eds., *Picket Pins and Sabers: The Civil War Letters of John Burden Weston* (Ashland, KY: privately published, 1971), 49.

35. Billings, *Hardtack and Coffee*, 366; Gause, *Four Years with Five Armies*, 384.

36. Susan P. Lee, *Memoirs of William Nelson Pendleton* (1893; reprint, Harrisonburg, VA: Sprinkle, 1991), 146; J. Albert Monroe, "Battery D, First Rhode Island Light Artillery at the Battle of Antietam," *Personal Narratives of Events in the War of the Rebellion*, 3rd ser. (Providence: Soldiers and Sailors Historical Society of Rhode Island, 1886), 23, 25.

37. Rhodes, "Cavalry Battles and Charges," in *Photographic History of the Civil War*, 4:257; The Survivors' Association, *History of the 118th Pennsylvania Volunteers* (Philadelphia: J. L. Smith, 1905), 189; Blackford, *War Years with Jeb Stuart*, 150; "The Battle-field at Murfreesboro," *Waynesboro (PA) Village Record*, April 10, 1863, 1.

38. Fannie A. Beers, *Memories: A Record of Personal Experience and Adventure during Four Years of War* (Philadelphia: J. B. Lippincott, 1888.), 153; Beatty, *Memoirs of a Volunteer*, 160, 267; "The Battlefield of Chickamauga," *Atlanta Daily Intelligencer*, October 6, 1863, 1.

39. "Rosecrans Seizing Horses," *Milwaukee Daily Sentinel*. May 14, 1863, 2; Meigs to Rosecrans. May 18, 1863, E9, vol. 68, RG 92, NARA; Meigs to Hooker, May 29, 1863, *OR*, ser. 1, 25(2):544; Court of Inquiry, August 17, 1863, ibid., 27(2):93.

40. Ford, *Cycle of Adams Letters*, 2:3–5; "Arrivals from the North," *Daily Richmond Examiner*, June 17, 1864, 2; Sawtelle to Meigs, May 26, 1863, *OR*, ser. 1, 25(1):1069; Stephen Z. Starr, ed., "The Wilson Raid, June, 1864: A Trooper's Reminiscences," *Civil War History* 21 (1975): 223–24; Elias H. Beck, "Letters of a Civil War Surgeon," *Indiana Magazine of History* 27 (March 1931), 134.

41. Meigs to Stanton, November 3, 1864, *OR*, ser. 3, 4:888–90; Root to McCook, August 5, 1864, ibid., ser. 1, 38(2):776, 786; "Wheeler's Raid," *Fayetteville (TN) Observer*, October 29, 1863, 1; Reunion Committee, *Ninety-Second Illinois Volunteers* (Freeport, IL: Journal Steam Publishing House, 1875), 181–82; David Evans, *Sherman's Horsemen: Union

*Cavalry Operations in the Atlanta Campaign* (Bloomington: Indiana University Press, 1996), 228–29.

42. Bustead to Stanton, December 16, 1863, E74, RG 108, NARA; "Offices and Duties of Veterinary Surgeons," *Prairie Farmer*, March 12, 1864, 169–70; "The Importance of Veterinary Education," *Prairie Farmer*, July 9, 1864, 22; Louis A. Merillat and Delwin Campbell, *Veterinary Military History of the United States*, vol. 1 (Kansas City, MO: Haver-Glover Laboratories, 1935), 75.

43. Rucker to Meigs, December 22, 1862, E9, vol. 65, RG 92, NARA; Rucker to Meigs, September 29, 1863, E225, ibid.; "The Quartermaster's Depot," *National Intelligencer* (Washington, DC), July 7, 1864, 3; Stoneman to Marcy, September 17, 1861, E1469, RG 393, NARA; Collins to Lincoln, September 9, 1861, E301, RG 92, ibid.; "Loss of Army Horses," *American Stock Journal*, January 1862, 27; "Loss of Horses," *Evening News* (Gold Hill, Nebraska Territory), December 21, 1863, 2; "Destruction of Horses during the War," *Vermont Transcript* (St. Albans), September 30, 1864, 1.

44. Bustead to Cameron, August 30, 1861, E301, RG 92; Bustead to Lincoln, December 23, 1861, ibid.; "Army Horses," *Prairie Farmer*, January 2, 1864, 6; General Order No. 73, March 24, 1863, *OR*, ser. 3, 3:93; Thomas M. O'Brien and Oliver Diefendorf, eds., *General Orders of the War Department 1861, 1862, 1863*, vol. 1 (New York: Derby & Miller, 1864), 32728; Baker to Bixby, [1863], *The Illustrated Horse Doctor*, National Sporting Library and Museum, Middleburg, VA.

45. "Giesborough Camp," *National Intelligencer* (Washington, DC), August 26, 1863, 3; "The Cavalry Bureau," *Army and Navy Journal*, August 29, 1863, 3; General Order No. 236, July 28, 1863, *OR*, ser. 3, 3:580–81; Stoneman to Kelton, October 30, 1863, ibid., ser. 1, 29(2):399; Sawtelle to Ekin, February 25, 1865, E225, RG 92; Thomas to Stanton, September 22, 1863, ibid.; Browning to Ekin, March 23, 1865, ibid.; Stoneman to Stanton, December 23, 1863, E69, RG 108, ibid.; DuPuy to Ekin, January 25, 1864, E1270, RG 92, ibid.; Rhodes, "Mounting and Remounting of the Federal Cavalry," in *Photographic History of the Civil War*, 4:328; John Thomas Scharf, *History of Saint Louis City and County from the Earliest Periods to the Present Day*, vol. 1 (Philadelphia: Louis W. Everts, 1883), 444–46; "A Model Establishment," *Wilkes' Spirit of the Times*, November 5, 1864, 152–53.

46. Munford to Lee, July 18, 1864, E68, RG 109, ibid.; Runge, *Four Years in the Confederate Artillery*, 116; Pendleton to Lee, February 11, 1863, *OR*, ser. 1, 25(2):619; Pendleton to Cole, February 18, 1864, ibid., 33:1189–90; "Glanders and Farcy in Horses," *Special Reports of the Department of Agriculture for 1879 and 1880* (Washington, DC: Government Printing Office, 1881), 205–8.

47. "The Horse Infirmary in Georgia," *Richmond Times Dispatch*, February 3, 1864, 1; Pendleton to Lee, February 17, 1864, *OR*, ser. 1, 33:1183–84; Pendleton to Cole, February 18, 1864, ibid., 1189–90; G. Terry Sharrer, "The Great Glanders Epizootic, 1861–1866: A Civil War Legacy," *Agricultural History* 69 (Winter 1995): 79–97.

48. Smith to Loughborough, July 10, 1863, *OR*, ser. 1, 24(2):393–94.

49. Hale to Ekin, January 30, 1864, E1270, RG 92, NARA; DuPuy to Office Depot Quartermaster, February 8, 1864, ibid.; Ekin to Rucker, July 4, 1865, E1261, ibid.; Meigs to Rucker, April 7, 1863, E9, vol. 67, ibid.; "Military Affairs," *Boston Daily Advertiser*,

October 12, 1864, 1; "What Becomes of Dead Horses," *Milwaukee Daily Sentinel,* January 15, 1864, 2; "The Value of Dead Horses," *Pittsburgh Presbyterian Banner,* March 23, 1864, 4; "The Contract for Dead Horses," *Milwaukee Daily Sentinel,* June 22, 1864, 2.

50. Consolidated Report of Cavalry, March 1865, E74, RG 108, NARA; Sales of Horses and Mules, 1865–67, E1286, RG 92, ibid.; Brightbill to Meigs, October 12, 1865, E1270, ibid.; Stanton to Johnson, November 14, 1866, *OR,* ser. 3, 5:1032; "Supplement," *National Intelligencer* (Washington, DC), May 29, 1865, 5; "Questions of Finance," *Milwaukee Daily Sentinel,* May 15, 1865, 2.

51. Meigs to Thomas, August 29, 1865, E9, vol. 86, RG 92, NARA; General Orders No. 61, October 10, 1865, E225, ibid.; Helper to Colfax, December 14, 1865, ibid.; Ekin to Meigs, June 12, 1865, E1261, ibid.; Ekin to Meigs, October 6, 1865, ibid.; Harris to Ludington, November 4, 1902, January 4, 1904, E862, ibid.; "Frank Furness," E496, RG 94, NARA.

52. "Bureau of Agriculture," *American Rail Road Journal,* May 21, 1864, 489; ibid., May 20, 1865, 469; Dept. of the Interior, *Ninth Census of the United States* (Washington, DC: Government Printing Office, 1872), 75.

53. Frank Aretas Haskell, *The Battle of Gettysburg* (N.p.: Wisconsin History Commission, 1910), 161–62; John M. Stayan, *A History of the Eight Regiment of New Hampshire Volunteers* (Concord, NH: Ira C. Evans, 1892), 361–62; Billings, *Hardtack and Coffee,* 363, 367; Thatcher, *A Hundred Battles in the West,* 369.

# The Artillery Horse as Warrior

EARL J. HESS

OF THE APPROXIMATELY 3 million equines used by the Union and Confederate armies in the Civil War, at least 261,672 were artillery horses.[1] The weight of the artillery piece and the certainty that these horses would come under fire meant they had to be carefully selected for their physical attributes and trained to endure the sounds of combat. They also had to work within a team of six horses, which was guided by three drivers, to maneuver the heavy gun over rugged terrain and often around the bodies of men and other horses littering the ground. Artillery horses used a specially designed harness because the mechanics of pulling the gun were quite different from pulling a wagon or carriage.

Artillery horses were animal warriors, although within the context of human experience, we have to admit they were draftees rather than volunteers. Most of them responded reasonably well to their specialized training and outfitting, becoming reliable warriors for the most part. Some artillery horses, however, never accepted their unrequested role as warriors and fought back against their drivers, who had the responsibility of feeding and caring for them as well as training them. The war service of artillery horses was a never-ending story of human-animal interaction from start to finish. It involved tragedy, too, as thousands of horses were killed or injured in combat, and many thousands more died of rampant equine diseases. But the story also is one of caring, even love, between some drivers and their horses. Equines were quite capable of forming bonds with at least some of their human counterparts, while experiencing nothing but neglect or cruel treatment from others. To a limited degree, artillery horses could exercise agency, but mostly that was by resisting or escaping army service altogether. Of all unsung heroes of the war, artillery horses rank high on the list of ever-present but rarely rewarded soldiers.

Most artillery officers of both armies would have agreed with Capt. Warren P. Edgarton of Battery E, 1st Ohio Light Artillery that horses were "the main dependence of a light battery." To that end the US Army artillery manual urged officers to "make themselves thoroughly acquainted with the natural history of the horse." This would help a great deal in feeding and caring for them, but it is doubtful that most officers took that advice seriously. The manual assured readers that artillery horses had a more difficult job than cavalry mounts and recommended a daily march rate of no more than sixteen miles in ten hours. Because of the weight of the gun, these animals worked with what was termed "quick draught," meaning that they pulled mostly through "the weight thrown into the collar than by muscular exertion." This required a certain standard of development in specified parts of the horse's anatomy. Officers sometimes spent hours selecting the right kind of equines from a lot of horses delivered by quartermasters for army use. Any assigned horses that were understrength were returned and others were acquired that better suited the particular needs of the artillery branch.[2]

Typically, there were nearly as many horses as men assigned to an artillery unit. When the 14th Massachusetts Battery began the Overland Campaign, it contained 120 horses compared to 132 men. But the loss of horses was significantly higher than the loss of personnel (for reasons that will be explained later), necessitating replacement animals. As a result, fewer artillerymen served in the Civil War than artillery horses. At least 208,644 soldiers North and South manned the guns, compared to at least 261,672 horses.[3]

Horses are among the mere dozen or so species that have been domesticated out of around four thousand known species during the past 10,000 years. That process of domestication, which started about 6,000 years ago, has created a tight bond between horses and people that is anything but domination of one species over the other. Both parties acquired something useful or important to them by agreeing to work with each other. Horses are natural bonding animals; they socialize a lot with each other, recognize a pecking order, understand the body language of that order, and respond to self-assurance and authority. They are apt pupils for training because they are sensitive to cues and respond to them readily.[4]

We should not think in terms of extremes when considering the horse-human relationship. It is not dominance by a person over a brute creature, nor does it consist of full independence by the animal. It is instead a working relationship between two sentient beings, a give and take that both have willingly engaged in. The relationship can run the gamut from one extreme to the other but far more often settles into a pattern somewhere in the middle of the spectrum that is comfortable for both horse and human. It has always been this way. Animal agency is often discussed in the literature of animal studies in a controversial manner. The extent to which it exists is the extent to which the relationship between animal and human is flexible enough to allow it at any given moment, but it is very real and needs to be considered within any interspecies relationship. Human agency within that relationship is also limited; there are only so many things a person can coax a horse into doing.[5]

Perhaps the best model for understanding horses in war, whether in the artillery or the cavalry, is the relationship between performance animals and the people who train them, ride them, or perform with them. Studies of racehorses and sea mammals at water theme parks show that intense training regimens produce results, but it is not because humans are compelling ignorant animals to perform by repetitive actions. Whether it is a racehorse or a dolphin, a great deal of intelligence and cooperation is offered by the animal. They learn quickly how to work with the trainer/performer. Within the performance there is room for variation. Racehorses often ignore the signals of their jockeys and run at the speed or pace of their own judgment, likely as not winning the race. Variations within the canned performance of a dolphin at a theme park often take place because the sea mammal wishes to relieve boredom, forcing the human coperformer to adjust his or her own routine. As one of these human participants has pointed out, if the animal is engaged in human-directed performance because they have been trained to do so for their food, then the person is in the same category as the animal. They also are doing this routine to make a living and are as much a cog in the entertainment machine as the horse or the dolphin.[6]

Training for war also involves a great deal of cooperation between animal and human. The cavalryman or artilleryman not only had to teach the horse what to do but also had to fight alongside the animal in battle. The horse was highly capable of learning the tactical formations and maneuvers, remembering the bugle calls, and supporting the rider and other horses in times of stress and danger. Whether it is performance on a racecourse or a battlefield, the similarities are striking.

The horse was highly amenable to careful training. It responded to immediate threats such as unusual noises or sights and therefore had to be acclimated to the experience of combat. Once trained, it was not more likely to run in battle than the average soldier. Horses responded to the voice of their drivers or to bugle calls. Frederick W. Wild of Alexander's Baltimore Battery, a Federal unit, learned through experience not to appear excited while harnessing his horses as the mood communicated easily to the animals. It was always necessary to be calm around them. "I learned to know the horses," Wild recalled. "Every horse had its peculiarities or character. Some were brave, some were cowards, some were nervous and easily frightened, some were exceedingly ambitious, others were indolent and lacked ambition, others were intelligent, some were absolutely ignorant."[7]

Horses capable and willing to perform the tasks of hauling artillery far outnumbered those who refused, but every battery had a handful of reluctant warriors. They balked and kicked repeatedly, disrupting other horses and throwing off the drivers who rode on their backs. Battery commanders sought ways to get rid of them by trading with another unit; sometimes the balky equines eventually weakened and died due to their confinement in artillery service. A couple of horses who "obstinately refused duty" with the 10th Massachusetts Battery "yielded the contest with their lives," wrote John D. Billings, "giving way in a few days to the rigors of a discipline to which they would not submit." It could be dangerous to be around such animals. More than one artilleryman was badly injured and some were killed by kicking horses.[8]

Much depended on the process of training. The artillery manual urged drivers to exercise "patience, kindness, and fearlessness" in dealing with horses. Punishment should be meted out only after an offense, and nothing should be done to the horse in the throes of anger. Drivers were to inspire them "with confidence" and gradually accustom them to the sounds of war. If the horse could stand twenty feet from a roaring piece without budging, a big part of the training had been accomplished. Jacob Roemer, commander of Battery L, 2nd New York Light Artillery, found that it took about two weeks to break the horses to their harness and accustom them to the formations and maneuvers necessary to move artillery.[9]

Most horses passing through the training period became reliable warriors. They could distinguish between different bugle calls and often responded to them accurately without urging by the driver. Artillerists carefully placed steeds within the six-horse team according to their personalities and physical attributes. The two in front were responsible for leading the rest, so agile and smart animals were needed. Heavy, plodding horses were best placed at the rear of the team, where brute strength was needed. Animals willing to go with the flow, or those of average ability, served in the middle. Three drivers, each sitting on the left-side horse of his team, managed his own horse and the one to his right.[10]

Accounts are filled with references to the love many drivers felt toward their animal charges. Lewis Sykes of the 1st Connecticut Battery "treated them as friends and cared for them as faithfully as he would have done for any human being." That loving care paid off in many cases, as horses who reacted badly at first to artillery service became calm and accepting. Stories of men crying when their horses were killed or wounded on the battlefield abound.[11]

Confident handling by the driver helped a great deal to impart confidence in the animal, but the reverse also could be true. One of Jacob Roemer's New York drivers "caught the 'cannon fever' and had lost control of his horses" under fire at Cedar Mountain. The animals refused urgings to move, becoming "totally deaf," as Roemer put it. He had to replace the driver and personally whip the horses before they pulled the piece out of danger.[12]

On many battlefields artillery horses lost their nerve and ran in panic, forgetting their training. They threw drivers, injuring them, or ran through lines of friendly infantrymen, hurting them as well. Horses became "perfectly ungovernable," as Harry Cushing of Battery H, 4th US Artillery wrote of their conduct on the second day at Chickamauga. When heavy fire descended on Fenner's Louisiana Battery during the North Anna phase of the Overland Campaign, the horses were the first to suffer. All the animals at one gun went down, and when three horses of another were shot, the rest "saved themselves by running away."[13]

Like their human comrades, artillery horses were fully capable of failing the test of battle. But for every instance of running from enemy fire, one can find a dozen instances of stoic endurance or actual bravery on the battlefield. Just as with soldiers, the overall performance of artillery horses varied.

Horses paid for their faithfulness, for they were large targets on the battlefield. The Staunton Artillery of Virginia lost thirty-one horses out of seventy-one (43 percent) at First Bull Run. Taking position only 150 yards from the Federal line, Marshall's Tennessee Battery lost forty-nine horses in ten minutes at Chickamauga. Battery E, 1st Rhode Island Light Artillery suffered a loss rate of 47 percent of its animals at Gettysburg, while the 9th Massachusetts Battery lost 77 percent of its horses in the same engagement.[14] These were among the highest loss ratios for artillery horses to be found in the Civil War.

Other batteries suffered a greater loss of horses than of men. Battery A, 1st Illinois Light Artillery lost thirty men and forty-eight horses at Shiloh. In the Confederate army, the 5th Company, Washington Artillery totaled its losses for most of the war, from Shiloh to Missionary Ridge, as eighty-three men and ninety-three horses.[15]

We do not have consolidated numbers of horses lost in battle for the entire war, but a handful of reports coming from command levels higher than the battery are available. The Army of the Cumberland started the Atlanta Campaign with 2,445 artillery horses and received 599 replacements by the time the city fell. But it lost 1,439 artillery horses during the operation, a loss rate of 47 percent over four months of difficult campaigning.[16]

Horses were the biggest living objects on Civil War battlefields, and when they became casualties, it often was very noticeable. Incoming rounds could literally go right through a horse's body, killing it instantly in a spectacle of gore. One shell hit a horse "right between its eyes" and exploded. The burst decapitated the animal and severed the hind legs of another one nearby. The driver who held the reins of the decapitated steed was "covered from his face to his knees with the brains and blood of the horse." On the third day at Gettysburg, a shell tore off the buttock of a horse as its team was making a turn on "a pretty grassy slope." Edward Porter Alexander remembered the event for the rest of his life. "I never saw so much blood fly, or so much grass painted red before," he later wrote.[17]

Battlefield losses produced severe emotional reactions among many artillerymen. Confederate Edward A. Moore of the Rockbridge Artillery saw it all through four years of arduous service. He witnessed some horses, "partially disemboweled, but still on their feet, turning round and round in one spot, till they lay down to die." Other wounded animals still tried to keep up with the team, "tossing the head up and down as they labored to follow on, but all too brave to utter other than a half suppressed groan." Fallen horses in the process of dying could rub a smooth place in the dirt "by the moving to and fro of his head and neck, or where he had thrown out convulsively his legs," noted Confederate Napier Bartlett of the Washington Artillery.[18]

FIG. 3.1. Combat and the Artillery Horse. The tragic price artillery horses had to pay for becoming warriors in the Civil War is vividly illustrated in this image of the effect of battle on teams that pulled artillery carriages and caissons. Many such images were produced during the war, along with photographic documentation of the impact of combat on military horses of all kinds. Whether these images moved viewers to a higher level of animal awareness and protection after the war is an open question. *Frank Leslie's Scenes and Portraits of the Civil War* (New York: Mrs. Frank Leslie, 1894), 403.

At some battles, such as Antietam and July 22 east of Atlanta, opposing troops deliberately targeted enemy artillery horses to immobilize batteries and render them ripe for capture. In these instances the slaughter of equine warriors could be extensive. Confederate skirmishers deliberately fired at Union artillery animals at the Battle of Reams's Station during the Petersburg Campaign. John Billings of the 10th Massachusetts Battery penned a poignant description of what followed. Hit by a bullet, many horses fell and lay a while, then stood up only to be hit again. Sometimes the animal shook his head "as if pestered by a fly" when a bullet plunged into the flesh but continued to stand "in bold relief above the slight earthworks." One with a broken leg stood on its other three legs until further rounds brought it down. Billings could hear the hollow snapping sound when a bullet broke the lower limb of an animal, and he counted seven balls received by one horse before it succumbed. The sharpshooters did their job with gruesome efficiency. Only four of fifty-seven horses belonging to the battery survived this deliberate destruction.[19]

"Words fail to convey an adequate idea of the fortitude displayed by our horses," Billings wrote.[20] In fact, it was a warrior's fortitude typical of many human soldiers as well. In Billings's mind and heart, the artillery horse was elevated to the same level as his stalwart comrades. But he spent more time and emotion in describing the horse's experience of battle at Reams's Station than he did the human experience at the same engagement. There was a natural tendency to be touched by the suffering of these animals because they had been forced into these horrible circumstances. Sensitivity toward their suffering among those soldiers who noticed and cared about it denotes an unstated realization that military men and their logistical needs had been responsible for placing the horses in this dangerous position, and many soldiers felt a bit guilty about it.

Injured horses usually were shot to put them out of their misery, although, as government property, two commissioned officers had to approve the act. But when Jacob Roemer arranged to have his men shoot "a beautiful gray horse" that had a bullet lodged deep in its shoulder, he called it off at the last minute. The animal "looked at me so pitifully that I had not the heart to give the order to fire." Roemer allowed the horse twenty-four hours to show signs of improvement. By that time, it could stand up, and a man could ride him within a few days. A surgeon cut out the ball seven months after the injury, and the horse recovered more quickly after the operation.[21]

Disposal of horse remains was a more difficult problem than burying the human dead because of the size and weight of the animal. When possible, they were buried on the spot. That proved virtually impossible at the Battle of Secessionville. Several horses of the 1st Connecticut Battery had been dismembered by artillery rounds, and pieces of horse carcasses were scattered over a wide area. "A leg in one place, another so mangled that it bore no resemblance to anything ever seen in the animal kingdom, a head lying far away from any other part of a body, while the entrails seemed to have been distributed in every direction." Often, horse carcasses were simply burned on the battlefield, using nearby sources of fuel to start the pyre.[22]

Combat was only one source of attrition that wore down artillery animals in both armies. Diseases exacted a terrible toll on horses in all branches of the service. The worst ailment to hit artillery horses was an outbreak of glanders, a communicable disease that produces high fever and thick nasal mucus. Tens of thousands of horses in all branches of the service, Union and Confederate, died of this illness during the war.[23]

Providing the animals with proper feed became a major logistical problem. Horses require far more subsistence than men. The artillery manual specified twelve pounds of grain (oats, corn, or barley) and fourteen pounds of hay every day in addition to four gallons of water. Both grain and hay were essential for a healthy horse; it could not thrive on either of them alone. Too much grain often led to scours, a condition chiefly associated with diarrhea. Charles Wainwright referred to the artillery horse when he wrote, "his belly must be filled and he can no more improve in condition on oats and corn alone than a man can on beef extract, or any other concentrated food."[24]

Handlers relied on local sources to provide water for their artillery horses and sometimes could forage for grain and hay in the countryside. But the army's logistical system had to provide most of the animal feed they needed. Not only was this a large amount (compared to three pounds of food for every soldier per day), but hay constituted the bulkiest material hauled on military transportation during the Civil War. Some of it was bailed into compact rectangles for easier shipment, but the majority of hay was hauled loose in railroad cars and river steamers, taking up a great deal of precious space. Moreover, the demands of war led to periodic hay shortages, even for the agriculturally rich northern states. If hauling room was short, horse feed was the first item to be dropped on the assumption that it could be found in local areas wherever troops were stationed. That assumption often proved to be false. Artillery animals were simply forced to do without adequate food if their handlers could not find alternate sources of grain and hay in the countryside.[25]

Ironically, horse-food shortages often occurred during an active campaign as the military transportation system became more strained. This happened exactly when the artillery horses were stressed to their utmost to perform in the field, especially during extended campaigns. The combination of hard work and little feed created a high rate of attrition during long operations. Battery C, 1st Rhode Island Light Artillery lost fifteen horses in twelve days during the Maryland Campaign due to "want of food and overwork." Excessive heat oppressed artillery horses and lowered their immunity. Rapid marching also was tough on the animals. Contending with Sterling Price's Missouri Raid in the fall of 1864, Battery H, 2nd Missouri Light Artillery marched over 1,200 miles, fought in ten engagements, and lost eighty horses—twenty-five killed, thirty wounded, fifteen captured, and ten that were "worn out and abandoned on the road." There are reports of artillery horses literally dropping while in harness, "utterly incapable of being moved," in some campaigns.[26]

In addition to overwork, food shortages, and disease, the other major factor in horse attrition was the wear and tear of the harness on animal skin. During extended campaigns, it was not unusual for an artillery horse to be in harness for days at a time. It was important to take off the heavy rigging and properly water, feed, and curry the animals. But the demands of the service (and careless drivers) often intruded. The horses of Battery A, 1st Ohio Light Artillery remained in harness for six days during the Chickamauga Campaign, and the commander feared he would lose twenty-five animals as a result. Treatment like this often caused skin sores that took weeks to heal.[27]

Replacing artillery horses became a major problem. The manual specified in detail what to look for in an artillery animal. It should be five to seven years old, fifteen hands and three inches tall, and weighing 1,100–1,200 pounds. Moreover, the steed should be "well broken to harness, free from vice, perfectly sound in every respect, full chested, . . . full barreled, with deep broad loins, . . . [and] solid hind quarters." It should have large hoofs and good feet. Any animal that was "restive, vicious, or *too free* in harness" should be rejected.[28]

It might have been possible to honor all of these requirements in peacetime or in the early days of the war, but the lengthening conflict placed increasing demands on the country's equine supply. Battery commanders, especially in the Confederate army, very often had to make do with whatever animals their quartermasters could find. They consolidated teams and gave up a gun or two if necessary, reclaiming the pieces when additional horses could be found. Higher-level commanders granted permission for artillery officers to take horses from cavalry units and ambulances to make up shortages. When Quartermaster General Montgomery C. Meigs asked William T. Sherman if he needed additional horses after completing his March to the Sea, the general reported that he had no need for anything except good artillery animals "of a size and weight which cannot be found in this country."[29]

Meigs had a good chance to fulfill Sherman's desire. The Quartermaster Department bought 20,714 artillery horses from September 1, 1864, to May 9, 1865. It paid $161 to $185 each for them, a price range a bit higher than that paid for cavalry and draft horses but not as high as that paid for mules (the primary draft animal of the war). A total of 434 artillery horses died of disease in depots during that time, indicating that the health of horses sometimes left much to be desired. Charles Wainwright, artillery chief of the First Corps, Army of the Potomac, reported in detail the condition of ninety replacement horses he received after the Battle of Gettysburg. Two-thirds of them were "really good," but twenty of the others were "entirely worthless." Wainwright nevertheless considered this a good showing. He thought that typically half of the replacement horses he received were "totally unfit for artillery use."[30]

The Confederates faced far more difficulties in procuring artillery horses than did the Federals. By the midpoint of the war, those problems became critical. The loss rate combined with limited numbers of equines fit for artillery service led to serious shortages. On occasion Confederate authorities resorted to pressing horses from civilian owners, and battery commanders learned how important it was to post guards at their horse lines and corrals to prevent other Confederates from stealing them. The horse shortage contributed to a decision by Robert E. Lee to reduce his batteries from six to four guns each in 1863.[31]

The 13th Virginia Battalion in Lee's Army of Northern Virginia lost 219 horses from August 1, 1864, to March 9, 1865. Of that number, 58 were condemned and returned to the quartermaster. Another 35 were sent to a recovery camp near Lynchburg, and 64 died as a result of disease or were abandoned as worthless to the army. Another 2 horses were lost because they "strayed." None were listed as perishing from combat because the battalion's batteries were safely lodged in heavy earthworks along the Richmond–Petersburg lines. Food shortages and disease accounted for most of the battalion's equine losses during this phase of the war.[32]

Mules were not considered a fit substitute for horses in the artillery arm. They were viewed as too nervous to withstand the noise and confusion of battle. Mules were effective at pulling the wagon and forge for a battery but not the guns or caissons. Only when dire necessity dictated did officers use these animals to pull ordnance. In the retreat from Lenoir's Station to Knoxville, Capt. William W. Buckley of Battery D, 1st Rhode Island Light Artillery was forced to use mules to pull his six Napoleon guns because of the muddy, rutted roads. But when pursuing Confederates offered battle at Campbell's Station, Buckley found that the mules caused too much trouble—half the team tried to run, while the other half stood still.[33]

In contrast to the mule, the artillery horse was a stalwart soldier. As a rule, when well trained and cared for, it was reliable, knew its role, and was willing to play it. While these animals received little credit from the public at large, they garnered a great deal of love and affection from many if not most of the artillery men assigned to handle them. Bonds of comradeship were formed between man and animal similar to those formed between human comrades within the same unit. Many horses returned the affection and the loyalty.

The horse was indispensable to the modern artillery arm of the mid-nineteenth century. Before this, field artillery typically had been pulled by oxen (usually driven by hired civilians) when on the march and then manhandled into place on the battlefield by the soldiers who fired the weapon. The difficulties of relying on civilians led to the use of soldier-drivers by the early nineteenth century, and the need to find animals that could pull ordnance faster led to the replacement of the ox with the horse. The Civil War witnessed the transition from light 6-pounders to heavier ordnance, with 12-pounders and 20-pounders becoming common on the battlefield. This placed an even greater demand on artillery horses, straining them physically even as the supply of replacements became problematic. Especially in the Confederate army, many artillery horses wore themselves out in long campaigns trying to pull heavier guns with fewer partners. Although oxen were used on a couple of occasions, with mules tried a bit more often than oxen, horses were called on to shoulder the bulk of pulling ordnance in the field during the Civil War.[34] They fulfilled that call as well as the humans who fired the guns.

## NOTES

1. There are no readily available statistics on the number of artillery horses used by either side in the war. I arrived at this figure by counting the number of batteries in both armies and using Jacob Roemer's statement that his battery used about 400 horses during the war. I also assumed that most Union batteries had six guns and most Confederate batteries had four pieces. This formula (460 Union batteries with 400 horses each and 292 Confederate batteries with 266 horses each) resulted in 184,000 Union artillery horses and 77,672 Confederate artillery horses. Jacob Roemer, *Reminiscences of the War of the Rebellion, 1861–1865*, ed. L. A. Furney (Flushing, NY: Flushing Journal, 1897), 300, 317. For an estimate of the total number of horses and mules used in the war, see Gene C. Armistead, *Horses and Mules in the Civil War: A Complete History with a Roster of More Than 700 War Horses* (Jefferson, NC: McFarland, 2013), 3.

2. Warren P. Edgarton to James Barnett, June 25, 1863, *The War of the Rebellion: A Compilation of the Official Records of the Union and Confederate Armies*, 70 vols. in 128 parts (Washington, DC: Government Printing Office, 1880–1901), ser. 1, 20(1):300 (hereafter *OR*, all citations to series 1 unless otherwise stated); *Instruction for Field Artillery* (Philadelphia: J. B. Lippincott, 1860), 46–47; Chamberlayne to mother, April 23, 1863, John H. Chamberlayne, *Ham Chamberlayne—Virginian: Letters and Papers of an Artillery Officer in the War for Southern Independence, 1861–1865*, ed. C. G. Chamberlayne (Richmond: Dietz, 1932), 169; Henry M. Cist to James H. Wilson, February 4, 1865, *OR*, 49(1):649.

3. Joseph W. B. Wright to not stated, n.d., *OR*, 36(1):922. I calculated the average number of men in a Union battery as 319 and the average number of men in a Confederate

battery as 212 based on comparing reports of total enrollments in A. J. Bennett, *The Story of the First Massachusetts Light Battery* (Boston: Deland and Barta, 1886), 185–86; Philip S. Chase, *Battery F, First Regiment Rhode Island Light Artillery in the Civil War, 1861–1865* (Providence, RI: Snow and Farnham, 1892), 249–79; and Roemer, *Reminiscences,* 317. Those should be considered minimum average numbers per battery.

4. Stephen Budiansky, *The Nature of Horses: Exploring Equine Evolution, Intelligence, and Behavior* (New York: Free Press, 1997), 9, 18, 20, 40–41, 81–85, 147–67, 263.

5. Andria Pooley-Ebert, "Species Agency: A Comparative Study of Horse-Human Relationships in Chicago and Rural Illinois," in *The Historical Animal,* ed. Susan Nance (Syracuse, NY: Syracuse University Press, 2015), 150–52; Natalie K. Waran and Rachel Casey, "Horse Training," in *The Domestic Horse: The Origins, Development, and Management of Its Behaviour,* ed. D. S. Mills and S. M. McDonnell (Cambridge, UK: Cambridge University Press, 2005), 186; Paul McGreevy and Andrew McLean, "Behavioural Problems with the Ridden Horse," ibid., 198–99.

6. Shelly R. Scott, "The Racehorse as Protagonist: Agency, Independence, and Improvisation," in *Animals and Agency: An Interdisciplinary Exploration,* ed. Sarah E. McFarland and Ryan Hediger (Leiden, The Netherlands: Brill, 2009), 45–65.

7. Ann Norton Green, *Horses at Work: Harnessing Power in Industrial America* (Cambridge, MA: Harvard University Press, 2008), 153; John H. Rhodes, *The History of Battery B, First Regiment Rhode Island Light Artillery in the War to Preserve the Union, 1861–1865* (Providence, RI: Snow and Farnham, 1894), 21; Frederick W. Wild, *Memoirs and History of Capt. F. W. Alexander's Baltimore Battery of Light Artillery, U.S.V.* (Loch Raven, MD: Maryland School for Boys, 1912), 18, 207.

8. Herbert W. Beecher, *History of the First Light Battery Connecticut Volunteers, 1861–1865,* vol. 1 (New York: A. T. De La Mare, [1901]), 154; William T. Shepherd to mother, August 11, 1861, in *To Rescue My Native Land: The Civil War Letters of William T. Shepherd, First Illinois Light Artillery,* ed. Kurt H. Hackemer (Knoxville: University of Tennessee Press, 2005), 55; J. E. Boos, ed., "Civil War Diary of Patrick H. White," *Journal of the Illinois State Historical Society* 15, nos. 3–4 (October 1922–January 1923): 642–43; John D. Billings, *The History of the Tenth Massachusetts Battery of Light Artillery in the War of the Rebellion, 1862–1865* (Boston: Hall and Whiting, 1909), 42; Allan Nevins, ed., *A Diary of Battle: The Personal Journals of Colonel Charles S. Wainwright, 1861–1865* (New York: Harcourt, Brace, and World, 1962), 55; George Lewis, *The History of Battery E, First Regiment Rhode Island Light Artillery, in the War of 1861 and 1865, to Preserve the Union* (Providence, RI: Snow & Farnham, 1892), 359.

9. *Instruction for Field Artillery,* 141; Reed to mother, November 12, 1862, in *"A Grand Terrible Dramma" from Gettysburg to Petersburg: The Civil War Letters of Charles Wellington Reed,* ed. Eric A. Campbell (New York: Fordham University Press, 2000), 46–47; Roemer, *Reminiscences,* 24.

10. William Terry Moore Reminiscences, Special Collections, University of Mississippi, Oxford; Rhodes, *History of Battery B,* 20.

11. Beecher, *History of the First Light Battery,* 420; George C. Sumner, *Battery D, First Rhode Island Light Artillery in the Civil War, 1861–1865* (Providence: Rhode Island Printing, 1897), 74; Wild, *Alexander's Baltimore Battery,* 209.

12. Roemer, *Reminiscences*, 51.

13. Levi Baker, *History of the Ninth Mass. Battery* (South Framingham, MA: J. C. Clark, 1888), 22; Thomas A. Davies to Kennett, October 18, 1862, *OR*, 17(1):259; George Estep to Race, January 4, 1863, ibid., 20(1):476; Richard N. Griffin, ed., *Three Years a Soldier: The Diary and Newspaper Correspondence of Private George Perkins, Sixth New York Independent Battery, 1861–1864* (Knoxville: University of Tennessee Press, 2006), 97; Harry Cushing to Mendenhall, September 26, 1863, *OR*, 30(1):800; Fannie A. Beers, *Memories: A Record of Personal Experience and Adventure during Four Years of War* (Philadelphia: J. B. Lippincott, 1888), 237.

14. John D. Imboden to Whiting, July 22, 1861, *Supplement to the Official Records of the Union and Confederate Armies*, 100 vols. ed. Janet B. Hewett (Wilmington, NC: Broadfoot, 1993–2000), pt. 3, 1:261 (hereafter *SOR*); Lucius G. Marshall to Hood, December 4, 1866, John B. Hood Papers, National Archives and Records Administration, Washington, DC; Lewis, *History of Battery E*, 210; John Bigelow, "Account of the Engagement of the 9th Mass. Battery," in *The Bachelder Papers: Gettysburg in Their Own Words*, ed. David L. Ladd and Audrey J. Ladd, vol. 1 (Dayton, OH: Morningside, 1994), 177.

15. Peter P. Wood to Taylor, April 9, 1862, *OR*, 52(1):24; "Order Book, 5th Company, B. W. A.," 158, Box 12, Folder 1, Civil War Papers, Battalion Washington Artillery Collection, Louisiana Research Collection, Special Collections, Tulane University, New Orleans.

16. John M. Brannan to Barry, October 1, 1864, *OR*, 38(1):186.

17. Robert Stiles, *Four Years under Marse Robert* (New York: Neale, 1903), 196; William H. Runge, ed., *Four Years in the Confederate Artillery: The Diary of Private Henry Robinson Berkeley* (Chapel Hill: University of North Carolina Press, 1961), 98; Gary W. Gallagher, ed., *Fighting for the Confederacy: The Personal Recollections of General Edward Porter Alexander* (Chapel Hill: University of North Carolina Press, 1989), 253.

18. Edward A. Moore, *The Story of a Cannoneer under Stonewall Jackson* (Lynchburg, VA: J. P. Bell, 1910), 258; [Napier Bartlett], *A Soldier's Story of the War: Including the Marches and Battles of the Washington Artillery, and of Other Louisiana Troops* (New Orleans: Clark and Hofeline, 1874), 74.

19. Dumas to Pickens, July 25, 1864, *SOR*, pt. 1, 7:123; Bragg to Wood, September 21, 1862, *OR*, 19(1):255; Billings, *Tenth Massachusetts Battery*, 315–16.

20. Billings, *Tenth Massachusetts Battery*, 315.

21. Roemer, *Reminiscences*, 260–261; *History of the Fifth Massachusetts Battery* (Boston: Luther E. Cowles, 1902), 143.

22. Wildey to Dewey, October 9, 1864, *OR*, 42(1):787; Herb S. Crumb and Katherine Dhalle, eds., *No Middle Ground: Thomas Ward Osborn's Letters from the Field (1862–1864)* (Hamilton, NY: Edmonston, 1993), 48; Beecher, *First Light Battery*, 154.

23. G. Terry Sharrer, "The Great Glanders Epizootic, 1861–1866," *Agricultural History* 69, no. 1 (Winter 1995): 79–97.

24. *Instruction for Field Artillery*, 47–48; William L. Ritter, "Sketches of the Third Maryland Artillery," *Southern Historical Society Papers* 11 (1883): 437; Nevins, *Diary of Battle*, 500.

25. Earl J. Hess, *Civil War Logistics: A Study of Military Transportation* (Baton Rouge:

Louisiana State University Press, 2017), 164; Charles Dana Gibson, "Hay: The Linchpin of Mobility," *North & South* 2, no. 2 (January 1999): 51–53; Bragg to Johnston, April 13, 1864, *OR*, ser. 4, 3:293.

26. Waterman to Martin, October 4, 1862, *OR*, 12(2):468; Record of Events, 4th Ohio Battery, May–June 1862, *SOR*, pt. 2, 50:387; Montgomery to Cole, November 14, 1864, *OR*, 41(1):461; Bramhall to De Russy, July 5, 1862, ibid., 11(2):106.

27. Goodspeed to Schmitt, September 27, 1863, *OR*, 30(1):554; Beecher, *First Light Battery*, 126.

28. *Instruction for Field Artillery*, 46.

29. Shoemaker to not stated, December 25, [1864], *SOR*, pt. 1, 7:614; Griffin, *Three Years a Soldier*, 236–37; Special Orders No. 41, Headquarters, Army of the Mississippi, April 26, 1862, Special Orders, January 2, 1862 to August 27, 1862, 123–24, Container 22, G. T. Beauregard Papers, Manuscript Division, Library of Congress, Washington, DC; Davis to Dechert, April 9, 1865, *OR*, 47(3):144–45; Sherman to Meigs, December 25, 1864, ibid., 44:807.

30. Meigs to Stanton, November 8, 1865, *OR*, ser. 3, 5:220–21; Nevins, *Diary of Battle*, 269.

31. Lee to Pendleton, April 25, 1863, *OR*, 25(2):749; Pendleton to Alexander, May 19, 1863, ibid., 808; Johnston to Bragg, March 16, 1864, Joseph E. Johnston Papers, Rubenstein Rare Book and Manuscript Library, Duke University, Durham, NC; Larry J. Daniel, *Cannoneers in Gray: The Field Artillery of the Army of Tennessee, 1861–1865* (Tuscaloosa: University of Alabama Press, 1984), 71; James Robert Maxwell, *Autobiography of James Robert Maxwell of Tuskaloosa, Alabama* (New York: Greenberg, 1926), 217; Spencer Jones, "The Influence of Horse Supply upon Field Artillery in the American Civil War," *Journal of Military History* 74, no. 2 (April 2010): 373.

32. "Consolidated Horse Report of the Thirteenth Virginia Artillery Battalion, from August, 1864, to March, 1865," *OR*, 46(2):1306.

33. John D. Billings, *Hardtack and Coffee; or, The Unwritten Story of Army Life* (Boston: George M. Smith, 1887), 281; Wells to Marshall, October 27, 1864, *OR*, 39(3):468; Martin to Cumming, June 25, 1863, ibid., 24(3):965; Sumner, *Battery D*, 93–94.

34. Pendleton to Cole, March 31, 1863, *OR*, 25(2):695; P. C. Hoy, *A Brief History of Bradford's Battery, Confederate Guards Artillery* (Petersburg, VA: N.p., 1903), 256.

# War Horses

*Equine Perspectives on the Confederacy*

**ABRAHAM GIBSON**

IN 1974 THE IDEA that animals might have a history was considered so absurd that it was openly mocked in scholarly journals.[1] Now, less than fifty years later, the field of animal history has not only arrived, it has "triumphed."[2] The canon is much too large to summarize in such limited space, but a few of the broader trends warrant mention. For example, many of the classics in animal history examine humanity's relationship with domestic animals in different times and places.[3] More recently, though, a growing number of scholars have also studied wild animals, insects, and even sponges.[4] Meanwhile, just as the topics have grown more diverse, so too have the methods. Perhaps most notably, numerous historians have embraced an "evolutionary" turn. Michael Pollan first examined the evolutionary implications of plant domestication in *Botany of Desire*, and others have since applied the same method of analysis to animals.[5] Edmund Russell has called for an entirely new field to study humanity's profound influence on the evolutionary trajectory of other species and the ramifications of this human-induced evolution on society and culture.[6] Several scholars have already answered the call.[7]

As one might expect, numerous historians have examined the role that animals played in the Civil War. Horses have proven an especially popular topic, which is understandable given their integral place in the war effort.[8] Some of the earliest studies amounted to little more than glowing hagiographies of various cavalrymen, though Charles Ramsdell's excellent study of the Confederate horse supply is an exception.[9] More recently, Gene Armistead has provided an exhaustive description of Civil War horses and mules, but his straightforward analysis makes no effort to engage with recent scholarship in animal studies. By comparison, Ann Norton Greene embraces the evolutionary perspective in her work on Civil War horses and thus belongs on the vanguard of animal history, but her analysis is limited to northern horses exclusively.[10]

A brief examination of the history of horses in the South during the Civil War, while neither exhaustive nor authoritative, nevertheless illustrates that animal history has value precisely by allowing us to reexamine familiar topics from a new perspective. Horses were present for every major event in the war, but their experiences were anything but uniform. Shifting winds of fortune placed them in a variety of different categories during the conflict, each with its own life-or-death implications. One might think that the short timeframe would preclude any meaningful engagement with evolutionary history, and that is certainly true in a sense; after all, there were no speciation events during the Civil War. Even so, there is still much we can learn from the evolutionary perspective. Horses had already coevolved with people for thousands of years by the 1860s, and they were entangled in many of the same ecological relationships. As a result, studying horses necessarily sheds light on the people with whom they engaged.

## LUXURY IMPORT

It was obvious from the start that the fledgling Confederate States of America would face significant challenges during the Civil War, but one area where white southerners presumed to hold an advantage was horses. Most of the horses in the northern states were draft animals that were used to pull carriages, but there were not enough miles of improved roadways to warrant a large number of carriages in the South. Instead, white southerners were more likely to ride their horses in the saddle, which better prepared them for military service as mounted cavalry. In 1866, Union soldier Samuel Ringwalt admitted that the horses of the northern states had proved "sadly deficient" for mounted warfare, and he bemoaned "the lamentable inefficiency of our cavalry in the early days of the war."[11]

Historians generally agree, ascribing an early advantage to the southern mounted arm. As Ted Steinberg writes, "it was no secret that the Confederate troops retained a significant edge during the early years of the war in terms of horsemanship, a benefit bestowed on them at least in part by climate, specifically the mild winters that allowed them to spend nearly the entire year outside practicing their skills while their adversaries kept warm by the fire."[12] Greene makes a similar point. "Many northerners subscribed to a romantic image of southerners as cavaliers riding the finest pure-blooded horses. If horses were military hardware and horsemanship was military software, many Americans believed that the Confederates were cutting-edge."[13]

Southern soldiers may have had more experience in the saddle, but from a strictly numerical standpoint, the Union possessed an undeniable equine advantage. When we include those slave states that never seceded among the Union tally, the northern states had access to a far greater number of horses. Whereas the Union states contained more than 3,170,000 horses on the eve of war, the future Confederacy contained just 1,740,000. Granted, it is true that the southern states contained an absolute numerical advantage when it came to mules. In 1860 the future Confederacy contained more than 800,000 mules, over 70 percent of the nation's total. Yet this surplus was hardly enough to overcome the South's relative dearth of horses. When one combines the number of all equine types, the Union had more than 4,640,000 head, while the future Confederacy contained fewer than 2,570,000.[14]

Ecological conditions help explain this remarkable imbalance. High-nutrient pasture grasses were scarce and hard to grow across large swaths of the South. Instead, many white southerners found it more cost effective to import horses and mules from breeding operations in Tennessee and Kentucky, where there was ample forage and range. Cumulative statistics are difficult to come by, but even snapshot testimonies bear witness to the large volume of equine traffic that crossed the Appalachian Mountains from west to east before the construction of railroads. In 1831 more than 4,000 horses left Kentucky via the Cumberland Gap, ultimately destined for Virginia and North Carolina.[15] Thousands of additional horses followed the exact same route every year throughout the 1830s.[16] Meanwhile, traders bound for markets in South Carolina and Georgia traveled along the French Broad River. In 1839 James Silk Buckingham estimated that 10,000 horses and mules traveled this route into South Carolina every year.[17] In 1843 the state-sponsored agricultural survey of South Carolina acknowledged that

"Kentucky supplies the most of our horses and mules."[18] These animals eventually served as farm equipment, modes of transportation, ornaments of prestige, instruments of sporting leisure, and near-constant companions.

## INSTRUMENTS OF WAR

The South's longstanding reliance on horses from the Ohio River valley left the southern states vulnerable when the Civil War broke out, though their looming crisis was not immediately apparent. During the first year of war, Confederate quartermasters could still procure horses from Virginia and North Carolina, relatively close to the front.[19] Mules were also conscripted into service, but their smaller size proved a disadvantage. According to contemporary sources, a six-mule team was only equivalent in strength to a four-horse team.[20] Meanwhile, the Confederate government mandated that a mounted volunteer provide his own horse. According to Ramsdell, "this provision, adopted partly in the interest of economy and partly in the belief that the men would furnish better mounts than the government and that they would take better care of their own property, was later the cause of much difficulty in procuring remounts for the cavalry in Virginia."[21]

It did not take either side long to realize that horses conveyed extraordinary military advantages. Accordingly, soldiers on both sides increasingly aimed for their enemies' horses, which contributed to an enormous number of equine casualties. "There was constant attrition of army horses in the never-ending skirmishes and campaigning that defined much of the Civil War military action," Greene writes.[22] And since horses do not just disappear when they die, their carcasses became a seemingly ubiquitous symbol of war. In September 1862 J. J. McDaniel described the horrendous aftermath of one battle in northern Virginia: "The stench was dreadful from the dead horses and men."[23] While some of the Confederacy's equines were being killed, others were being captured. Tennessee, which contained the second-highest population of horses in the Confederacy after Texas, had fallen by the summer of 1862.[24]

Not surprisingly, white southerners began to worry about how long their supply would hold out. "The Army of Northern Virginia initially enjoyed a better supply of horses, but as early as June 1862 the quartermaster general warned that lack of animals and forage meant that his department could not sustain any increase in artillery strength," Spencer Jones writes.[25] Quartermaster agents from the eastern and western theaters found themselves in competition for Georgia's supply of horses.[26] To help the situation, Confederate forces conducted raids in Union territory. One such raid in October 1862 netted more than five hundred horses, but that would not offset losses.[27] Officials struggled to produce viable ideas. In late 1862 Secretary of State Judah P. Benjamin suggested rounding up herds in Texas to send to Virginia, but nothing ever came of the idea.[28]

Making matters worse, horses required enormous amounts of forage to survive. By the winter of 1862–63, the lands surrounding the Army of Northern Virginia had been exhausted.[29] By February 1863, fodder was so scarce that General Robert E. Lee was compelled to scatter his army. "Artillery horses were sent as far away as was safe—some towards the James and others to the lower Rappahannock; part of the cavalry was moved to Page County in the Shenandoah Valley," Ramsdell writes.[30] On April 25, 1863, Lee drafted a letter to Brigadier General William N. Pendleton in which he openly worried about the availability of replacements: "The destruction of horses in the army is so great that I fear it will be impossible to supply our wants. There are not enough in the country."[31] Edmund Ruffin, who was not only one of the South's most learned agriculturalists but also one of its most zealous patriots, voiced similar concerns that spring:

> It seems to me that our country & cause are now, for the first time during the war, in great peril of defeat—& not from the enemy's arms, but from the scarcity & high prices of provisions, & the impossibility of the government feeding the horses of the army, which is even much more difficult than to feed & support the men. In the cavalry brigade to which my grandson belongs, the horses have rarely had any feed but corn for some months—& are generally without any hay or other long provender, & for weeks together. Horses cannot live on grain alone, even if plentifully supplied with it. As might be expected, the horses are reduced very low in flesh & strength, & many are dying, & more failing entirely. I do not know but infer that this brigade is not worse supplied than all others of our cavalry in eastern Virginia. And if so, the cavalry and the wagon & artillery teams cannot be capable of performing hard or even immoderate service.[32]

A decisive victory at Chancellorsville (May 1863) improved Confederate morale and boosted Lee's confidence, but it did little to bolster the army's dwindling supply of equids. All of these facts compelled Lee and the Army of Northern

Virginia to charge northward into Pennsylvania's Cumberland Valley. The general hoped that invading the Union would weaken its resolve, of course, but there were other, more pragmatic, reasons behind his offensive. Three years of intense warfare had left the landscape of northern Virginia utterly denuded, whereas Pennsylvania's fertile countryside had scarcely been touched. Charging northward, therefore, promised bountiful forage for human and horse alike. It also afforded the southern army an opportunity to loot the Union's agricultural riches. "Exactly how many head the Confederates took is impossible to know," Mark Fiege writes, adding that "the total surely was in the tens of thousands."[33] The Confederate and Union armies clashed at Gettysburg on July 1, beginning three days of intense combat. All told, more than three thousand horses died during the battle. "Lying for days in the warm, moist air, the remains—an estimated six million pounds, or three thousand tons—fed a disgusting orgy of decomposition," Fiege writes.[34]

## PORTENTS OF GLOOM

After Gettysburg, both sides were forced to abandon their broken-down animals, and it was not uncommon to find abandoned horses in the armies' wake.[35] Scarcely a month after Gettysburg, Union bugler Oliver Wilcox Norton reported that horses were being discarded with staggering frequency. "Every day since we returned to Virginia, every day we have marched, Battery D, Fifth United States, has turned out to die from four to ten horses."[36] In many cases the desperate farmers of northern Virginia were only too happy to reclaim these equine rejects in hopes of rehabilitating them. If indeed these animals actually recuperated, however, they were invariably reconscripted. "When such a brute got to be pretty lively once more, unless he was concealed, he would soon fall into service again in one of the armies, and possibly another gasping skeleton left in his place," John D. Billings recalled.[37] More often, however, weary horses simply fell by the wayside. "Everywhere we march there is a dead horse or mule on the road every bad place we come to, and often there are three or four. I tell you hot weather and heavy guns use up artillery horses," Norton wrote.[38]

The destruction of southern horses had grown impossible to ignore and, for many white southerners, difficult to stomach. Ruffin knew that they had only themselves to blame for the Confederacy's dearth of horses. In August 1863 he wrote:

> The waste & destruction of horses in our cavalry service are enormous—& enough to destroy the efficiency of that branch of the army, as well as to increase both public and private expenses beyond all calculation for new supplies of horses. It was one part of our general bad system of southern economy to raise very few horses, & to buy nearly all, & all our mules, from the western states. A change of this general system of buying to rearing animals, cannot be changed, even under favorable circumstances for obtaining breeders, &c. in less than three years—& the war, & the dangers of every farmer's stock made the circumstances very unfavorable for a change. Therefore there has been little increase in the breeding of horses & mules—the supply by purchases from abroad totally cut off—the waste, by want of food & great hardships & abuse, in our army, made us destructive—as can be conceived—& the raids & robberies of the enemy, in addition, have stripped much of the country of the before diminished & insufficient stock of horses & mules for agricultural labors. This alone is a very serious subject for gloomy anticipations.[39]

The dwindling number of horses necessarily shaped Confederate strategy. On August 24, 1863, Lee wrote to Confederate president Jefferson Davis: "Nothing prevents my advancing now but the fear of killing our artillery horses." He explained that the animals were already half-starved and that Virginia's denuded landscape offered little reprieve. Some days the horses subsisted on little more than a pound of corn; other days they subsisted on none. "Everything is being done by me that can be to recruit the horses," the general assured Davis, but "you can judge of our prospects."[40]

Lee's already dampened optimism was even more muted by the time he wrote Lieutenant General James Longstreet on January 16, 1864. "You know how exhausted the country is between here and the Potomac; there is nothing for man or horse," he lamented. "After you get into Kentucky, I suppose provisions can be obtained. But if saddles, etc. could be procured in time, where can the horses be? They cannot be obtained in this section of country, and, as far as my information extends, not in the Confederacy."[41] That month Lee was compelled to disband three regiments of cavalry for lack of forage.[42]

Ruffin, who may have possessed more agricultural acumen than anyone else in the South, was similarly dispirited. "Our cavalry is almost worthless for fighting, because of the broken-down condition of a large proportion of the horses, & the inability to replace them from any surplus stock of the country, & the impossibility of providing half enough provender," he wrote in his diary on May 27, 1864.[43] One month later he recorded the failure of Confederate cavalry to pursue some Federal raiders, commenting: "This is regularly the case in all raids of the enemy. They, by stealing fresh horses, & other facilities, are able to keep better mounted, & their horses better fed, & cannot often be overtaken, or matched in battle, by our cavalry, on half-starved & failing horses."[44]

On July 5, 1864, Lee wrote to Davis with what was probably his most forthright assessment of southern horses to date:

> Mr. President, The subject of recruiting and keeping up our cavalry force, has occupied much of my thoughts, especially since the opening of the present campaign. The enemy is numerically superior to us in this arm, and possesses greater facilities for recruiting his horses and keeping them in serviceable condition. In the several engagements that have taken place between the cavalry of the two armies, I think great loss has been inflicted upon him, but it has been attended with a diminution of our force which we were less able to bear. Could I sweep his cavalry from the field, or preserve a fair proportion between its numbers and our own, I should feel that our present situation was in a measure secure. But in view of the disparity that exists, and the difficulty of increasing or even maintaining our force, I cannot but entertain serious apprehensions about the safety of our southern communications. Should we be unable to preserve them, I need not point out the consequences.

Lee was so confounded that he actually suggested procuring horses from Texas and swimming them across unobserved points along the Mississippi River. Other than that far-fetched idea, the general was at a loss. "I hope your Excellency will be able to devise some means of obtaining an increase of our supply of horses, and recruiting our cavalry, as upon that in a great measure I believe, depends the issue of the campaign in Virginia."[45]

## HARBINGERS OF DOOM

By comparison, the Union army had access to far more horses, and this influenced their prosecution of the war in significant ways. Beginning in 1864, impatient Union forces adopted an increasingly unforgiving strategy. Toward that end, late in the summer of 1864, Lieutenant General Ulysses Grant placed an army of more than 50,000 soldiers under the direction of Major General Philip Sheridan and charged them with conquering the Shenandoah Valley.[46] After a slow start, the campaign began routing Confederate forces with increasing consistency. They famously spared nothing that might be used by the Confederate army, especially domestic animals. One southern farmer recalled Sheridan's army marching through the Valley, "horses were taken and carried away, whether needed by the army or not."[47] By late October, Union forces had effectively conquered the Shenandoah. During the course of a few short months, Sheridan's troops had appropriated more than four thousand horses and mules from the Valley's farmers.[48]

Sheridan's march through the Shenandoah was a preamble to Major General William Sherman's more famous march through the heart of Georgia. Sherman's forces entered the northwestern corner of the state in May 1864 and had conquered Atlanta by September. While occupying that city, Sherman prepared a custom map of Georgia. Using information from the 1860 agricultural census, he scribbled how many animals and crops he expected to find in each of the counties that lay between his forces and the Atlantic Ocean.[49] He then decided to abandon the troublesome supply lines linking him to the Tennessee Valley and to instead live off the land. To accomplish this task, he famously directed his forces to "forage liberally."[50]

Technically speaking, "foraging" was the process whereby soldiers appropriated what they needed to survive from the local population. Sherman showed little sympathy for Georgia's homefront population, who were not yet privy to the horrors of war. "They don't know what war means," he wrote.[51] Indeed, the strategy was designed to destroy the South's agricultural foundations.[52] This proved successful, and Union soldiers loved it. "This is probably the most gigantic pleasure excursion ever planned," one man wrote, adding that foraging troops were "finding lots of horses and mules."[53] George Sharland reported much the same. "It is invariably the case that in traveling through the enemy's country, all classes of foragers make it their ruling object to be always on the alert for horses and mules, which they find in large numbers, in going through such a country as Georgia."[54] When foragers found worn-out horses they deemed unfit for stealing, it was policy to kill those animals. "This is a very unpleasant duty for those upon whom it falls, but like many other disagreeable duties, it is a necessity and must be done," one soldier reasoned, "the object being to cripple the enemy in every possible resource." He added, "should we leave the cripples and worn out stock, they would endeavor to recuperate them for future use." As a result, soldiers sometimes killed hundreds of horses in a single day.[55]

As Sherman's forces drew closer to their destination, Savannah, some of the soldiers tried to calculate just how much they had foraged. "We were talking over last night what this army had cost the Confederacy since the 4th of October last," Charles Wright Wills wrote in his diary on December 6, 1864, before finally estimating that Sherman's men had captured or killed some 15,000 horses and mules.[56] Ten days later, with his army perched on the outskirts of Savannah, the general also attempted to tally the damages:

> As for our mules and horses, we left Atlanta with about two thousand five hundred (2,500) wagons, many of which were drawn by mules which had not recovered from the Chattanooga starvation; all of which were replaced, the poor mules shot, and our transportation is now in superb condition. I have no doubt the State of Georgia has lost by our operations fifteen thousand (15,000) first-rate mules. As to horses, Kilpatrick collected all his remounts, and it looks to me, in riding along our columns, as though every officer has three or four led horses, and each regiment seems to be followed by at least fifty (50) Negroes and foot-sore soldiers, riding on horses and mules. The custom was for each brigade to send out daily a foraging party of about fifty (50) men on foot, who invariably returned mounted.

So many horses had been stolen, he continued, that "great numbers of these were shot by my orders, because of the disorganizing effect on our infantry of having too many idlers mounted."[57]

Although Sherman's "March to the Sea" remains one of the most famous campaigns of the Civil War, his campaign through the Carolinas was no less important. Sherman directed his forces north out of Savannah in January 1865, scarcely a month after they had arrived. They continued foraging through the Carolinas, with attendant consequences for local horses. On February 2 Dexter Horton wrote in his diary: "Up at daylight and went aforaging. Found a drove of nine (horses), very wild. Had a hard race in getting them or six of them. Pretty near played our horses out."[58] Later that month Oscar Lawrence Jackson noted that the Union army had appropriated a huge number of horses while passing through South Carolina. "We are gathering immense herds of horses and mules," he wrote.[59] By March 7, Jackson wrote that South Carolina's horses "have been entirely cleaned out."[60] By March 22, the army had reached the Neuse River near Goldsboro, North Carolina, where "lots of mules and horses (were) captured."[61]

As Sherman tore through the Carolinas, Grant chased Lee across Virginia. By the spring of 1865, Grant had more horses than his opponent had soldiers.[62] In March 1865 Lee wrote to Secretary of War John C. Breckinridge that "unless the men and animals can be subsisted, the army cannot be kept together, and our present lines must be abandoned."[63] Lee surrendered the Army of Northern Virginia to Grant on April 9, and General Joseph E. Johnston surrendered the armies of the Carolinas, Georgia, and Florida to Sherman later that same month. The conditions of surrender allowed the ex-Confederate soldiers to retain their horses. Rather than some grand gesture of respect, however, the decision was instead intended to stabilize the social and domestic spheres of the South. According to agricultural censuses conducted immediately before and immediately after the war, the southern states lost more than a third of their horses during the Civil War. In some places losses were even more acute. Virginia's horse population decreased by 40 percent, while Georgia's horse population shrank by 45 percent.[64]

## CONCLUSION

In many ways the equine version of the Civil War mirrors the human version. After all, horses were present for every major event. They were the tip of the spear during Major General George Pickett's ill-fated charge up Cemetery Ridge, and they later bore silent witness at Appomattox Court House. But their presence in the historical record also yields previously unexpected lessons. Consider, for example, that the end of the conflict was not the end of the story. Most of the war horses retired back to their homesteads, but some took up residency in the southern wilds. More than twenty years after the end of the Confederacy, bands of feral (free-ranging) horses roamed the marshy wilds of western Tennessee. Locals explained that these animals had survived the carnage of the Fort Pillow massacre, having persisted in the wilderness for more than two decades thereafter. When news of these feral equines was published in the papers, several local hunting parties set out to find the animals, kill them, and eat them.[65]

Animal history provides a new perspective on familiar topics.[66] This can tell us about the animals themselves, of course, but it can also tell us about their human partners. Serving as both a lens and a mirror, equines offer new ways of thinking about the Civil War, the historical enterprise, and humanity's relationship with the rest of nature.[67]

## NOTES

1. Charles Phineas, "Household Pets and Urban Alienation," *Journal of Social History* 7 (1974): 338–43.

2. Joshua Specht, "Animal History after Its Triumph: Unexpected Animals, Evolutionary Approaches, and the Animal Lens," *History Compass* 14 (2016): 326–36.

3. See, for example, Robert Darnton, *The Great Cat Massacre: And Other Episodes in French Cultural History* (New York: Basic, 1984); Harriet Ritvo, *The Animal Estate: The English and Other Creatures in the Victorian Age* (Cambridge, MA: Harvard University Press, 1987); Virginia DeJohn Anderson, *Creatures of Empire: How Domestic Animals Transformed Early America* (New York: Oxford University Press, 2004); Sandra Swart, *Riding High: Horses, Humans, and History in South Africa* (Johannesburg: Wits University Press, 2010); Alan Mikhail, *The Animal in Ottoman Egypt* (New York: Oxford 2013); Tiago Saraiva, *Fascist Pigs: Technoscientific Organisms and the History of Fascism* (Cambridge, MA: MIT Press, 2016).

4. See, for example, Robert Kohler, *Lords of the Fly: Drosophila Genetics and the Experimental Life* (Chicago: University of Chicago Press, 1994); Charlotte Sleigh, *Six Legs Better: A Cultural History of Myrmecology* (Baltimore: Johns Hopkins University Press, 2007); Tania Munz, *The Dancing Bees: Karl von Frisch and the Discovery of the Honeybee Language* (Chicago: University of Chicago Press, 2016); Andrea Smalley, *Wild by Nature: North American Animals Confront Civilization* (Baltimore: Johns Hopkins University Press, 2017); Peter Godfrey-Smith, *Metazoa: Animal Life and the Birth of the Mind* (New York: Farrar, Straus, & Giroux, 2020).

5. Michael Pollan, *Botany of Desire: A Plant's-Eye View of the World* (New York: Random House, 2001).

6. Edmund Russell, *Evolutionary History: Uniting History and Biology to Understand Life on Earth* (New York: Cambridge University Press, 2011); Russell, *Greyhound Nation: A Coevolutionary History of England, 1200–1900* (New York: Cambridge University Press, 2018).

7. Sam White, "From Globalized Pig Breeds to Capitalist Pigs: A Study in Animal Cultures and Evolutionary History," *Environmental History* 16 (January 2011): 94–120; Ann Norton Greene, *Horses at Work: Harnessing Power in Industrial America* (Cambridge, MA: Harvard University Press, 2008); Abraham Gibson, *Feral Animals in the American South: An Evolutionary History* (New York: Cambridge University Press, 2016); Joshua Specht, *Red Meat Republic: A Hoof-to-Table History of How Beef Changed America* (Princeton, NJ: Princeton University Press, 2020).

8. Joseph W. A. Whitehorne, "Issues of Horse and Mule Logistics in the Civil War," in *From These Honored Dead: Historical Archaeology of the American Civil War*, ed. C. R. Geier, D. D. Scott, and L. E. Babits (Gainesville: University Press of Florida, 2014), 177–90; Gene C. Armistead, *Horses and Mules in the Civil War: A Complete History with a Roster of More than 700 War Horses* (Jefferson, NC: McFarland, 2013); Gervase Phillips, "Writing Horses into American Civil War History," *War in History* 20 (2013): 160–81; Spencer Jones, "The Influence of Horse Supply upon Field Artillery in the American Civil War," *Journal of Military History* 74 (2010): 357–77; Ann Norton Greene, "War Horses:

Equine Technology in the Civil War," in *Industrializing Organisms: Introducing Evolutionary History*, ed. Susan R. Schrepfer and Philip Scranton (New York: Routledge: 2004), 143–66; Larry Sawers, "U.S. Army Procurement of Draft and Pack Animals in the Civil War Era," *Eastern Economic Journal* 29 (Winter 2003): 59–67.

9. Charles W. Ramsdell, "General Robert E. Lee's Horse Supply, 1862–1865," *American Historical Review* 35 (July 1930): 758–77.

10. Greene, "War Horses," 143–66.

11. Col. Samuel Ringwalt, "The Horse—from Practical Experience in the Army," *Report of the Commissioner of Agriculture for the Year 1866* (Washington, DC: Government Printing Office, 1867), 324.

12. Ted Steinberg, *Down to Earth: Nature's Role in American History* (New York: Oxford University Press, 2002), 90.

13. Greene, *Horses at Work*, 88.

14. Joseph C. G. Kennedy, *Agriculture of the United States in 1860: Compiled from the Original Returns of the Eighth Census* (Washington, DC: Government Printing Office, 1864), 184–85.

15. "Quantity of Livestock," *Georgian* (Savannah), February 25, 1832, 2.

16. Robert Byron Lamb, *The Mule in Southern Agriculture* (Berkeley: University of California Press, 1963), 23.

17. James Silk Buckingham, *The Slave States of America*, vol. 2 (London: Fisher, Son, 1842), 203–4.

18. Edmund Ruffin, *Report of the Commencement and Progress of the Agricultural Survey of South Carolina*, app., sec. 8 (Columbia: A. E. Pemberton, 1843), 7.

19. Ramsdell, "General Robert E. Lee's Horse Supply," 759.

20. Ringwalt, "The Horse—from Practical Experience in the Army," 328.

21. Ramsdell, "General Robert E. Lee's Horse Supply," 758.

22. Greene, "War Horses," 154.

23. J. J. McDaniel, "Diary of J. J. McDaniel, September 1862," in *Diary of Battles, Marches, and Incidents of the Seventh S.C. Regiment* (Privately published, 1862), 10.

24. Ramsdell, "General Robert E. Lee's Horse Supply," 759.

25. Jones, "Influence of Horse Supply upon Field Artillery," 371.

26. Ibid., 369.

27. Thomas T. Ellis, "Diary of Thomas T. Ellis, October 1862," in *Leaves from the Diary of an Army Surgeon; or, Incidents of Field, Camp, and Hospital Life* (New York: John Bradburn, 1863), 308.

28. Ramsdell, "General Robert E. Lee's Horse Supply," 760.

29. Mark Fiege, *The Republic of Nature: An Environmental History of the United States* (Seattle: University of Washington Press, 2012), 208.

30. Ramsdell, "General Robert E. Lee's Horse Supply," 761.

31. Robert E. Lee to William N. Pendleton, April 25, 1863, *The War of the Rebellion: A Compilation of the Official Records of the Union and Confederate Armies*, 70 vols. in 128 parts (Washington, DC: Government Printing Office, 1880–1901), ser. 1, 25(2):749 (hereafter *OR*, all citations to series 1 unless otherwise stated).

32. Quoted in Ramsdell, "General Robert E. Lee's Horse Supply," 762.

33. Fiege, *Republic of Nature*, 212. See also Kent Masterson Brown, *Retreat from Gettysburg: Lee, Logistics, and the Pennsylvania Campaign* (Chapel Hill: University of North Carolina Press, 2005), 387.

34. Fiege, *Republic of Nature*, 220.

35. Jones, "Influence of Horse Supply upon Field Artillery," 366.

36. Oliver Wilcox Norton, "Letter of August 5, 1863," in *Army Letters, 1861–1865* (Chicago: Deming, 1903), 171.

37. John D. Billings, *Hardtack and Coffee: The Unwritten Story of Army Life* (Philadelphia: Thompson, 1888), 236.

38. Norton, "Letter of August 5, 1863," 171.

39. Quoted in Ramsdell, "General Robert E. Lee's Horse Supply," 762–63.

40. Robert E. Lee to Jefferson Davis, August 24, 1863, in *OR*, 29(2):664.

41. Robert E. Lee to J. Longstreet, January 16, 1864, in *Memoirs of Robert E. Lee: His Military and Personal History, Embracing a Large Amount of Information Hitherto Unpublished*, ed. Armistead Lindsay Long and Marcus Joseph Wright (New York: J. M. Stoddart, 1887), 637–38.

42. Elizabeth L. van Lew to Benjamin Franklin Butler, January 25, 1864, in *Private and Official Correspondence of Gen. Benjamin F. Butler, during the Period of the Civil War*, vol. 3 (Springfield, MA: Plimpton, 1917), 332.

43. Quoted in Ramsdell, "General Robert E. Lee's Horse Supply," 768.

44. Ibid. (quote).

45. Robert E. Lee to Jefferson Davis, July 5, 1864, in *Lee's Dispatches: Unpublished Letters of General Robert E. Lee, C.S.A., to Jefferson Davis and the War Department of the Confederate States of America, 1862–65*, ed. Douglas Southall Freeman (New York: G. P. Putnam's Sons, 1915), 273–74.

46. Lisa Brady, "Wilderness of War: Nature and Strategy in the American Civil War," *Environmental History* 10 (July 2005): 431.

47. Ibid., 434 (quote).

48. G. Terry Sharrer, *A Kind of Fate: Agricultural Change in Virginia, 1861–1920* (Ames: Iowa State University Press, 2000), 31.

49. Robert Christopher Welch, "Forage Liberally: The Role of Agriculture in Sherman's March to the Sea" (PhD diss., Iowa State University, 2011), 3.

50. Special Field Orders No. 120, Headquarters, Military Division of the Mississippi, November 9, 1864, *OR*, 39(3):713–14.

51. Brady, "Wilderness of War," 436.

52. Ibid., 428.

53. Welch, "Forage Liberally," 93–94.

54. George Sharland, *Knapsack Notes of Gen. Sherman's Grand Campaign through the Empire State of the South* (Springfield, IL: Jackson & Bradford, 1865), 25.

55. Sharland, *Knapsack Notes*, 25.

56. Welch, "Forage Liberally," 161.

57. William Tecumseh Sherman to Ulysses S. Grant, December 16, 1864, in *History of*

*the Army of the Cumberland: Its Organization, Campaigns, and Battles, Written at the Request of Major-General George H. Thomas Chiefly from His Private Military Journal and Official and Other Documents Furnished by Him*, ed. Thomas B. Van Horne, vol. 2 (Cincinnati: R. Clarke, 1875), 296.

58. Clement Eaton, "Diary of an Officer in Sherman's Army Marching through the Carolinas," *Journal of Southern History* 9, no. 2 (May 1943): 242.

59. Oscar Lawrence Jackson, "February 13, 1865," *The Colonel's Diary* (N.p., ca. 1922), 180.

60. "March 7, 1865," ibid., 188–203.

61. Eaton, "Diary of an Officer in Sherman's Army," 250.

62. Sharrer, *Kind of Fate*, 10.

63. Robert E. Lee to John C. Breckenridge, *OR*, 46(2):1295.

64. *Compendium of the Tenth Census* (Washington, DC: Government Printing Office, 1883), 675–76, 681; Isaac Newton, "Report of the Commissioner of Agriculture," in *Report of the Commissioner of Agriculture for the Year 1866*, 13.

65. "Wild Horses at Fort Pillow," *Abbeville (SC) Press and Banner*, February 17, 1886, 7.

66. Harriet Ritvo, "History and Animal Studies," *Society & Animals* 10 (2002): 404.

67. Specht, "Animal History after Its Triumph," 327.

# III

# Interaction with Wildlife during THE Civil War

# Wildlife
## AND THE
# Civil War

EARL J. HESS

THE ANIMAL WORLD is defined as all sentient creatures of any size or shape, including humans. Domesticated animals tend to be uppermost in our consciousness, while the creatures that live in the wild, or in a state that is somewhere between wild and domesticated, tend to be relatively obscure. Wildlife ranges from large mammals to microscopic organisms, and Civil War soldiers encountered many of these wild creatures. When the men commented on wildlife, they admired it, felt threatened by it, were pestered by it, or looked at it as a source of food. Ironically, several types of insect life, not to mention the odd alligator, also looked on the soldiers as a source of food. When armies invaded a natural habitat, they brought the war home to wildlife with devastating results. Wild animals coexisted with Civil War soldiers, and many greatly suffered from wartime conditions. But some species, such as insects, benefited from the presence of soldiers in their environment.

The Civil War lessened the divide between men and wildlife by placing millions of soldiers in the countryside, where they lived and fought in closer touch with the environment than was normal. The conflict, therefore, offers a significant window into popular attitudes toward and interactions with the wild environment and the animals that it sustained.

At heart, this essay is an initial exploration of the possibilities inherent in studying war service and the wild. It describes the context and characteristics of soldier awareness and contact with wild animals and, to a degree, with the natural environment. Surveying a wide variety of diaries, letters, and memoirs written by Federals and Confederates and supplemented by Kelby Ouchley's statistical study of environmental awareness among soldiers, we get an idea of the different attitudes and approaches to the wild among soldiers. From these, one can speculate on whether soldier action during the war, especially organized military operations and hunting, had significant consequences on wildlife populations. Finally, one also can speculate on whether the war experience was connected to the natural-conservation movement that began in the Civil War era, or whether soldiers were indifferent to that movement.

## AWARENESS OF WILDLIFE

The theater of military operations during the Civil War encompassed the southeastern United States from Texas to Virginia and from Missouri to Florida. Ouchley has concluded that 575 species of "terrestrial (land-dwelling), vertebrate fauna" existed in this territory. These included 102 species (18 percent) of mammals, 112 species (19 percent) of reptiles, 130 species (23 percent) of amphibians, and 231 species (40 percent) of birds. In addition, close to 500 species of freshwater fish lived in this large region. Millions of species of invertebrates such as insects, mollusks, and worms lived there as well.[1]

During the four years of war, three million soldiers in both armies became more intimately exposed to the natural world than ever before. Farming families worked in a combined natural and built environment for a living, but their residence in houses separated them from it as well. Campaigning in the field literally meant living in woods, fields, and near streams. Especially for soldiers recruited from urban areas, army life thrust thousands of young men into an environment most only dimly understood, and even soldiers recruited from rural areas had to adjust to living in the field.

Soldier awareness of the environment and its animals derived from their prewar experience as civilians. Most antebellum Americans tended to view nature as an entity separate from themselves, something to be conquered, exploited, and changed to suit human needs. Despite the publication of Henry David Thoreau's *Walden* in 1854 and George Perkins Marsh's *Man and Nature* ten years later, there was little change in the predominant way of thinking about nature during the Civil War era.[2]

Ouchley examined 359 Union and 148 Confederate soldier accounts to gauge their environmental awareness not only of animals but also of plants. The most common reference to both flora and fauna related to food. Thirty-six percent of Union soldiers and 57 percent of Confederates viewed animals as part of their diet. Seeing animals as part of the human environment, which could be interpreted as the most positive expression of environmental awareness, occurred for only 17 percent of the Federals and 4 percent of the Confederates. Viewing animals as a curiosity, which could also be seen as a positive expression of environmental awareness, occurred for 26 percent of the Union soldiers and 22 percent of the Confederates. But seeing animals as pests also was evident in Ouchley's survey. This occurred 20 percent of the time among Union soldiers and 16 percent of the time for Confederates.[3]

## AWARENESS OF BIRDS

Birds filled the air that Civil War soldiers breathed, not only on battlefields but also in camps and along marching routes. There were more than 700 kinds of birds in North America in the 1860s, 230 species alone inhabiting the theater of Civil War operations. Birds tended to be noticed, admired, and coveted by soldiers. Robert Fletcher Winn, a private in the 3rd Kentucky Cavalry (US), was detailed for most of the war as an assistant to his regimental surgeon. He illustrated several of the 175 letters he wrote to his sister with finely executed drawings of birds and other animals. On October 16, 1864, Winn drew pictures of two women plus a red-tufted hawk, a young buffalo, a dog, a ground pheasant, and three snails. A few days later he drew the bust of an unnamed soldier alongside drawings of a woodcock, a horned pheasant, and a third bird that he did not label. The animal and human drawings are made with minute detail.[4]

Birds adapted to living in close proximity with humans even on the battlefield. They appear in soldier accounts as a stark contrast to the noise and confusion of combat. Jerome B. Dann of the 20th Illinois recalled the presence of birds while waiting to advance during the assault against Vicksburg on May 22, 1863. "I remember seeing birds fly over us and noted the unusual quiet." More than a year later, John C. Arbuckle of the 4th Iowa recalled the morning of July 22, 1864, as peaceful east of Atlanta, just before the Confederates launched a surprise attack at noon. "The pine forest in our rear was vibrant with the song of birds," he wrote.[5]

## AWARENESS OF REPTILES

Civil War soldiers interacted with many other varieties of wildlife between battles, especially when camped in environments that were rich habitats for diverse species. During the hot summer of 1863, while waiting out the slow process of besieging Vicksburg, Charles Dana Miller of the 76th Ohio had daily visits from a lizard that was about six inches long. It changed its light green color "to darker shades of green or to dark and mottled brown" as camouflage. He was fascinated by its neck, a "delicate pink color which it could stretch out to about an inch in diameter." Miller's lizard became "quite tame or domesticated," visiting him at regular times. He "perched himself on a camp stool, throwing out his pink film and winking his beautiful little bead-like eyes."[6]

Few soldiers became friendly with snakes, although forty-seven species of them lived in Civil War territory; seven of those species were poisonous. The normal reaction to them was fear, aggression, or avoidance. Andrew Jackson McConnell of the 17th South Carolina killed "a very large Rattle Snake" one evening in Mississippi. He pulled the eight rattles off and cut the fangs, which were three-quarters of an inch long, saving all of them as trophies. August Bondi of the 5th Kansas Cavalry noted in his memoirs that his comrades enjoyed swimming in the Mississippi River near Helena during the summer of 1863. One day the men saw a large cottonmouth snake swimming toward the bank, "its mouth open and showing the white foam, it was killed as it reached the bank."[7]

Alligators filled soldiers with a similar desire to kill. The American alligator is the biggest reptile in North America. Males are capable of growing up to thirteen feet in length and weighing six hundred pounds. They mostly live in Florida and Louisiana but range all the way to North Carolina, central Texas, Arkansas, and Tennessee.[8]

Thousands of Union soldiers saw their first alligators during the Siege of Vicksburg while stationed on the bluffs overlooking the Mississippi Delta north of the city. "It was awful to look at," wrote Iowan John A. Loveless of an eight-foot long specimen near Haynes' Bluff. Many soldiers in both armies automatically used them for target practice. "The boys had great Sport Shooting aligators," wrote C. Pearson of the 37th Alabama. "I wish you could see one. They are the worst looking yet except a yankey." Soldiers of the 19th Iowa killed an alligator in a lake near Port Hudson, Louisiana, and cooked it "by way of experiment." The men who tasted the meat pronounced it "very good."[9]

But alligators turned the tables on many soldiers, viewing them as potential food as well. "Quite a number" of Union soldiers were bitten by alligators, and one man was killed by them in the bottomland of the Yazoo River just north of Vicksburg. The problem became so widespread that Colonel Reuben Williams read an order prohibiting swimming in the Yazoo to his regiment, the 12th Indiana, one evening. The next morning he found that a man in another regiment had violated the order immediately after it had been promulgated. The soldier was bitten so badly in the leg that the limb had to be amputated and he later died in the hospital.[10]

## AWARENESS OF INSECTS

In terms of sheer numbers, soldiers encountered insects far more often than any type of animal. Often only dimly perceived or not noticed until they bit, insects constituted the silent majority of all animal life in Civil War country. They multiplied by the millions, and their lives were greatly enriched by the presence of massed numbers of warm human bodies, horses, and mules. Insects of many types fed not only on those mammalian bodies but also on the refuse created by soldiers and army animals. The most dangerous insect, the mosquito, spread diseases that sapped regimental strength. One also wonders how much the ordinary fly devastated armies by lighting on human and animal feces and then flying to see what a soldier was eating, spreading digestive ailments to hapless men of both armies.

All insects are invertebrates—animals with no backbones. To date, there are one million known species of insects, but that number is believed to be "only a small fraction of the total kinds present." The known species of insects constitute 98 percent of all animals in the world.[11] It is humbling to pause and consider the significance of the fact that vertebrates (mammals, birds, fish, reptiles, and amphibians) compose only 2 percent of the world's animal population.

"You never seen such a country as this for *Bugs*," wrote Will P. Henderson of the 17th Illinois during the Siege of Vicksburg. A year later Abraham J. Seay of the 32nd Missouri was greatly bothered by swarms of flies during the Atlanta Campaign.[12]

Flies, the most common insect encountered by Civil War soldiers, are classified in the order Diptera, which includes insects with one pair of wings, along with mosquitoes and gnats. There are 120,000 species of Diptera in Civil War country. The life cycle typically goes from egg to larva (with maggots in some species), pupa, and then adult. All of these species can transmit disease to humans.[13]

Flies may have been more numerous, proliferating by the millions because of unsanitary army camps, but mosquitoes spread far more disease. The impact of mosquito-borne illness on soldier health has been the subject of extensive study by health historians and Civil War scholars. Malaria and yellow fever were the most significant such diseases, draining victims physically and sapping their morale.[14] Flies fed from the waste products soldiers and animals produced, while mosquitoes fed on the men and animals themselves.

Three types of lice, another category of insects that used troops as sources of nourishment, afflict humans. Body lice were often called "gray backs" because of their appearance. They have three life stages, starting with eggs, or nits, which need thirty days to hatch. The next stage is nymphs, in which the creatures look like miniature versions of an adult louse. The adults, like the nymphs, feed on people and are the size of a sesame seed. They die in about a week if they have no source of nourishment. Lack of personal hygiene is the essential environment for these tiny creatures. They thrive on filthy bodies and spread through close contact in crowded conditions, laying eggs along the seams of clothing and feeding from the host's blood. Cleanliness is the cure.[15] Because armies tend to be a prime target population (soldiers live in the field, crowd together, and often have few opportunities for bathing), body lice have been a feature of military history for centuries, not just of the Civil War.

"Scarcely a man in the Regiment has a change of shirts with him," wrote Unionist George B. Carter during the Vicksburg siege, "and as 'grey backs' are one of the natural productions of the soils, found everywhere and on everything, we have our share." Within the Confederate works at Vicksburg, Chaplain William Lovelace Foster called lice "*body guards*." The "ditches were alive with these crawling pests and to escape was impossible," he informed his wife. Even cavalrymen, who were constantly on the move, did not escape them. George Dallas Mosgrove of the 4th Kentucky Cavalry (CS) recalled that body lice were more bothersome on warm and sunny days. They tended to remain quiet when the soldier was active, but when he tried to rest, they annoyed him so much it was impossible to sleep. No remedies seemed to work. "Boiling his clothes, the using of mercurial ointment, red precipitate and other devices were of no avail," Mosgrove asserted.[16]

A truly captive population stuck in an unsanitary environment such as a prison suffered the most. Survivors of Andersonville described the place as "alive with gray-backs," as Edwin R. Mason noted. "You could not take up a handful of sand without picking up more or less of these animals. We had to [de]louse our shirts twice a day to live at all."[17]

Chiggers were another category of insect that widely bothered soldiers. Very small red bugs, they are the larval stage of a group of tick-like creatures called harvest mites. Chiggers burrow under the skin, "inject the host with digestive enzymes, and ingest the resulting brew for nutrition." This sounds gruesome, but chiggers are more harmless than it sounds. They normally do not infect the host with disease, unlike ticks. Ironically, when chiggers reach the adult stage, they lose interest in human flesh and feed on plants. Chiggers thrive all across Civil War country, but their population fluctuates every year depending on humidity, environment, and temperature. They reach their larval stage in late spring and early summer, exactly when Civil War armies were most active as well.[18]

"There is a little red insect about the size of a fine grane of sand that gets on a fellow and bites like sixty," wrote George R. Buck of the 17th Illinois. "They are called chegars and are tolerable thick." John Q. A. Campbell of the 5th Iowa knew what Buck was talking about. He recalled sitting on grass inside a small ravine near his regimental camp at Vicksburg "and got chiggers on me, from which I suffered intensely for three nights." Then a comrade suggested rubbing pork fat on the affected skin, which took care of the problem. Federal soldiers engaged in the Atlanta Campaign also were affected by chiggers, but an ointment issued by regimental surgeons seemed to ease their suffering.[19]

Ticks are closer in origin to spiders than to other insects such as body lice, but they are potentially more harmful to humans in terms of spreading disease. Their life cycle goes from larva to nymph and then adult. Feeding on blood is necessary to go from one stage to the next. The entire cycle can take up to two years. They prefer to live in leaf clutter and will attach themselves to humans and animals at the first opportunity. Ticks are less often noted in Civil War soldier accounts than chiggers and body lice. When discussed, soldiers often mentioned countermeasures. They had to be "Smoked with Tobacco," reported W. A. Dickerman of the 103rd Illinois. Turpentine also proved effective.[20]

A widespread skin condition caused or made worse by mites was commonly termed "camp itch" or "army itch" in the Civil War. It had prewar and postwar histories as well. The condition appeared by the late 1850s in the West and was then called "prairie itch," "Missouri itch," "Illinois itch," or "Western itch." Reported by early 1862 among western troops, it spread throughout both armies pretty rapidly. Officially, 35,236 cases of this condition were reported, but Thomas G. Cropley, a modern physician who has studied the situation, believes it was much more common. Cropley estimates that from 175,000 to 245,000 cases, or 11–15 percent of the entire Union army, were affected by the itch. He also believes Confederate soldiers suffered from it at a higher rate.[21]

Contemporary observers reported camp itch as a very complex condition but tended to associate it with scabies. Cropley agrees with that conclusion. Scabies is a skin condition caused by mites. The females burrow under human skin and lay eggs. After hatching, the young feed on the flesh, creating burrow tracks that cause blisters and bumps on the skin, usually where it folds. This microscopic mite has eight legs and eventually burrows to the surface of the skin to mature and spread to other parts of the body and to other people. Human scabies is a different type from the condition that affects other animals. The human affliction has been recorded as far back as 2,500 years ago in Egypt and the Middle East.[22]

Physicians of the Civil War era thought scabies originated with organisms embedded in the soil and that returning Union soldiers spread it to northern communities after their discharge. Aggressive treatments with "sulphur-based alkaline ointments or washes" were needed to reduce its occurrence over time. Army surgeon George M. Sternberg thought he had a good cure. Stationed at Jefferson Barracks near Saint Louis, he reported nearly two hundred cases of army itch in late 1865 and early 1866. But a mixture of lime, sulphur, and boiled water provided a "speedy cure." Sternberg blamed the "crowded manner in which soldiers live in their tents or barracks, and the carelessness that exists among them in regard to personal cleanliness" for the spread of the condition. Ridding affected northern communities of the army itch was a slow, tough battle that extended into 1867 before occurrences ceased.[23]

Not all soldiers considered insects to be pests. A few who were fascinated by these creatures examined unusual specimens and tried to collect them. Charles W. Wills of the 103rd Illinois caught "a small scorpion" and "a reddish brown bug." The latter was quite aggressive when bothered. Wills wanted to send them to his sister, "I know you'd like em." But capturing and preserving insects was hardly feasible for soldiers in the field. Surgeon Edwin Hutchinson of the 137th New York tried to do so, but the insects emitted a foul odor and tended to "break up when I under take to save them." A large bug three inches long, black with a bright red color under the wings and two yellow stripes, fascinated Hutchinson. It was impossible to preserve it. All he could do was put "one little bug" in the envelope that contained a letter to his mother.[24] What she did with it is not known.

The urge to collect bugs was part of a more general tendency for Civil War soldiers to capture wild animals for a variety of reasons. Whether it was to keep them as pets, to study their bodies for scientific information, or to eat them, technology has enabled man to become the supreme predator species.

## AWARENESS OF SEA LIFE

Many Union soldiers who were transported by coastal shipping or were stationed on the coast became exposed to sea life for the first time. Often, the first thought was to catch some of these unusual fish and see how they tasted. Members of the 15th New Hampshire trailed a line with a hook for two or three days behind their vessel, the *James S. Green,* while shipping from New York to New Orleans in December 1862. Their first catch was a Spanish mackerel.[25]

Other soldiers merely observed sea life without trying to kill it. Those who saw flying fish considered them an oddity. Jonathan Huntington Johnson of the 15th New Hampshire closely examined one that landed on board his vessel. "They are about 6 inches long with two wings,—a very pretty fish." William Shelly of the 176th New York shared Johnson's respect for sea life and the ocean environment. He marveled at the beautiful sunrise one morning, the phosphorous that sparkled in the water during the night, and the schools of fish that played around his vessel. Unusually large fish drew his special attention, as did flying fish.[26]

Soldiers were well aware of sharks and tended to assume a belligerent attitude toward them. Charles Musser and his comrades of the 29th Iowa enjoyed bathing in the Gulf waters along the coast of Texas soon after the war. Whenever a shark appeared, "you ought to see the scatterment among the boys." But the shark, according to Musser, "invariably gets cropped by a Minnie ball or two before he gets out of reach of our rifles."[27]

Members of the 2nd Rhode Island Cavalry tried to fish for sharks while on their way to New Orleans on the *Belle Wood* but got no nibbles. Their own horses were dying rapidly during the voyage, probably due to disease, and the men were dumping so many carcasses overboard that the sharks were having a feast and they could not be bothered by a little bit of meat attached to a hook in the water.[28]

The voyage of the *Belle Wood* demonstrates not only an instinctive desire by soldiers to harvest exotic sea life but also the symbiotic nature of virtually all interactions between the army and wildlife in general. There were gives and takes on many levels. Disease that affected horses on board the vessel provided a rich boon for meat-eating sea life that was far more beneficial to the creatures of the deep than the occasional fish that a soldier managed to snare for his dinner was to human life. If soldiers felt threatened by a shark, they in turn threatened it with their weapons of destruction.

## THE IMPACT OF COMBAT

The extent to which human battle devastated wildlife is impossible to estimate because of a lack of data, but Ouchley convincingly argues that wildlife populations were able to deal with human intrusion without much long-term damage to its numbers. Natural events such as wildfires, tornados, and floods also afflicted their habitat and killed individual animals locally. All wildlife populations are spread out over extensive areas, however, limiting the overall damage from any one local disaster. Numbers always bounce back once the natural or human event has ended. “Plant and animal populations exhibit remarkable resilience in their abilities to recover from disturbance,” Ouchley concludes.[29] But while overall numbers may recover, the individual animals killed or traumatized in natural or human events deserve to be considered as sentient, feeling creatures for their own sake as well as within the context of human history.

The great majority of all Civil War combat took place in the countryside, on cultivated fields and in natural woods. Humans literally invaded the homeland of wild animals to kill each other, and in the process, they inadvertently killed wild animals as well, or at least terrified them with the noise and confusion of battle. Soldiers noticed this phenomenon more easily on some battlefields than others, but it is safe to assume that literally every engagement produced an animal element in its history whether soldiers reported it or not.

Wildlife caught in the vortex of battle suffered greatly while the human event was taking place in their once peaceful homes. The Battle of Stones River on December 31, 1862, serves as a good case study of this phenomenon. An unusually high number of Union and Confederate soldiers noticed and commented on how combat disturbed wildlife of all kinds. About half the battlefield, located just north and west of Murfreesboro, Tennessee, consisted of forest that was dominated by dense cedar brakes with limestone outcroppings. Although the Federals had maneuvered into this locality with heavy skirmishing over a couple of days before the battle, the wildlife had settled down into the woods and fields very near the quiet battle lines by the evening of December 30. Wild animals were literally only a short distance behind the Union position, feeling safe in the brush, when the Confederates launched a surprise attack on the Federal right wing. The rebels began to drive it back in bitter fighting on the morning of December 31, pushing the retreating soldiers right into the unsuspecting wildlife.[30]

Animals added to the confusion and astonishment experienced by the Union soldiers as they tried to stop the Confederate attack. Wild turkeys and rabbits seemed to be everywhere. "Smaller birds fluttered, and shrieked unnaturally and piteously, so great was their consternation and fear," wrote the soldier-historian of the 73rd Illinois. This veteran felt that "never before . . . had the natural and peaceful occupants of the dense cedar thickets been disturbed by a commotion so great, so unnatural, and appalling, as that created, on that day." Many birds seemed to be too disoriented to fly and hopped along on the ground instead, joining wild turkeys and rabbits in moving through one waiting line of battle to the reserve line at the rear. The men in the reserve line dropped their weapons and tried to catch them, taking up their guns again when the Confederates approached their position.[31]

Several Federals saw their comrades catch wild turkeys during the battle. One of the captors sold his bird to a staff officer who tied it to the saddle of his horse. Soon after, a stray bullet cut the string, dropping the turkey to the ground, and the staff officer lost his purchase. Some men of the 94th Ohio caught a turkey while the regiment was moving at the double-quick through a cedar brake. Later that day they gave the bird to hospital attendants to be eaten by their wounded comrades.[32]

Any variety of bird could be taken that day, according to a Texas Confederate, because so many of them were benumbed that "they could not fly." Many animals sought refuge with the men nearby, snuggling close to them while battle lines were stationary and the troops lay prone on the ground. But many other birds retained their ability to fly and used their unique talents to escape from the sudden eruption of human combat. Federal soldiers a short distance from the fighting noticed with amazement that thousands of birds of all kinds flew over their heads.[33]

Birds of a rare species appeared on the battlefield as well. William E. Patterson of the 38th Illinois saw a bald eagle on a tall tree that "quietly maintained his position in spite of shot and shell."[34] One wonders what drew the eagle's attention most; the noisy martial display on the ground or the rush of prey escaping from the battlefield across open ground.

The fields and woods near Murfreesboro were full of rabbits. While Philip Sheridan's Union division held its position in the cedar woods, the men lying on their stomachs to minimize exposure to fire, their mood was lightened by a rabbit that ran along the length of the line, jumping on the backs of the soldiers. Other rabbits took refuge with the prone men, snuggling close to their feet or hiding under the cape of their heavy overcoats.[35]

Confederate soldiers also commented on the large number of rabbits to be seen. While advancing, a pet dog named Frank, which belonged to a man in the 2nd Kentucky (CS), scared up a rabbit two hundred yards from the Union line and chased it toward the Federal position. Many rebels yelled to encourage Frank in the chase, and Gervis D. Grainger reported that the Unionists fired a volley too early because of this yelling, with most of the balls flying harmlessly over the Kentuckians' heads. The rabbit circled back before reaching the Federals and ran through the advancing Confederate line, with Frank in hot pursuit. "Run, cottontail, run!," yelled a rebel named Big Tom Wilson. "Had I no more reputation to sustain than you, I would run too."[36]

Wilson's shout at the rabbit became a trope among veterans of the battle at Stones River, repeated nostalgically for years to come.[37] It made of the rabbit a metaphor that represented a sane and practical kind of cowardice—and a major comment on what the soldier wanted to do but could not.

Six months after Stones River, participants in the Battle of Chancellorsville near Fredericksburg, Virginia, noticed a similar rush of wildlife from the field. When Thomas J. Jackson conducted a surprise attack on the Union right wing on the evening of May 2, 1863, he scared up thousands of animals from their peaceful rests in the thick woods. Oliver O. Howard, commander of the Union corps that was attacked, described this rush as similar to "a cloud of dust driven before a coming shower." In it were "startled rabbits, squirrels, quail, and other game flying wildly hither and thither in evident terror, and escaping, where possible, into adjacent clearings." The tactical and environmental conditions at Chancellorsville were quite similar to those at Stones River and produced one of the more memorable effects on wildlife during the war.[38]

## THE IMPACT OF FISHING AND HUNTING

Soldier accounts are studded with reports of men fishing to supplement their army rations. Sometimes those reports admit that little was caught, but at other times the haul was tremendous. The Mississippi River provided access to fresh fish for thousands of soldiers. Men rigged up fishing equipment from whatever they could find. August Bondi and John Gerth of the 5th Kansas Cavalry managed to create a fishing line 250 feet long with a dozen hooks on it and caught so many Mississippi perch, as Bondi called them, that they sold some of their catch to comrades. One day a large gar caught Bondi, in a manner of speaking. He was swimming in the Mississippi near Helena, Arkansas, when a fish six feet long bit his arm and held on. Bondi managed to get to the bank, the giant fish finally letting go only when half its length was exposed out of water. Bondi carried the scars of its teeth marks for the rest of his life.[39]

Soldiers hunted a wide variety of game, often taking random shots even when it was impossible to retrieve the carcasses. While being transported along the Tennessee River on steamboats, members of the 27th Alabama took potshots at any ducks and geese they saw on islands in the stream. This random firing usually failed to hit anything. The waterfowl "got out of the way too soon," reported Robert Lewis Bliss. Members of the 1st Maryland Artillery (CS) used flocks of ducks on the Potomac River as target practice for their canister rounds. They killed many and retrieved most of them to eat. James Robert Maxwell of the 34th Alabama reacted instinctively when a quail suddenly flew near him as his unit was marching through the countryside two days before the Battle of Stones River. He reached out and managed to strike the bird in midair, knocking it to the ground, where another man picked it up for him. Maxwell broke the quail's neck and put it into his haversack. That evening he "stuffed it with biscuit crumbs and little pieces of fat bacon, took my silk cord hat band, and hung the stuffed quail before hot coals, with a slice of fat bacon between its legs at the top." After roasting it well, Maxwell shared his feast with Col. Julius Mitchell as a supplement to their normal "broiled beef and toasted crackers."[40]

Hunting trips were not assured successes. Many Civil War soldiers reported coming up with nothing despite spending hours in search of wild game. Bradford Nichol of Rutledge's Tennessee Battery bagged one rabbit, but only because he tracked it in the snow. His relative lack of success may have been due to the scarcity of game within reach of such a large concentration of men. But that was

FIG. 5.1. Foraging for Food. This image of Federal soldiers vigorously foraging for provisions on a southern farm demonstrates a key component of food support for the Union army during the Civil War. Domesticated animals were easily available to soldiers desiring supplements to the army ration. In turn, that ready availability reduced human pressure on the far-less-available wildlife near army camps and along routes of march through the Confederacy. The impact of soldier hunger on farm animals was tremendous in comparison with what we can surmise about its impact on wild animals. *Frank Leslie's Scenes and Portraits of the Civil War* (New York: Mrs. Frank Leslie, 1894), 459.

not always the case. J. E. Thomas of the 1st Tennessee Cavalry (US) admitted that the woods near Eastport, Mississippi, seemed to be full of wild turkey and deer, but whenever his comrades went out on a hunt, they usually returned empty handed. Soldiers who sought possums often failed to catch one even when they managed to tree the creatures. But when Charles Wills took a shotgun and went into the woods near Waterford, Mississippi, he killed seven squirrels and a raccoon in one hour.[41]

Many factors, including the proximity of game, the type of animal hunted, and the hunter's skill at stalking and shooting, influenced the success of a man's outing. Most men reported higher levels of success when hunting rabbits, especially in areas where the numbers happened to be high. Using snow cover to track them, as did Nichol, helped a great deal. Using a hunting dog also was a tremendous aid.[42]

But the most successful mode of rabbit hunting was to gather comrades and perform a military-like operation. "The greatest wholesale slaughter I ever witnessed" in the war, wrote George Dallas Mosgrove, was not a battle between humans but a massive rabbit hunt staged by the Confederates of McLaws's Division in East Tennessee during the winter of 1863–64. About 2,000–3,000 men took part, surrounding an open field of sage grass one hundred acres in extent. At the tap of a drum, they marched toward the center, with ramrods ready to strike down any rabbit that tried to escape. When the four lines neared at the center of the field, Mosgrove found it "a pitiful and a ludicrous sight to see the countless little animals, timid and frightened, vainly trying to escape." After the slaughter ended, officers carefully divided the mound of dead rabbits between all companies involved, "just the same as if issuing ordinary rations."[43]

Given the chronic food shortages the Confederates in East Tennessee suffered, it is hardly surprising that they took advantage of the abundant rabbit population. Organized hunts such as this devastated a local wildlife population on a temporary basis far more than did individual hunts by men acting not only on hunger but also on the impetus of the hunting culture so prevalent in mid-nineteenth-century America. Yet there is no reason to believe that fishing and hunting adversely affected wildlife populations on a large scale or in the long term during the Civil War. Except for unusual cases as that described by Mosgrove, neither was done on an organized basis by large numbers of soldiers.

There is no doubt that the overwhelming majority of soldiers North and South hungered for more food, and for a wider variety, than they could find in the army ration. Their impulsive need to seek it could have led to a higher level of individual and even organized hunting of wildlife, except that there was a large population of domesticated animals much more readily available to them. Foraging the stock to be found on farms and plantations became the focus of food gathering for the majority of soldiers. It was far easier to snatch a cow, a pig, or a chicken from the nearest farm than to track down a deer, a squirrel, or a rabbit across the countryside. The ready availability of domesticated farm animals saved many wild creatures during the Civil War.

## A BOON TO CONSERVATION?

One cannot easily summarize the contours and characteristics of soldier contact with wild animals and the natural environment during army service because that experience was rich and varied. The best summary might be to conclude that soldiers encountered wild animals, thought about and commented on them, killed them for food, or just killed them for sport, without giving too much further consideration for them.

But that assessment may be a bit unfair. If Ouchley is on the mark, up to 43 percent of Union soldiers and 26 percent of Confederates expressed views of wildlife and of the environment that could be considered positive, appreciative, and a basis for supporting animal and natural conservation to some degree. If we assume that men who held aggressive and destructive attitudes toward nature retained them by war's end, then we must assume that soldiers who held positive and protective attitudes retained those as well.

These latter men may have looked favorably on the origins of the natural conservation movement, which began at about the time of the Civil War. Thoreau and Marsh have already been mentioned, and to them one can add the start of efforts to preserve Yosemite Valley in May 1864. In fact, it is tempting to link conservation efforts with the effects of the Civil War. Andrew Sachs sees a metaphor in the devastation of four million acres of trees during the conflict and the stumps of amputees, a link fostered by artists and intellectuals in the aftermath of the war.[44]

But the average soldier, one most likely to see wild animals as food, would hardly have been aware of the conservation movement, have read Thoreau or Marsh, or have seen the link between tree stumps and human appendages. I am not aware that a leader or worker in the conservation movement served in the Civil War. As for John Muir, perhaps revulsion against the war, rather than service in it, was the true connection between the Civil War and the leaders of conservation efforts. Muir was appalled by the destruction attending the conflict, calling the Civil War "so unsightly a monster." His younger brother, Dan, left for Canada to escape the Wisconsin state draft, and John followed him, concerned about his own chances of being conscripted. John Muir did not return to the United States until 1866.[45]

Whether the war acted as a catalyst for the conservation movement has yet to be proven. But one thing is sure: the country needed something constructive to focus on after the guns fell silent. As Frederick Law Olmsted has pointed out, nature had soothing, healing qualities for those who sought its sanctuary. Americans needed that balm in 1865, but we have no idea how many of them heard or understood Olmsted's point.[46]

## NOTES

1. Kelby Ouchley, *Flora and Fauna of the Civil War: An Environmental Reference Guide* (Baton Rouge: Louisiana State University Press, 2010), 111.

2. Ibid., 1–2, 8.

3. Ibid., 9.

4. Ibid., 121; Bao Bui, "An Englishman in a Kentucky Regiment: The Civil War Letters of Robert Winn," *Ohio Valley History* 17, no. 2 (Summer 2017): 71–72, 74.

5. Jerome B. Dann, "Ft. Hill June 25, 1863," March 12, 1902, 20th Illinois Folder, Vicksburg National Military Park, Vicksburg, MS (hereafter VNMP); John C. Arbuckle, *Civil War Experiences of a Foot Soldier Who Marched with Sherman* (Columbus, OH: N.p., 1930), 69.

6. Stewart Bennett and Barbara Tillery, eds., *The Struggle for the Life of the Republic: A Civil War Narrative by Brevet Major Charles Dana Miller, 76th Ohio Volunteer Infantry* (Kent, OH: Kent State University Press, 2004), 106.

7. Ouchley, *Flora and Fauna,* 175; Andrew Jackson McConnell Diary, July 2, 1863, Coleman, Feaster, and Faucette Families Papers, South Caroliniana Library, University of South Carolina, Columbia; August Bondi Reminiscences, August Bondi Papers, Kansas Historical Society, Topeka.

8. Ouchley, *Flora and Fauna,* 115.

9. Loveless to wife, June 22, 1863, John A. Loveless Papers, Military History Institute, US Army Heritage and Education Center, Carlisle, PA; C. Pearson to cousin, June 10, 1862, Pearson and Danielly Family Papers, Alabama Department of Archives and History, Montgomery; Timothy Phillips Diaries, July 29, 1863, Wisconsin Historical Society, Madison.

10. Andrea R. Foroughi, ed., *Go If You Think It Your Duty: A Minnesota Couple's Civil War Letters* (St. Paul: Minnesota Historical Society Press, 2008), 175–76; Sally Coplen Hogan, ed., *General Reub Williams's Memories of Civil War Times: Personal Reminiscences of Happenings That Took Place from 1861 to the Grand Review* (Westminster, MD: Heritage Books, 2004), 97–98.

11. Ouchley, *Flora and Fauna,* 184.

12. Will P. Henderson to friend, July 11, [1863], 17th Illinois Folder, VNMP; Abraham J. Seay Diary, July 13, 1864, Abraham J. Seay Collection, Western History Collections, University of Oklahoma, Norman.

13. Ouchley, *Flora and Fauna,* 149.

14. For examples, see Andrew McIlwaine Bell, *Mosquito Soldiers: Malaria, Yellow Fever, and the Course of the American Civil War* (Baton Rouge: Louisiana State University Press, 2010); Paul E. Steiner, *Disease in the Civil War: Natural Biological Warfare in 1861–1865* (Springfield, IL: Charles C. Thomas, 1968); Rhonda M. Kohl, "'This Godforsaken Town': Death and Disease at Helena, Arkansas, 1862–63," *Civil War History* 50, no. 2 (June 2004): 109–44.

15. Ouchley, *Flora and Fauna,* 133; "Louse," Wikipedia, last edited May 10, 2021, https://en.wikipedia.org/wiki/Louse.

16. George B. Carter to Bill, June 9, 1863, 33rd Wisconsin Folder, VNMP; Foster to Mildred, June 20, 1863, William Lovelace Foster Letter, Special Collections, University of Alabama, Tuscaloosa; George Dallas Mosgrove, *Kentucky Cavaliers in Dixie: Reminiscences of a Confederate Cavalryman* (Jackson, TN: McCowat-Mercer, 1957), 187–88.

17. [Henry A. Rood], *History of Company "A," Thirteenth Iowa Veteran Infantry, from September 12th, 1861, to July 21st, 1865* (Cedar Rapids, IA: Daily Republican, 1889), 18.

18. Ouchley, *Flora and Fauna*, 137.

19. Buck to Dolly, June 9, 1863, George R. Buck Letters, Old Court House Museum, Vicksburg, MS; J. Q. A. Campbell to William Rigby, January 13, 1905, 5th Iowa Folder, VNMP; David Gould and James B. Kennedy, eds., *Memoirs of a Dutch Mudsill: The 'War Memories' of John Henry Otto, Captain, Company D, 21st Regiment Wisconsin Volunteer Infantry* (Kent, OH: Kent State University Press, 2004), 268.

20. Ouchley, *Flora and Fauna*, 135; [W. A. Dickerman], June 16, 1863, 103rd Illinois Diaries, Special Research Collections, University of California, Santa Barbara.

21. Thomas G. Cropley, "The 'Army Itch': A Dermatological Mystery of the American Civil War," *Journal of the American Academy of Dermatology* 55, no. 2 (2006), 302–3; "Scabies," Wikipedia, last updated April 19, 2021, https://en.wikipedia.org/wiki/Scabies.

22. Cropley, "'Army Itch,'" 307.

23. Ibid., 303, 305–7; George M. Sternberg, "Scabies—'Army Itch,'" *Medical and Surgical Reporter* 14, no. 15 (April 14, 1866): 298.

24. Charles W. Wills, *Army Life of an Illinois Soldier* (Washington, DC: Globe Printing, 1906), 282; Hutchinson to mother, August 10, 1864, Edwin Hutchinson Papers, Louisiana and Lower Mississippi Valley Collections, Louisiana State University, Baton Rouge.

25. Charles McGregor, *History of the Fifteenth Regiment New Hampshire Volunteers, 1862–1863* (N.p.: Fifteenth Regiment Association, 1900), 173.

26. Alden Chase Brett, ed., *The Letters and Dairy of Captain Jonathan Huntington Johnson* (N.p., 1961), 20; William Shelly Diary, February 4, 6, 9, 11, 1863, Louisiana and Lower Mississippi Valley Collections, Louisiana State University, Baton Rouge.

27. Barry Popchock, ed., *Soldier Boy: The Civil War Letters of Charles O. Musser, 29th Iowa* (Iowa City: University of Iowa Press, 1995), 215.

28. Stevens to Molly, February 1, 1862 [*sic*, 1863], William H. Stevens Letters, Southern History Collection, University of North Carolina, Chapel Hill.

29. Ouchley, *Flora and Fauna*, 195.

30. For general studies of the battle, see Peter Cozzens, *No Better Place to Die: The Battle of Stones River* (Urbana: University of Illinois Press, 1990); and Larry J. Daniel, *Battle of Stones River: The Forgotten Conflict between the Confederate Army of Tennessee and the Union Army of the Cumberland* (Baton Rouge: Louisiana State University Press, 2012).

31. *A History of the Seventy-Third Regiment of Illinois Infantry Volunteers* (N.p.: Regimental Reunion Association, [1890]), 141; William F. G. Shanks, *Personal Recollections of Distinguished Generals* (New York: Harper and Brothers, 1866), 342–43.

32. *Proceedings of the Eighth Annual Session of the Survivors of the Battle of Stone's River* (N.p.: Survivors of the Battle of Stones River, [1908]), 43; Shanks, *Personal Recollections*, 343; John A. Duncan, *Diary of My Life*, 3rd Ohio Regimental File, Stones River National

Battlefield, Murfreesboro, TN; Francis M. Carlisle Autobiography, 10, 42nd Indiana Regimental File, ibid.; *Record of the Ninety-Fourth Regiment Ohio Volunteer Infantry, in the War of the Rebellion* (Cincinnati: Ohio Valley, n.d.), 30.

33. P. R. Jones, "Recollections of the Battle of Murfreesboro," *Confederate Veteran* 31 (1923): 342; Irving A. Buck, *Cleburne and His Command* (New York: Neale, 1908), 80; James Fenton Diary, 72, Abraham Lincoln Presidential Library, Springfield, IL.

34. William E. Patterson Diary, January 1, 1863, Missouri History Museum, St. Louis.

35. Thomas B. Roughton to [Sarah Roughton], February 13, 1863, Lane and Wheller Family Papers, Western Reserve Historical Society, Cleveland, OH; P. H. Sheridan, *Personal Memoirs*, vol. 1 (Wilmington, NC: Broadfoot, 1992), 234; Thomas J. Ford, *With the Rank and File* (Milwaukee: Evening Wisconsin, 1898), 9; Fenton Diary, 72.

36. Gervis D. Grainger, *Four Years with the Boys in Gray* (Franklin, KY: Favorite Office, 1902), 16.

37. David Urquhart, "Bragg's Advance and Retreat," in *Battles and Leaders of the Civil War*, ed. Robert Underwood Johnson and Clarence Clough Buel, vol. 3 (New York: Thomas Yoseloff, 1956), 609.

38. Oliver O. Howard, "The Eleventh Corps at Chancellorsville," in Johnson and Buel, *Battles and Leaders*, 3:197.

39. Mark Grimsley and Todd D. Miller, eds., *The Union Must Stand: The Civil War Diary of John Quincy Adams Campbell, Fifth Iowa Volunteer Infantry* (Knoxville: University of Tennessee Press, 2000), 123; Boughton to Augustus, June 4, 1863, Clement Abner Boughton Papers, William L. Clements Library, University of Michigan, Ann Arbor; Bondi, Reminiscences.

40. Bliss to mother, December 30, 1861, Robert Lewis Bliss Papers, Alabama Department of Archives and History, Montgomery; Tunstall Smith, ed., *Richard Snowden Andrews, Lieutenant-Colonel Commanding the First Maryland Artillery (Andrews' Battalion) Confederate States Army.* ([Baltimore]: Sun Job, 1910), 43; James Robert Maxwell, *Autobiography of James Robert Maxwell of Tuskaloosa, Alabama* (New York: Greenberg, 1926), 161.

41. Bradford Nichol Memoir, February 11, 16, 1862, Tennessee State Library and Archives, Nashville; J. E. Thomas Diary and Daybook, January 23, 1865, Special Collections, University of Tennessee, Knoxville; Thomas D. Mays, ed., *Let Us Meet in Heaven: The Civil War Letters of James Michael Barr, 5th South Carolina Cavalry* (Abilene, TX: McWhiney Foundation, 2001), 171; Wills, *Army Life*, 138.

42. Bush to wife, January 17, 1863, Andrew Bush Letters, Old Court House Museum, Vicksburg, MS.

43. G. W. F. Harper Diary, October 29, 1864, G. W. F. Harper Papers, Southern History Collection, University of North Carolina, Chapel Hill; J. Ferrell Colton and Antoinette G. Smith, eds., *Column South with the Fifteenth Pennsylvania Cavalry from Antietam to the Capture of Jefferson Davis* (Flagstaff, AZ: Northland, 1960), 34; Mosgrove, *Kentucky Cavaliers*, 186–87.

44. Judkin Browning and Timothy Silver, *An Environmental History of the Civil War* (Chapel Hill: University of North Carolina Press, 2020), 195, 197; Lisa M. Brady, *War upon the Land: Military Strategy and the Transformation of Southern Landscapes during the*

*American Civil War* (Athens: University of Georgia Press, 2012), 136–37; Aaron Sachs, "Stumps in the Wilderness," in *The Blue, the Gray, and the Green: Toward an Environmental History of the Civil War*, ed. Brian Allen Drake (Athens: University of Georgia Press, 2015), 96–112.

45. Donald Worster, *A Passion for Nature: The Life of John Muir* (New York: Oxford University Press, 2008), 85–86, 90–93.

46. Olmsted quoted in Browning and Silver, *Environmental History*, 195.

# All the Buzz

*Why Bees Mattered in the Civil War*

MARK SMITH

APICULTURE—living with and cultivating bees—was deeply embedded in American life before the Civil War. It was so pervasive that it shaped the way Confederate and Union participants experienced and made sense of America's bloodiest and costliest conflict. The very ubiquity of bees and their close relationship with humans throughout Western history hardly makes this connection unique. Bees litter scripture, appear in the political philosophy of classical thinkers from Pliny to Cicero, and animate the thinking of moderns from Bernard Mandeville to Robert Baden-Powell. For centuries, honey was the main source of sweetness available to humans, and bees had long been admired for their industriousness and their self-governance. What is perhaps surprising is the extent to which apiculture—understood in both material and metaphorical terms—permeated so many aspects of the American Civil War. Contemporaries drew on bees—their hives, their governance, their apparent habits, their sounds, even their emotions—to invest secession, mobilization, politics, political economy, and the very fighting of the war with meaning. Although little evidence supports the idea that they were used in a militarized fashion (unlike today, when deploying bees to reconnoiter for chemical weapons is actively being explored by the US military), no insect occupied such a resonant place in the minds and experience of people during the war. Interpretively, human-bee interaction might reside on the "ragged edge" of Civil War historiography; historically, it occupied a surprising center.[1]

While people—soldiers and civilians alike—during the war experienced and understood bees in multiple ways (and with several of their senses), it was through sound, listening, and hearing that human-bee interaction took on heightened and often very precise meaning. While not unmindful of the many other ways people interacted with bees, to advance our understanding of the human meaning and experience of the Civil War, we can listen to people listening to bees.[2]

The buzz of war was context specific and indebted to the relationship between humans and insects. In the Civil War, bees served as an interface between soldier and environment, at once nourishing and attacking the human body, their presence on the field, on the home front, and in literature and culture providing ways to understand myriad political, economic, and military developments. While historians of the Civil War have been relatively slow to think fully about the role of insects generally, what has been written, albeit in a largely popular vein, reaffirms the idea that apiculture was important in helping soldiers and civilians mediate their experience of the conflict. What we need to understand in addition is how bees allow us to think more broadly about what constitutes the environment, specifically the Civil War environment. They did not just interface with humans in the most obvious sensory ways (tasting honey, stinging skins), they also helped constitute the soundscape of antebellum America and the war itself. Their buzz was both literal and figurative during these years, allowing soldiers and civilians to use apiarian acoustic metaphors to better make sense of their wartime experience. Bees helped humans express the violent experience of war; their sound, their "buzz," once understood predominantly as a signifier of antebellum American identity, evolved into the sound of wincing pain and possible death. No sound quite captured combat's authenticity as the "buzz" of bees; in this way, humans lived through the environmental soundscape created by these insects to help them understand the experience of warfare.[3]

To appreciate fully how bees informed the experience of participants in the Civil War, it is necessary to examine the presence of apiarian culture in antebellum America. Knowledge about honeybees, in particular, was not the purview of specialists. Although there are thousands of bee species in North America, when people talked about bees, they seemed to have meant the honeybee. By 1860, newspaper readers could learn about the origins of the honeybee (not native to the United States but introduced probably in the seventeenth century by European immigrants) and their geographic extent. Honeybees eat nectar and pollen and convert it into honey. "There are but few bees in the new territories," claimed one apiary expert at the beginning of the war, although the 1860 US census shows that California was home to fifty-nine "apiarists" that year. More commonly, beekeeping appears to have been part and parcel of farming. It was not without its challenges. For much of the antebellum period, the bee moth threatened bees, and keepers tried to limit their damage by using different types of hives.[4]

Books on the topic were popular among antebellum Americans. Frederick Butler's *The Farmer's Manual, including a Treatise on the Management of Bees* (S. G. Goodrich, 1828) received popular airing courtesy of reviews in the *North American Review* and local newspapers, such as *The Repertory* of Saint Albans, Vermont. The focus was on the honeybee, *Apis mellifica:* "From the commencement of history to our own day, bees have been an object of attention, honey has been used, and wax has been an article of commerce." The nature of the bee-human relationship was important. "Man has never been slow to appropriate to himself the physical powers of the inferior animals," argued the reviewer, pointing out, "but of all those which have been subdued to his use the bee alone has preserved its independence." The habit of bees remained unchanged. Their "instinct," their predictability, rendered them useful. Humans could capitalize on this unwavering habit by introducing hives, which in turn bees populated. Bees never changed their food, always made hives, always defended what was there, were always led by a queen, maintained the same cells, retained the same hierarchy, and were respected for their attendant economy and sagacity. Moreover, there was money in bees, quite a lot in fact. In Ohio alone, the total value of apiculture was over one million dollars in 1861.[5]

Industriousness was at the heart of the American antebellum conceit, and the bee was the perfect proxy. A Pennsylvania newspaper from 1812 gave apiarian voice to the emerging credo that time was money, that industriousness was an American virtue. Bees were busy, time was their currency, and they seemed to understand that not making the most of an hour could be perilous to the overall health of the hive. Prosperous citizens were bee-like. By the 1830s, Massachusetts was boasting, in hyperbolic fashion, "The 'busy bees' possess not only the political and social power, but ninety-nine hundredths of the property of the State."[6]

Northerners framed westward expansion in apiarian terms. New Englanders described their antebellum towns as hives and colonies. The inhabitants were not drones but workers who, with their queen bee, made "the rude western hives . . .

resonant with the happy hum of merry, young life." Northerners were analogous to bees and were, in their thinking, the custodians of the idea that western lands should be populated by the free and industrious.[7]

But the comparison had limits. A republic, after all, was no place for monarchs, queen bees included. American voters were "as liable to be agitated and moved by a single demagogue, as are the tenants of the hive of the Queen Bee." Ever vigilant, Americans were wary of the "queen bee of the caucus," a political concentration that could coordinate power to undermine liberty. Queen bees could not be replaced but only nurtured from within the hive, with drones and workers happy to "suffer themselves to be governed by her."[8]

The United States was no monarchy, and it was the worker bees that Americans celebrated. A close cousin of Jeffersonian vigilance was the insects' reactiveness and the emotion of anger. Bees, while naturally productive and focused on their own business, should not be provoked. In 1808 certain classes, such as merchants, were deemed essential to the working of the new republic but better off left alone: "self-interest is continually before them: and a bee-hive should seldom be disturbed." Bees could be justly angry when disturbed, having something of a human emotion about them, and the "buzz of angry bees" could be heard North and South. When attacked, Americans felt justified in their anger. Whether or not bees possess emotions remains unclear; what is apparent is that antebellum Americans believed bees capable of emotion, anger specifically.[9]

This connection between bees, humans, and anger is rather more important than it might appear at first blush. As Michael Woods has shown, that emotion, especially in the context of emerging sectional consciousness, was not one widely encouraged or tolerated. Anger, he shows, was the enemy of reason and, as such, enjoyed a limited currency in civil discourse. "Throughout the generation preceding the Civil War, Americans waged a 'steady war' against anger in domestic life because they believed that the emotion threatened the relationships idealized by the cult of domesticity," maintains Woods. He goes on to elaborate: "This aversion to anger extended into politics, particularly among those who conceived of the nation as a family writ large. In a country knit together by 'mutual harmony and good feeling among all its members,' emotions which destroyed those harmonious feelings, as anger was liable to do, were politically unacceptable." Plainly, though, it was displayed, anger did matter, and it did have currency in antebellum America and during the war itself, despite the prevalence of bourgeois discursive structures working to contain and limit its expression. For anger to be expressed, an intermediary was needed. Bees helped fulfill that role. They provided antebellum Americans a safe but accurate metaphor allowing for the articulation of righteous anger and locating its cause—provocation—with precision. Bees, then, performed important emotional labor for antebellum Americans and allowed them to mediate and express a feeling otherwise excluded from their traditional lexicon.[10]

Given their importance to antebellum society, it is hardly surprising to find bees featuring heavily during the war. The very process of mobilization was apiarian, not least because it borrowed heavily from the antebellum hum-of-industry metaphor as well as a connection to the only other war available to most living memories, the US–Mexican War (1846–48). The *Baltimore Sun* reported in 1845: "Supplies of ammunition are forwarded from the arsenal by almost every conveyance to the South. Destined for Texas. The workshops resemble a beehive." This was US industry gearing up for that earlier conflict. Now, the sheer scale of the Civil War—tens of thousands of men and women, tightly coordinated—invited apiarian comparisons. During the secession crisis, it was the "buzz of conversation" about volunteering and the "buzz of business" that prevailed.[11]

The firing on Fort Sumter in April 1861 rallied northern white men to the Union cause, not like bees around honey but in the more martial fashion of having been provoked into anger. "The North indeed, is like a bee-hive swarming with its thousands that are rallying in defense of the flag of our country," exclaimed one newspaper. Angered by the attack, northern men were like bees coming to the defense of their hive. Efficient hospitals "buzzed like a bee-hive." The Greenpoint, New York, shipyard building Union ironclads was "like a human beehive," a place so busy that "ears are worthless when once you get inside." The Confederacy was not without its apiary comparisons. Mobilizing the South's cotton economy for wartime clothing entailed repurposing and expanding existing factories. As one report stated, the "Clothing Bureau in Richmond," Virginia, was "a very extensive establishment, is in full work, and presents a bee-hive appearance." Confederate soldiers returning from the front were delivered by train to Atlanta, where "the depot works like a beehive, with a busy, jostling crowd." Mobilization, something that persisted throughout the war, assumed a similar register—"the clink of hammers and the buzz of machinery," the "buzz of saws," the "buzz of sewing machines, and the hum of industry"—as both sides geared up to fight. The very idea of mass mobilization was intimately tied to the martial and productive beehive.[12]

In more material ways, bees proved important to soldiers during the war. Honey was a source of sweetness during these most bitter years and of sustenance and nourishment, too. During the war, consuming "beehive syrup" was common in both North and South. Soldiers on picket duty snagged honey from hives, supplementing their army rations. When not in battle, Confederate and Union troops foraged for a treat. The sweetness lured men, and some "tramped many a mile by night in quest of these depositories of sweets." Destroying enemy resources meant also taking their honey. Troops from an Ohio regiment in 1862 not only shot pigs, sheep, and calves on one southern farm but happily ate the honey from its beehives. The soldiers even opened "a hive full of beautiful honey, . . . though they were already surfeited." It was important for civilians, too, so much so that Confederate women booby-trapped their hives by tying them together, making it difficult for Union soldiers to steal them. Beeswax was also prized, as soldiers used it to make a salve for soothing sore feet.[13]

Honey hunting was not without its dangers, and the gustatory delight of sweetness was often paid for in the tactile currency of the sting. In great numbers, bees were a martial force. As one newspaper article from 1861 put it, "The stings of the little owners are more formidable than an entrenched army." Untested soldiers at the Battle of Antietam (September 17, 1862), most notably the 132nd Pennsylvania Volunteers, found themselves under attack not only from Confederates but also from honeybees. A rebel battery (perhaps deliberately) fired on farmer Roulette's bee yard, creating havoc not only for the insects but also among the Union troops who were stung by the angered swarm. Soldiers were seen "rolling in grass, running, jumping, and ducking." Fearing the spread of panic to other units, officers ordered a double-quick march in an effort to outdistance them. If bees did not get soldiers, wasps and hornets could. Foraging soldiers could mistake hornet nests for hives, and some found themselves stung viciously as a result. Part of soldiering involved clearing nearby hives so that troops could march or camp without fear of being stung.[14] Bees were a sometimes common enemy of humans on both sides, their loyalties naturally nonexistent.

Bees informed wartime thinking about politics and political economy just as they had in the antebellum period. Again, it was their sound that came to the fore. On the home front, the US Senate—a chamber, no less—was described as bustling, active, and productive. Its deliberations made a "noise . . . like that of an immense beehive." During the war, northern Copperheads—Democrats anxious to end the war—were considered "like a drone in the beehive—of no use to either friends or foe." "The Queen Bee of the Copperhead hive [Clement Vallandigham, leader of the antiwar Democratic faction in the North] has been arrested, tried, found guilty, and instead of being hung, as he deserved, has been sent South to his friends. This has stirred up the whole nest, and they are buzzing about as spitefully as so many wasps." Dangerous figures became wasps. The Union was a beehive, but the proper functioning of the body politic was dependent on not only industriousness but also a dedicated, unified purpose. Division from within could not be tolerated.[15]

In camp and on the battlefield, apiarian metaphors served to inspire. The men of the 1st Michigan, camped at Manassas, Virginia, were unhesitatingly compared to bees. The three beehives they maintained were valued less for their honey produced and more for the patriotism they inspired: "The industrious little creatures work on daily. No one disturbs them, nor do they offer any hostility to anybody within the encampment." Naturally, "It is presumed they are Union-loving insects, for while their owners are hostile, they manifest entire friendship for all of us, attending daily to their own affairs, the same as though law and order reigned supreme, as though there were no 'traitors' to tread the *sacred soil of Virginia,* to desecrate the land that gave birth and burial to illustrious patriots in the days of its glory." Here was the industrious, noble Yankee minding his own business, working hard, roused to action only when attacked.[16]

Apiarian metaphors entered the political discourse of the war, distinguishing slavery from freedom. Henry Ward Beecher made the distinction clearly in an 1864 essay, "How to Manage Men": "When you want to manage men, do as bee-keepers do when they want to manage bees." The imperious man—the slaveholder—says, "I own these bees, and I am going to divide and move them," and "thrusts his hand rudely in the[ir] midst"; the less imperious man—the northerner—soaks his hand with sugar and water, making it, like the free market, invisible to the bees. Gently, quietly, he inserts his hands, scooping up as many bees as he desires, directing their labor calmly, purposely, and, presumably, profitably.[17] Adam Smith's invisible hand was also sweet.

Union progress toward victory lent further voice to the association between free labor and bees. "Why, what a people you are!" a captured Confederate said. "You swarm like a bee hive. When I entered Ohio I found every valley bristling with arms, and every hill picketed with riflemen." Northerners concurred with his assessment, believing themselves to be like bees. Confederates, said Union men, erred by starting the war; they "had formed no conception of the mighty power of the free States, with the dense populations, and their millions of intelligent and industrious working men, as able to feed a war as to fight themselves." Dense. Millions. Intelligent. Industrious. Self-reliant. Free. This was the Union hive.[18]

How soldiers heard the war was very much contingent on their environment, which, in turn, was informed by how they understood and represented the sounds around them. From Morris Island, South Carolina, Union soldier Richard Jewett wrote to his wife and catalogued what he heard daily. "No one who has not been under fire can realize how one feels in listening to the varied sounds made by the different kinds of missiles with which the air is filled," he explained. "The deep tones of the heavy shot with the 'whirring' sounds of grapes & canister and the sharp 'whistle' of the Minnie ball—these sounds are from the missiles not the thunder of the explosions which send them." Real-time events intervened as he wrote, "Just at the instant I made the dot after the word then a shell exploded over our works."[19]

With the First Battle of Bull Run came new sounds, those of the cannon, rifle, musket, and bullet, that few of the men had heard before; what better way to make sense of them than to appeal to old metaphors, even when they did not quite fit. Newspapers reported on the "buzz of cannon-balls" at Manassas. Participants, however, tended to differentiate the sounds with greater precision. One Union soldier recounted "the booming of cannon and the rattle of iron hail" but heard the "whistling buzz of a shell, or the more shrill whirr of a rifled cannon shot." It was the buzz of the bee that helped many soldiers make the best sense of hot fighting, especially the experience of being fired upon. John C. Gregg of the 2nd Michigan ran out of reliable metaphors for the sound of Minnie balls being fired at him during First Bull Run—only the sounds of bees made sense: "I cannot compare them to anything else than a lot of Bumble Bees flying by only a great deal faster." For George Miller of the 3rd Michigan, it was "the cannon shot" that "whirred over heads like a shower of bumble bees." Throughout the war, bee buzz functioned as metaphor. On one level, it was used to denote activity—mobilization and a general "buzz of the camp." But in martial moments it served as a way to convey the depths of sound, the vibrational—almost tactile—quality of the noise generated by warfare. Cannon could buzz so resonantly that "the earth quivers!"[20]

It is worth remembering that the most brutal military encounters, those places riddled with pain and agony, were closely associated with the pain of stinging. At the Battle of Shiloh, the viciousness of the Confederate attack was so pronounced that one part of the battlefield came to be known as the "Hornet's Nest." At once efficient and angry, buzz denoted speed and pain—and sometimes death. "The bullets sang like swarming bees, and their sting was death," recalled one soldier from the 93rd New York of the fighting at Spotsylvania Court House.[21]

Sensory metaphors reveal much about prevailing forms of technology and economy. Sometimes they help people make sense of how to incorporate new developments into preexisting categories. This was true in the early republic, when workers in the earliest factories braided the sound of nature with the emerging register of antebellum industrial society. A loosely understood process of industrialization was shaped in part by the way workers listened. Later, more conspicuously industrial societies spoke of the "dull static-like humming" of grenades and the electrical popping of gunfire. For their part, Civil War soldiers, Union and Confederate, elected to attach a natural metaphor to the sound of imminent or near death: the buzz they associated with bees. This is not especially surprising if we keep in mind that these soldiers, regardless of sectional loyalty, were still a product of largely rural societies. Their commitment to understanding the sound of the bullets in apiarian terms is a helpful reminder that this war was not simply between an industrializing North and an agricultural South, it was between two largely rural regions.[22]

That these metaphors were insect inspired highlights, with unusual precision, the intersectionality of animal-human relations. Contemplating the depth and extent to which bees were embedded in American antebellum culture generally, and in Civil War culture specifically, helps us better understand how participants not only experienced war but also how they thought of themselves in their material and metaphorical environment. It was an environment that not only depended on physical engagement with bees but also relied a great deal on how apiarian emotions (notably, justifiable anger), organization, and politics were both reflective of human relations and constitutive of them. Soldiers' sensory engagement with insects—how they heard them especially—allowed participants to measure the progress of mobilization, mark military progress, and index the nature of pain and death. If one of our principal challenges is to better understand the experience of the Civil War, we could do worse than listen to soldiers listening to bees, than to civilians thinking about apiary culture. Without bees and their buzz, Civil War participants would have been left with an impoverished vocabulary for understanding the experiential core of what it was like to endure the making of war and the violence of warfare. And without animal studies, we would be hard pressed to access that experience in the first place.

## NOTES

1. Neville Morley, "Civil War and Succession Crisis in Roman Beekeeping," *Historia: Zeitschrift für Alte Geschichte* 56 (2007): 462–70; Sidney Mintz, *Sweetness and Power: The Place of Sugar in Modern History* (New York: Viking, 1985); "Bee Killers," UC-Berkeley Social Science Matrix, December 27, 2014, http://matrix.berkeley.edu/research/bee-killers; Lisa Jean Moore and Mary Kosut, "Bees, Borders, and Bombs: A Social Account of Theorizing and Weaponizing Bees," in *Animals and War: Studies of Europe and North America*, ed. Ryan Hediger (Leiden, The Netherlands: Brill, 2012), 27–43; Stephen Berry, ed., *Weirding the War: Stories from the Civil War's Ragged Edges* (Athens: University of Georgia Press, 2011).

2. On the need for sensory history to take animal studies seriously, see Mark M. Smith, *A Sensory History Manifesto* (University Park: Penn State University Press, 2021), 65–66.

3. Donald R. Griffin, *Animal Minds: Beyond Cognition to Consciousness* (Chicago: University of Chicago Press, 2001); Brian Massumi, "What Animals Teach Us about Politics," in *Senses and Sensation: Critical and Primary Sources*, ed. David Howes, vol. 3, *Biology, Psychology and Neuroscience* (New York: Bloomsbury, 2018), 279–89; Margo DeMello, *Animals and Society: An Introduction to Human-Animal Studies* (New York: Columbia University Press, 2012), 17–18, 284–90; Gary L. Miller, "Historical Natural History: Insects and the Civil War," *American Entomologist* 43, no. 4 (Winter 1997): 227–45, http://www.montana.edu/historybug/civilwar2.html. Environmental historians have been particularly sensitive to the sensory texture and context of the environment and have done pioneering work on environmental soundscapes especially. More recently, Civil War scholars have addressed directly the sensory signatures of the war. See Peter A. Coates, "The Strange Stillness of the Past: Toward an Environmental History of Sound and Noise," *Environmental History* 10 (October 2005): 636–65; Mark M. Smith, *The Smell of Battle, the Taste of Siege: A Sensory History of the Civil War* (New York: Oxford University Press, 2014); and Evan A. Kutzler, *Living by Inches: The Smells, Sounds, Tastes, and Feeling of Captivity in Civil War Prisons* (Chapel Hill: University of North Carolina Press, 2019).

4. *Cleveland Daily Leader*, February 5, 1861, 1; *1860 Census: Population of the United States. Recapitulation of the Tables of Population, Nativity, and Occupation*, 656–57, https://www.census.gov/library/publications/1864/dec/1860a.html. See also *Burlington (VT) Weekly Sentinel*, January 17, 1862, 4.

5. Quotations from *Repertory* (Saint Albans, VT), January 1, 1829, 1; and *Cleveland Daily Leader*, February 5, 1861, 1.

6. *Gleaner* (Wilkes-Barre, PA), July 3, 1812, 4; second quotation from *Adams Sentinel* (Gettysburg, PA), March 13, 1837, 2.

7. *Berkshire County Eagle* (Pittsfield, MA), December 3, 1863, 1.

8. *Maryland Gazette* (Annapolis), December 18, 1823, 2; *New England Farmer* (Boston), April 27, 1827, 3; *Mineral Point (WI) Democrat*, April 25, 1845, 4.

9. *Pittsburg Weekly Gazette*, October 19, 1808, 3; *Times-Picayune* (New Orleans), August 28, 1851, 2; *Sandusky (OH) Clarion*, January 22, 1849, 2; Griffin, *Animal Minds*.

10. Michael E. Woods, "'The Indignation of Freedom-Loving People': The Caning of

Charles Sumner and Emotion in Antebellum Politics," *Journal of Social History* 44 (Spring 2011): 689–705 (quotation, 692).

11. *Detroit Free Press,* September 6, 1845, 3; *Philadelphia Inquirer,* April 22, 1861, 3; *Pittston (PA) Gazette,* January 17 1861, 2; Mark M. Smith, *Listening to Nineteenth-Century America* (Chapel Hill: University of North Carolina Press, 2001), 37–47, 93.

12. *Tiffin (OH) Tribune,* May 3, 1861, 2; *Plymouth (IN) Democrat,* October 24, 1861, 1 (the story in the *Democrat* quotes extensively from one originally published in the *Richmond Enquirer*). On the buzz of machinery, see *Daily Exchange* (Baltimore), April 27, 1861, 1; and *Alexandria (VA) Gazette,* April 29, 1861, 2. On saws, see *Evansville (LA) Daily Journal,* August 14, 1861, 2; and *Monroe (WI) Sentinel,* October 9, 1861, 3. On the hospital and shipyard, see *Cleveland Daily Leader,* October 2, 1862, 1; and *Daily State Record* (Topeka, KS), February 2, 1862, 3. On Atlanta, see *Memphis Daily Appeal,* May 7, 1864, 2; and Smith, *Smell of Battle,* 9–38. African American men were not eligible to serve in the Union army until 1863.

13. *Wisconsin State Journal* (Madison), January 2, 3, 12, 1861, 3; *New England Farmer* (Boston), April 13, 1861, 1; *Democratic Watchtower* (Talladega, AL), January 30, 1861, 3. On foraging, see *Orleans Independent Standard* (Irasburgh, VT), December 6, 1861, 4. On beeswax, see *New Orleans Crescent,* July 4, 1861, 1; Miller, "Historical Natural History"; and *M'arthur (OH) Democrat,* January 23, 1862, 4.

14. *New Orleans Crescent,* July 4, 1861, Miller, "Historical Natural History"; *Cincinnati Daily Press,* September 28, 1861, 2.

15. *Baltimore Sun,* March 4, 1861, 4; *Janesville (WI) Daily Gazette,* June 25, 1863, 2; *Chicago Tribune,* May 30, 1863, 2.

16. *Detroit Free Press,* June 27, 1861, 1.

17. *Weekly Marysville (OH) Tribune,* February 8, 1865, 1.

18. *Pittsburg Gazette,* September 21, 1863, 2.

19. Richard Jewett to Lizzie "Eliza" Jewett, August 3, 1863, folder 41, box 1, Richard H. L. Jewett Letters, Boston Athenaeum, Boston, MA (my thanks to Prof. Kathleen Hilliard for sharing this source).

20. *Chicago Tribune,* July 29, 1861, 1; *Lansing (MI) Republican,* July 31, 1861, 2; John C. Gregg to "Friend Heber," Arlington Heights, July 25, 1861, 1, Dr. Peter Schmitt Collection, Western Michigan University Archives and Regional History Collections, Kalamazoo, MI; George Miller to "Dear Parents," Bull Run, July 20, 1861, 2, John F. Lane Collection, ibid.; *Indianapolis Star,* October 18, 1865, 4; *Philadelphia Inquirer,* January 16, 1863, 3.

21. Quoted in Miller, "Historical Natural History."

22. See Mark M. Smith, "The Garden in the Machine: Listening to Early American Industrialization," in *The Oxford Handbook of Sound Studies,* ed. Trevor Pinch and Karin Bijesterveld (New York: Oxford University Press, 2011), 39–57; J. Martin Daughtry, *Listening to War: Sound, Music, Trauma, and Survival in Wartime Iraq* (New York: Oxford University Press, 2015), 2; Smith, *Listening to Nineteenth-Century America,* 147–94, 261–69; and Mark M. Smith, "Krieg," in *Handbuch Sound,* ed. Daniel Morat and Hansjakob Ziemer (Stuttgart, Germany: J. B. Metzler, 2018), 391–95.

# IV

# Animals as Food IN THE Civil War

# Root Hog or Die

*Southern Pigs and Confederate Independence*

JASON PHILLIPS

IN JULY 1865 the CSS *Shenandoah* passed south of the Aleutian Islands into warmer Pacific waters. The last ship to fly the Confederate flag, the cruiser sailed toward California and Mexico to capture merchant steamers running between Panama and San Francisco. As westerly winds thawed the masts and rigging, thirty-seven hogs sunned themselves on the ship's deck. Gathered from prize ships and island traders, the hogs had spanned the globe with their Confederate companions. Lieutenant James Waddell watched a sailor "scratching a hog to sleep in order to use him as a pillow." The officer considered the sight funny and filthy. "A sailor bathes all over every morning, and that is cleanliness," he explained, "but he is nevertheless a dirty fellow" because he associates with pigs. When Waddell recorded the relationship between the hog and sailor, he reduced the animal to a possession made for man's comfort. A better way to understand their unexpected bond is to recognize that they napped together. The man's caress calmed the animal to sleep, and the pig's stillness allowed the sailor to rest. Neither would have slept without a partner, and whoever woke first surely roused the other.[1]

By exploring relationships between southern hogs and people during the Civil War era, one can explain how animal agencies and human dependencies affected various subjects at the heart of nineteenth-century America, including slavery, western expansion, sectionalism, secession, Civil War, emancipation, memorialization, and Reconstruction. More than an "imagined community," the Confederacy was a material world inhabited by hogs and other animals that shaped its intellectual, economic, cultural, and political possibilities. As Linda Nash argues, "our stories might be different if human beings appeared not as the motor of history but as partners in a conversation with the larger world, both animate and inanimate, about the possibilities of existence." For example, instead of explaining southern secession as a political effort that fell short for human reasons alone, one can understand southerners' bid for independence as a web of relationships between people and animals that tested the possibilities of national existence and failed. Looking beyond Civil War historiography, focusing on this web connects animal exploitation to human oppression and capitalism to ecology.[2]

During the Civil War era, southern and northern hogs lived and died differently. "Root hog or die," an antebellum idiom attributed to David Crockett, refers to the southern practice of releasing livestock to fend for themselves on the open commons of woodlands, meadows, and swamps. Northern and European travelers criticized southern husbandry as cruel, irresponsible, and wasteful. Southern hogs were underfed, unsupervised, and free to destroy unfenced fields. White southerners believed nature would provide for them and their pigs; things, including livestock, would take care of themselves. Keeping pigs on the open range provided mountaineers, poor whites, and even slaves a way to acquire wealth without land or labor. By 1860, the South's livestock was twice as valuable as its cotton crop. Sprawling across the region and covering millions of acres, the commons changed the environment as hogs feasted on nuts and buds.[3]

By the time Crockett coined his phrase, northerners had already closed their commons and penned their animals. "Root hog or die" contrasted with the North's hog idiom of the Civil War era, "pork-barrel politics." Northerners corralled, fattened, slaughtered, and packed pigs to maximize production and anticipate future needs. While southerners expected the land to provide for them, northerners trusted the public and the government to sustain them. Before corruption scandals in the 1870s tainted the term, the "pork-barrel" symbolized how northern society prepared for challenges by storing goods. Edward Everett Hale first expressed this notion in his 1863 story "The Child of the Public." "I needed the money," his narrator explains, "and I put my hook into the pork-barrel,—that is, I trusted the Public." Northern farmers relied on nature, too, but their "pork-barrel" represented the enterprise, invention, and good sense of northern democracy and capitalism. Hale believed that citizens in need would receive what they deserved from the region's "pork-barrel." During the greatest national crisis, it fed 1.5 million Union soldiers who, according to William Cronon, "consumed over half a billion pounds of packed meat." Providence seemed to favor the North's political economy.[4]

White southerners insisted that God preferred their way with pigs. Per capita, southern hogs outnumbered northern and western swine in 1860. Southerners pointed to this booming population, as they noted their naturally growing slave society, as proof that their political economy was harmonious and superior. James De Bow argued that the South's open range, like slavery, erased class conflict in the region. Poorer whites prospered by raising hogs on the commons and selling them to planters, who relied on salted pork to feed their slaves. According to the *Southern Cultivator*, "Bacon, from long experience, is known to be the most healthy meat diet in the world, particularly for negroes, who do most of the labor on cotton plantations." Feeding slaves bacon supposedly lowered their mortality rates. The southern relationship between hogs and slaves seemed divinely ordained for "religion and humanity."[5]

The open range accelerated western expansion by increasing southern demands for pastureland. Since colonial times, hogs served as the vanguard of white settlement by invading Native Americans' territory and consuming their corn. Expanding the commons contributed to the Indian Removal Act of 1830, which pushed Native Americans from southern states to western territory. While Cherokees died along the Trail of Tears in 1838, South Carolina writer William Gilmore Simms explained, "the indian, who finds himself upon a hillock, has no more right to it, by nature, than the hog which burrows along its borders, until he proves his right by the exhibition of faculties superior to those which the hog possesses." His views support sociologist David Nibert's insight that animal domestication, especially pastoralism and ranching, has "engendered large-scale violence against and injury to devalued humans, particularly indigenous people."[6]

How white Americans related to animals also discriminated against Native Americans and African Americans by using science to claim natural hierarchies within the animal kingdom and among human races. Josiah Clark Nott, Samuel Morton, and other American scientists compared the skulls of Native Americans and African Americans to apes and debated whether nonwhites evolved differently over time or began as a separate species altogether, the "missing link" between apes and whites. Likewise, Simms defended slavery because it *was* discriminating. For him, human bondage, like the open range, recognized and accommodated natural orders of difference by placing creatures "in their proper places." Harmony in society and nature as well as in music required inequality to avoid "discord and monotony." For Simms, emancipation threatened an ontological crisis because leveling the races meant the "forfeiture of names to things, and all barriers of present distinction broken down." Abolishing slavery would end taxonomy as much as it would upend society. For white southerners, handling hogs, charting the animal kingdom, expelling Native Americans, and enslaving African Americans civilized the world by clarifying hierarchies that produced enlightenment and progress.[7]

Southerners oppressed African Americans by relating them to hogs and other beasts through language, punishment, and commodification. Former slave Moses Grandy recalled how "pickling" slaves was common practice in the South. "After they were flogged, pork or beef brine was put on their bleeding backs, to increase the pain." As a warning to others, owners suspended pickled people in the air, their feet barely touching the ground, resembling an animal hung to bleed. Masters also branded slaves with burns and cuts and displayed them on trading blocks, where potential buyers inspected their naked bodies, poked and prodded their flesh. Women on auction blocks were inspected and valued for their reproductive potential, just as livestock was.[8]

White Americans also degraded pigs and African Americans by grading their flesh for markets. Slave traders evaluated African American bodies along a five-point scale from 0 to 1 with fractional increments, 1 or A1 reserved for top field hands with healthy, conditioned musculature. When advertisements for slave auctions marketed bodies as "prime," "choice," or "select," they referred to specific qualities along this inspection scale. As historian Daina Ramey Berry notes, "the language used by today's USDA to rate meat uncomfortably mirrors the categories for rating enslaved bodies in the nineteenth century." This relationship was not coincidental. The federal government established the USDA in 1860 to evaluate pork processed by the meat-packing industry. A common language commodified people and animals in plantation ledgers, newspaper advertisements, government records, and market registers. Grading flesh degraded humans and hogs by creating an illusion of sameness and inferiority among them while elevating owners as discriminating experts. Lost in the process were unique characteristics and family ties that distinguished each devalued human and animal.

Owners insisted that this treatment did not harm pigs and slaves because such "lower beings" did not form strong relationships and lasting memories.[9]

When northern abolitionists challenged this dehumanizing system, southern secessionists argued that slaveowners, like southern hogs, needed open access to new lands or they would perish. As the Reverend Benjamin Palmer explained, God wanted slavery to "*root itself wherever Providence and nature may carry it.*" In 1861 masters gambled that they could thrive on their own as well as hogs survived on the commons. The phrase "root hog or die" appeared more frequently in 1861 newspapers and became the title of a popular secession song. "We'll have our Independence—I'll tell you the reason why," the song explains, "Jeff Davis he will make them sing 'Root Hog or Die'!" To inspire Confederate self-reliance, James Kilroy borrowed the tune and phrase for his song "Siege of Charleston." To win independence, white southerners must "shun all Yankee treachery" and "Root Hog or Die." When the 1st Georgia Infantry marched through Tennessee, a group of women expressed Confederate loyalties by singing "Root Hog or Die." In 1862 the *Macon Daily Telegraph* in Georgia urged Confederates to rely on their own resources instead of seeking foreign help. "Consign recognition and intervention to the dogs," it said. "We have got all our own fighting, feeding, clothing, and trade to provide for—we have our own independence to win, and it is now 'Root hog, or die' with us."[10]

As this rhetoric suggests, Confederates willingly compared their circumstances to that of their hogs on the open range because they believed their ecology and economy were natural, harmonious, and superior. Their arrangement would see them through the trials of war. But hogs might have known that "root hog or die" portended a dire future, a desperate life scrounging for basic needs, not a world of plenty. While the southern rallying cry from the American Revolution, Patrick Henry's "Give me liberty or give me death," expressed an urgent preference, "root hog or die" described an imposed predicament. The hog did not choose to live free on the open range; it was compelled to fend for itself by forces beyond its control. Confederates soon found themselves in a similar situation.[11]

Animal agencies frustrated Confederate agencies. Because hogs roamed free across the South, they created logistical nightmares during the war. Antebellum farmers rounded up their animals in the fall, fattened them on corn, and either slaughtered them or drove them to markets. Peacetime traffic, transportation, and economic networks accommodated this seasonal rhythm. Wartime demands did not. Denied access to the meatpacking capitals of Cincinnati and Chicago,

FIG. 7.1. Herding Cattle and Hogs. Union soldiers drive a herd of southern cattle and hogs in this illustration by Bavarian-born Adalbert J. Volck. A refugee of the failed revolutions of 1848, Volck settled in Baltimore, where he became a major player in the professionalization of dentistry, pioneering in the development of porcelain restorations. He also became a bitter critic of the Federal government and a strong supporter of the Confederacy. In addition to espionage and courier work, Volck drew many illustrations to promote his political views and to portray Confederate efforts to achieve independence. Library of Congress, LC-USZ62–100072.

Confederate quartermasters had to pay for every aspect of the hogs' journey from interior farms to army camps instead of simply buying pork barrels and shipping them to the front. Driving hundreds of hogs took time, men, and money. The account book of Quartermaster Charles Snyder details what the open range and its hogs cost the Confederacy. Snyder worked in southwestern Virginia, buying animals and sending them to towns where they boarded trains to the Army of Northern Virginia. On December 10, 1862, he purchased 336 hogs in Dublin and hired six hands (five drivers and one manager) to deliver the animals to Roanoke. The fifty-mile journey took five days. Snyder paid the hands wages and reimbursed local farmers for keeping the hogs, the men, and the manager's horse each night. Delivering the animals to Roanoke cost $391.90. Northern freight rates varied, but shipping pork barrels by rail, steamboat, or even wagon was a fraction of the cost that quartermasters paid to herd live animals to the Confederate army.[12]

The southern relationship between hogs and humans frustrated the Confederacy in other ways. The commons reduced the size and pedigree of regional hogs.

Snyder's animals averaged about two hundred pounds. By contrast, the average hog in Cincinnati's meatpacking plants weighed three hundred pounds in 1861. Also, the "disassembly line" in northern factories carved more meat from animals than southerners' traditional butchering practices. The closest Confederate comparison to Union pork cities was Smithfield, Virginia, a town that had been curing and shipping hams since the eighteenth century. William Forrest reported that Smithfield shipped "an immense amount of bacon" in 1853. When the railroads reached the county during the 1850s, they did not come to Smithfield. Instead, pork still traveled eighteenth-century water routes. As a result, the town's hams had a difficult time reaching Confederate mouths during the war. Union authorities recognized the importance of the place and used the naval blockade, army occupations, and raiding parties to disrupt the area's hog business.[13]

Despite its "root hog or die" mantra, the Confederacy, like the Old South, needed to import meat, but now through more precarious trade networks and with a weakening currency. The Old South had imported millions of northern pork barrels, a source of sustenance that disappeared after Fort Sumter. During the secession winter, southerners anticipated losing this critical food supply and bought more Yankee pork than ever before. In February 1861, during the Confederacy's founding, the *Nashville Banner* reported, "The amount of flour, corn, and bacon which has passed through this city en route for the Republics of Georgia, Alabama, Mississippi, and South Carolina is unprecedented." Before war erupted, southern states, private citizens, and the Confederacy imported 1.2 million of the 3 million hogs packed during the secession crisis, which happened to coincide with the packing season of 1860–61. That pork boom helped elect a southern sympathizer as mayor of Cincinnati in the spring of 1861. But when Kentucky, Maryland, and Missouri remained in the Union after Fort Sumter, the Confederacy lost access to one-third of the South's hogs with them. A year later the Bureau of Subsistence explained how the war's borders deprived the new nation of pork. In a report to the Confederate Congress, the bureau admitted that less than twenty thousand hogs were packed in 1860–61 at establishments within current Confederate territory. That amounted to less than 1 percent of America's pork-packing industry. This dire situation got much worse a month later when the surrender of Forts Henry and Donelson and Union occupation of Nashville disrupted pork production in Tennessee, the Confederacy's richest hog state. "So much for hogs," wrote L. B. Northrop, the commissary general of subsistence. After Fort Donelson fell, Kentucky farmers refused to sell pork for Confederate money. In the war's final months, the pounds of meat the Confederacy smuggled through the blockade equaled the combined weight of lead and saltpeter that it imported.[14]

Focusing on relationships between southern hogs and people during the war expands our understanding of the conflict's carnage because the open range harmed more pigs than people in the Confederacy. For four years the southern commons became America's battlefield. Contending armies marched, fought, and camped where free-ranging hogs inhabited. Soldiers in both armies referred to southern pigs as "bears" to justify killing and consuming them. Rebel guerrilla Andrew Walker caught a "big grunter" that simply walked into his camp in the Missouri brush. The 3rd Wisconsin Cavalry took a more systematic approach to foraging in that state, its men rounding up hogs on the open range and operating a butcher's shop in camp. Lieutenant James Drennan of the 25th Massachusetts Infantry reported "little success" in enemy territory until the regiment "came onto cattle and swine. We soon shot and dressed what we wanted and started for camp." In September 1864 Union Major General Philip Sheridan ordered his army to seize every hog the men needed from the Shenandoah Valley and kill the rest. Within months he reported that his troops captured or destroyed 15,000 swine and 12,000 pounds of pork. Meanwhile, Major General William Sherman's men slaughtered pigs as they marched through Georgia and the Carolinas. In addition to falling prey to armies, hogs died from cholera, which spread throughout the Confederacy when animals were penned together in large numbers for the first time. According to current estimates, at least 6,794,800 southern hogs perished during the Civil War, or about ten animals for every human fatality. They did not recover their antebellum population until the twentieth century.[15]

As the war worsened, white and Black southerners forecasted the fate of the Confederacy by focusing on their "root hog or die" dilemma. In April 1864 John B. Jones remarked that robbers stole animals from Richmond residents every night. Though he worked for the War Department, Jones did not know if Confederate armies were advancing, but he understood "Famine is still advancing, and his gaunt proportions loom up daily." Jones looked to the price of bacon as a portent of Confederate fortunes. He could afford to feed each family member only an ounce of meat per day.[16]

Instead of remarking on military fortunes, North Carolina slaveholder David Harris followed the war by keeping meticulous records of his hogs. In February 1861 he worried that a long, bloody conflict would spark a slave insurrection.

"The Lord save us from such a horrid war," he prayed. But God did not shield Harris or his hogs. During the difficult winter of 1864, his hogs ate one of his lambs, a fate unheard of during peacetime. A diehard rebel, Harris rationalized that at least the Yankees had not gotten it. That summer he vowed to root hog or die with the Confederacy. His slaves expressed different views by taking his livestock. In November 1864 Harris found a bloody hog skin in his lower field, where a thief had hastily slaughtered and skinned one of his animals. "I think our hogs are killed for revenge as well as gain," he surmised, because "we have insulted a negro who is too smart to be detected." The death of his hog convinced Harris that the future would bring "a general remodeling of every thing. *Every thing.*" He worried, "how many more losses and disappointments I am to have in the hog business." Two weeks later another hog skin appeared in his field.[17]

Across the Confederacy, African Americans asserted freedom by killing southern hogs. In May 1863 former slave Jack Banks led a group of Black men on a "hog hunt" in Virginia, which consisted of "catching hogs running at large in the woods and carrying them off to kill them." When one of the owners confronted them with a shotgun, both sides exchanged fire, resulting in the deaths of one of the Blacks and the white man. When Sherman's troops descended on his plantation, South Carolina geologist Joseph LeConte hid from them and waited for a report from his overseer after they passed. "Every living thing taken or destroyed," was what he learned, "all the horses, the mules, the hogs (of which there were 100 head), cattle, chickens, ducks." His slaves magnified the chaos by being "in a state of complete insubordination—no work of any kind done." As Simms had predicted, northern levelers were erasing everything. Anarchy prevailed as distinctions dissolved.[18]

The lives and deaths of southern hogs continued to shape history after Confederate surrender. Pigs that survived the war intensified sectional hatreds by rooting in the shallow graves of Union soldiers. Outraged northerners assumed that southerners released their animals on purpose to commit this offense when, in fact, the animals were merely surviving on the commons as they had for centuries. In May 1865 Union Brevet Brigadier General James Selfridge observed unburied Union dead near Spotsylvania, Virginia. He fumed that Confederates who left soldiers' remains "for their swine and dogs to revel over" were "desecraters of the dead, unfit to associate with the living." Reports of hogs consuming Union dead increased northern demands that the government account for all fallen soldiers and bury them in national cemeteries. In the end, the US government financed a four-million-dollar project to recover and reinter Union remains on the southern commons.[19]

After defeat, southern planters closed the range, not as an acknowledgment of superior northern husbandry, but in order to keep African Americans picking cotton instead of herding pigs. In August 1865 Alabama planter James Mallory took the oath of allegiance and noted "demoralization of every kind is in the order of the day" because "the yankees seem determined to put the negro over us, they do not understand their nature, they must be forced to work." Ending the commons across the region took decades, but it first happened during Reconstruction in places like Mallory's Talladega County and other Black-majority counties. Planters managed this feat against enfranchised Blacks by restricting the vote over the commons to property owners. Arguments for fence laws sometimes focused on environmental and agricultural concerns: the commons failed to collect rich manure for fields, intermingled hog populations diminished breeding stocks, corn-fed animals produced better meat, fencing fields wasted wood, and so on. While all of these arguments had been valid before the war, white southerners did not rally to close the commons until after emancipation. "All they need," wrote one fencing advocate about freedmen, "is a little to plant, their diminutive gangs of stock can herd it about over the woods, and are no expense to them." Ending the open range contributed to white supremacy, the sharecropping system, and debt peonage. As one Kentucky newspaper explained, the plan was to shackle freedmen to plantations. "The tune . . . will not be 'forty acres and a mule,' but . . . 'work nigger or starve,'" a song that sounded eerily similar to "root hog or die."[20]

The relationships between southern pigs and people reveal how nineteenth-century agriculture, capitalism, and ecology entangled and oppressed animals and humans. The environment affected how hogs lived and died in each region, but farmers' profits, not seasonal temperatures, proved the deciding factor. Southern commons and northern slaughterhouses exploited animals and workers to maximize earnings for owners. As J. L. Anderson explains, the history of American swine "is a story of power" in which humanity's repeated attempts to transcend limits "contained the seeds of failure." The same description applies to the far briefer history of the Confederacy. In its founding, defense, and defeat, the slaveholding republic epitomized humanity's brazen disregard for its material world—the people, earth, minerals, and animals that truly constituted the nation—in favor of wild illusions, widespread fears, and audacious egos. The differences between "root hog or die" and "pork-barrel politics" affected western expansion, sectionalism, slavery, the Civil War, and Reconstruction. But their similarities redound through the twenty-first century. Both systems and the war they fought enriched a few people at the expense of millions of animals and humans, depended upon laws and politics for protection and expansion, and rationalized their existence by claiming to be natural, beneficial, and even divine.[21]

## NOTES

1. James I. Waddell, Abstract Log of CSS *Shenandoah,* October 20, 1864–November 5, 1865, *Official Records of the Union and Confederate Navies in the War of the Rebellion,* 30 vols. (Washington, DC: Government Printing Office, 1894–1922), ser. 1, 3:832.

2. Benedict Anderson, *Imagined Communities: Reflections on the Origin and Spread of Nationalism* (London: Verso, 1983); Linda Nash, "The Agency of Nature or the Nature of Agency?" *Environmental History* 10 (January 2005): 69; Lucinda Cole, Donno Landry, Bruce Boeher, Richard Nash, Erica Fudge, Robert Markley, and Cary Wolfe, "Speciesism, Identity Politics, and Ecocriticism: A Conversation with Humanists and Posthumanists," *Eighteenth Century* 52 (Spring 2011): 87–106.

3. Virginia DeJohn Anderson, "Animals into the Wilderness: The Development of Livestock Husbandry in the Seventeenth-Century Chesapeake," *William and Mary Quarterly* 59 (April 2002): 377–408; Ted Steinberg, "Down to Earth: Nature, Agency, and Power in History," *American Historical Review* 107 (June 2002): 809; Whitelaw Reid, *After the War: A Southern Tour, May 1, 1865, to May 1, 1866* (Cincinnati: Moore, Wilstach, & Baldwin, 1866), 381; Dylan C. Penningroth, *The Claims of Kinfolk: African American Property and Community in the Nineteenth-Century South* (Chapel Hill: University of North Carolina Press, 2003), 93–95; Jack Temple Kirby, *Mockingbird Song: Ecological Landscapes of the South* (Chapel Hill: University of North Carolina Press, 2006), 123.

4. Edward E. Hale, *The Man without a Country and Other Tales* (Boston: Roberts Brothers, 1894), 212, 203–4; William Cronon, *Nature's Metropolis: Chicago and the Great West,* (New York: W. W. Norton, 1991), 230.

5. Sam Bowers Hilliard, *Hog Meat and Hoecake: Food Supply in the Old South, 1840–1860* (Athens: University of Georgia Press, 2014), 94; James D. B. De Bow, "The Interest in Slavery of the Southern Non-Slaveholder," in *Southern Pamphlets on Secession, November 1860–April 1861,* ed. Jon L. Wakelyn (Chapel Hill: University of North Carolina Press, 1996), 82; J. W. Jones, ed., *The Southern Cultivator,* vol. 1 (Augusta, GA, 1843), 115.

6. William Gilmore Simms, *Slavery in America: Being a Brief Review of Miss Martineau on that Subject* (Richmond: Thomas W. White, 1838), 67; David Nibert, *Animal Oppression and Human Violence: Domesecration, Capitalism, and Global Conflict* (New York: Columbia University Press, 2013), 2; Cary Wolfe, *Animal Rites: American Culture, the Discourse of Species, and Posthumanist Theory* (Chicago: University of Chicago Press, 2003).

7. Simms, *Slavery in America,* 65. Karl Jacoby, "Slaves by Nature? Domestic Animals and Human Slaves," *Slavery and Abolition* 15 (April 1994): 88–99; Margorie Spiegel, *The*

*Dreaded Comparison: Human and Animal Slavery* (New York: Mirror, 1996); Mark S. Roberts, *The Mark of the Beast: Animality and Human Oppression* (West Lafayette, IN: Purdue University Press, 2008).

8. Moses Grandy, *Narrative of the Life of Moses Grandy, Formerly a Slave in the United States of America* (Boston: Oliver Johnson, 1844), 23; Walter Johnson, *Soul by Soul: Life inside the Antebellum Slave Market* (Cambridge, MA: Harvard University Press, 1999).

9. Daina Ramey Berry, *The Price for Their Pound of Flesh: The Value of the Enslaved, from Womb to Grave, in the Building of a Nation* (Boston: Beacon, 2017), 68; Auction Notice, "Credit Sale of a Choice Gang of 41 Slaves!," 1856, Schomburg Center for Research in Black Culture, New York City, https://digitalcollections.nypl.org/items/510d47df-a264-a3d9-e040-e00a18064a99 (accessed February 6, 2018). Grading flesh also has sexual connotations. Anthropologist Margo DeMello makes this point by interpreting a tattoo of the USDA Choice meat symbol that is marketed to women. See DeMello, *Animals and Society: An Introduction to Human-Animal Studies* (New York: Columbia University Press, 2012), 264.

10. Benjamin Morgan Palmer, "The South: Her Peril and Her Duty," in Wakelyn, *Southern Pamphlets on Secession*, 71 (original italics), 75; Anon., "Root Hog or Die," *Dixie Land Songster* (Macon, GA: Burkey, Boykin, 1863), 5–6; James E. Kilroy, "The Siege of Charleston," Confederate States of America, ca. 1863–65, https://babel.hathitrust.org/cgi/pt?id=du11.ark:/13960/t6tx44t04;view=1up;seq=2 (accessed February 26, 2018); Oscar Alexander Cantrell, *Sketches of the First Regiment Ga. Vols., Together with the History of the 56th Regiment Georgia Vols., to January 1, 1864* (Atlanta: Intelligencer Steam Power Presses, 1864), 31; *Macon (GA) Daily Telegraph*, February 15, 1862.

11. "Root Abe or Die," *Fayetteville (TN) Observer*, December 12, 1861.

12. Charles Snyder Account Book, December 10, 1862, Johnston Family Papers, 1782–1973, Virginia Historical Society, Richmond; Earl J. Hess, *Civil War Logistics: A Study of Military Transportation* (Baton Rouge: Louisiana State University Press, 2017); Erin Stewart Mauldin, *Unredeemed Land: An Environmental History of Civil War and Emancipation in the Cotton South* (New York: Oxford University Press, 2019).

13. Cronon, *Nature's Metropolis*, 229; William Forrest, *Historical and Descriptive Sketches of Norfolk and Vicinity* (Philadelphia: Lindsay and Blakiston, 1853), 481. From November 25 to December 10, 1862, Snyder purchased 152 hogs weighing 32,362 pounds, roughly 212 pounds per animal. Charles Snyder Account Book, Johnston Family Papers; Timothy Cuff, "A Weighty Issue Revisited: New Evidence on Commercial Swine Weights and Pork Production in Mid-Nineteenth Century America," *Agricultural History* 66 (1992): 62.

14. *Nashville Banner*, February 8, 1861, quoted in Benjamin Franklin Cooling, *Forts Henry and Donelson: The Key to the Confederate Heartland* (Knoxville: University of Tennessee Press, 2003), 3; Edward Alfred Pollard, *The Lost Cause: A New Southern History of the War of the Confederates* (New York: E. B. Treat, 1866), 481; L. B. Northrop, Report on Commissary Supplies, November 18, 1862, *The War of the Rebellion: A Compilation of the Official Records of the Union and Confederate Armies*, 70 vols. in 128 parts (Washington, DC: Government Printing Office, 1880–1901), ser. 4, 2:193 (hereafter *OR*, all citations to series 1 unless stated otherwise); Stephen R. Wise, *Lifeline of the Confederacy: Blockade*

*Running during the Civil War* (Columbia: University of South Carolina Press, 1988), 7; J. L. Anderson, *Capitalist Pigs: Pigs, Pork, and Power in America* (Morgantown: West Virginia University Press, 2018), 19.

15. John D. Wright, *The Language of the Civil War* (Westport, CT: Oryx, 2001), 25; Joseph M. Beilein Jr., *Bushwhackers: Guerrilla Warfare, Manhood, and the Household in Civil War Missouri* (Kent, OH: Kent State University Press, 2016), 96; Anderson, *Capitalist Pigs*, 20; J. Waldo Denny to Jonathan Moschell, November 14, 1862, *OR*, 18:27; Philip Sheridan, General Orders, No. 16, September 8, 1864, ibid., 43(2):50; Philip Sheridan to Henry Halleck, November 24, 1864, ibid., 43(1):37; Lisa M. Brady, *War upon the Land: Military Strategy and the Transformation of Southern Landscape* (Athens: University of Georgia Press, 2012). According to Doug Hurt, the southern hog population in 1866 was 42 percent less than in 1860. I calculated hog deaths by subtracting 42 percent from the 1860 census totals for swine in the future Confederate states (16,178,096), which comes to 6,794,800 hogs. This figure includes West Virginia pigs but excludes all other border South animals. If hog fatalities in Missouri, Kentucky, and Maryland are included, the total number of southern hogs killed is 9,203,295. Joseph C. G. Kennedy, *Agriculture of the United States in 1860; Compiled from the Original Returns of the Eighth Census* (Washington, DC: Government Printing Office, 1864), 185, 192; R. Douglass Hurt, *Agriculture and the Confederacy: Policy, Productivity, and Power in the Civil War South* (Chapel Hill: University of North Carolina Press, 2015), 280. In 1866 the US Department of Agriculture estimated the South's hog population was 56 percent of its 1860 total. This was a year after farmers had worked to replenish their stock. No other species suffered such catastrophic losses. The 1866 cattle population was 65 percent of its 1860 total, while mules were 70 percent and sheep were 80 percent of their 1860 numbers. See Theodore Saloutos, "Southern Agriculture and the Problems of Readjustment: 1865–1877," *Agricultural History* 30 (April 1956): 61. The northern hog population declined from 19 million in 1860 to 13 million in 1865 due to military consumption and cholera. According to Joseph Anderson, "these losses, however, did not cripple northern agriculture, even in the great western pork-producing region." See Anderson, *Capitalist Pigs*, 20.

16. John B. Jones, *A Rebel War Clerk's Diary at the Confederate States Capital*, vol. 2 (Philadelphia: Lippincott, 1866), 185.

17. Philip N. Racine, ed., *Piedmont Farmer: The Journal of David Golightly Harris, 1855–1870* (Knoxville: University of Tennessee Press, 1990), 182, 203, 351, 352.

18. John Dix to Abraham Lincoln, May 13, 1863, *OR*, ser. 2, 5:601; Joseph LeConte, *'Ware Sherman: A Journal of Three Months' Personal Experience in the Last Days of the Confederacy* (Baton Rouge: Louisiana State University Press, 1999), 32; Mary Elizabeth Massey, *Ersatz in the Confederacy* (Columbia: University of South Carolina Press, 1952), 55–78; Joan E. Cashin, "Hungry People in the Wartime South: Civilians, Armies, and the Food Supply," in *Weirding the War: Stories from the Civil War's Ragged Edges*, ed. Stephen Berry (Athens: University of Georgia Press, 2011), 160–75.

19. James Selfridge to E. K. Buttrick, May 27, 1865, *OR*, 47(1):615–16; Drew Gilpin Faust, *This Republic of Suffering: Death and the American Civil War* (New York: Knopf, 2008), 73, 225.

20. Eric Foner, *Nothing but Freedom: Emancipation and Its Legacy* (Baton Rouge: Louisiana State University Press, 1983), 64, 48; Grady McWhiney, Warren O. Moore Jr., and Robert F. Pace, eds., *"Fear God and Walk Humbly": The Agricultural Journal of James Mallory* (Tuscaloosa: University of Alabama Press, 1997), 352; J. E. Williams and William Gilham, eds., *The Southern Planter*, vol. 21 (Richmond: August and Williams, 1861), 346, 367; Mauldin, *Unredeemed Land*, 114–27. For the scholarly debate over closing the range, see Forrest McDonald and Grady McWhiney, "The South from Self-Sufficiency to Peonage: An Interpretation," *American Historical Review* 85, no. 5 (December 1980): 1095–1118; J. Crawford King Jr., "The Closing of the Southern Range: An Exploratory Study," *Journal of Southern History* 48, no. 1 (February 1982): 53–70; Shawn Everett Kantor and J. Morgan Kousser, "Common Sense or Commonwealth? The Fence Law and Institutional Change in the Postbellum South," *Journal of Southern History* 59, no. 2 (May 1993): 201–42; Steven Hahn, "A Response: Common Cents or Historical Sense?," *Journal of Southern History* 59, no. 2 (May 1993): 243–58; and Kirby, *Mockingbird Song*, 129–31.

21. Anderson, *Capitalist Pigs*, 5.

# Meat-Eating IN THE Civil War

*A Vegetarian Perspective*

EARL J. HESS

IN 2009 SOCIOLOGIST Melanie Joy coined a new word, "carnism," to describe a major, historic feature of foodways. Described as a "belief system which supports meat eating," carnism has been around for a long time and stretches across the globe. In many societies throughout history, it has been "the dominant ideology surrounding food," in the words of Margo DeMello, and "is the unquestioned default." An ideology that advocates restraint from meat eating and promotes instead the consumption of fruits and vegetables, beans, and dairy products is the "strange alternative" and thus has to be defined, justified, and defended by those who criticize the mainstream food culture.[1]

Vegetarians have been the vanguard in attempts to wean people away from a meat-based diet to a plant-based approach to eating. In the United States a vibrant vegetarian movement began in the 1830s and approached this struggle on two primary fronts. Vegetarians deployed moral arguments against the wholesale slaughter of sentient animals to satisfy the human craving for meat, pointing out that a diet that overemphasizes meat has caused many health problems for a large percentage of individuals in society. By the latter, they really meant that minimizing or excluding fruits and vegetables in favor of protein-heavy foods created a serious nutritional imbalance that led to a variety of medical problems.

Unfortunately, vegetarianism never became the mainstream approach to diet in the United States. Carnism continued to hold sway into the Civil War era, shaping the army diet and influencing individual choices about what constituted a good meal. Despite some scientific evidence that man was born to eat vegetable matter rather than meat, the historical trend has been to veer toward an animal-based diet as soon as societies could afford the expense of providing it on a large scale. America had already achieved a high level of meat eating by the time of the Civil War. This was reflected in the army ration, which privileged meat over vegetables. Despite the fact that many Union and Confederate soldiers hungered for meat, many others had trouble digesting it properly or were equally hungry for vegetables and fruits. The ration failed to provide a balanced diet for soldiers, which led to serious health deficiencies that sapped their field effectiveness. Governments failed to learn the important lesson that carnism, a culinary culture based on meat eating, has many moral, institutional, and dietary deficiencies. As a result, Civil War soldiers North and South suffered.

Elisha Stockwell of Company I, 14th Wisconsin represented the meat eater in the army. Born in Massachusetts in 1846 but raised since childhood in Wisconsin, Stockwell was sixteen years old when his regiment participated in Ulysses S. Grant's North Mississippi campaign in the late fall of 1862. While writing his memoirs after 1927, he described foraging and eating all sorts of things but mostly detailed his never-ending quest for meat. One gets the impression that eating meat was the only thing on his mind.[2]

Stockwell and his comrades often broke ranks when no officer was looking and searched for hogs on farms and plantations. This practice became so widespread that officers held roll call every time the regiment halted and inspected the men's cartridge boxes three times a day to see if they were using their rifles to kill farm animals. In response, Stockwell and his chum George Reeder procured revolvers so they could shoot hogs without using their rifles. Many officers sympathized with the troops and "would look the other way when they heard a hog squeal."[3]

Toward the end of this campaign, Stockwell recalled a typical incident near Grand Junction, Tennessee: "There came an old sow and a nice litter of pigs. I and one of the other boys got clubs and got two nice pigs that weighed about thirty pounds apiece. We skinned them, and that was as nice meat as I ever ate. The hogs ran wild in the woods at this time and lived on nuts, of which there was an abundance this year. The meat had a nutty flavor. It tasted more like bear meat than pork."[4]

This was written like a true meat gourmet. Although still a teenager, Stockwell had enormous experience at tasting meat of all kinds, wild and domestic. Even today, pork producers cater to a select segment of the meat market by feeding pigs on nuts to create the taste that Stockwell so enjoyed.

Stockwell was joined in his food preferences by a large proportion of Union and Confederate soldiers. Andrew Bush of the 97th Indiana, who also was positioned near La Grange, Tennessee, joined with Jacob Nihart to obtain a dog from a farm for use in hunting rabbits. "Killed Beef Hogs," wrote English-born William E. Carpenter of the 124th Illinois: "Good Living for a few days." Even though he had been ill, True Morrill of the 38th Iowa went out of his way to find "the head of a beef and cut out the tongue and some other meat, and had some cooked for breakfast, and kept the rest for night and cooked it up and ate some of it."[5]

It is astonishing how often soldiers bypassed their commissaries to procure meat on their own initiative. But then many of the men developed an attitude that they deserved whatever they wanted. "We soon learned that the true way to soldier, was to take all we could get, and get all we could take," recalled C. W. Gerard of the 83rd Ohio. They practiced this particular art of soldiering with intensity. "Soldiers are like children, and eat, eat all the time," William T. Sherman told his wife.[6]

Of course soldiers can be forgiven an impulsive desire for food. They were young men doing much physical labor, and it is true that the stomach influences the emotions. To be well fed with satisfying food produces an uplift of spirits. John Haley of the 17th Maine supported Stockwell's approach to hunger. "We ate all we could get our hands on," he commented early in the Overland Campaign. "Once started filling their bellies with something besides rusty port and hardtack," Haley wrote of the thriving business done by army sutlers, "the men don't seem to know when to stop as long as money or credit holds out, at which time a rigid fast begins." One day Haley devoured his ration of fresh beef "in a jiffy" and went looking for more. He and his comrades cut out spleens from the entrails of slaughtered beef and tried them. "I have never heard before of eating such trumpery . . . , but necessity drives us to sample this disgusting filthy mess." On his discharge from the army, the first meal Haley ordered at a restaurant featured sausages.[7]

The desire for meat extended beyond Union army ranks. Naval personnel shared their comrades' hunger. Men manning the mortar boats that bombarded

Vicksburg during the siege complained that they ate meat only once per day. Confederate soldiers also pined for more good quality meat, especially fresh beef.[8]

Civil War archaeologists regularly document the presence of meat bones at campsites. On Folly Island, South Carolina, a camp occupied by the 55th Massachusetts, 1st North Carolina Colored Infantry, and 2nd US Colored Troops contained mostly hog and beef bones. Knife and saw marks on them indicated that those responsible for preparing the meat were well trained in how to butcher the carcass. Because of the absence of evidence for salted meats, archaeologists assume that cattle were delivered live to the island, killed, and the meat prepared on site.[9]

The findings at Folly Island confirm that a great deal of administrative effort went into providing meat to Union soldiers. This was part of what contemporaries thought was a generous attitude by the government. "There was nothing good enough for a Soldier that would leave his home and friends to fight the battles of his country," commented Charles O. Musser of the 29th Iowa. Even the ever-hungry Haley thought "no government under the sun ever made such generous provision for its soldiers."[10]

Federal officials were aware that their troops received the most liberal army ration of any military force in the world. This was linked to food ways prevalent in American society as a whole. "Americans consumed more food and a greater variety of food than did the people of any other nation," concludes historian Edgar W. Martin. He set the yearly per-capita consumption of meat in the United States as 183.9 pounds during the 1850s. Richard Delafield, member of a War Department commission to observe the Crimean War, noted the difference between the American army ration and that of other nations. In Europe "greater reliance is placed upon vegetable matter, studying the least consumption of animal food," while in the US Army, "meat constitutes a principal element of the ration, vegetable matter being secondary."[11]

Many Union soldiers recognized the largesse and were satisfied the government was taking good care of them. How much good-quality meat they received played the largest role in determining whether they were satisfied. David Brett of the 9th Massachusetts Battery told his wife that he received fresh meat four days a week. "On the whole we live well enough better than most of folks at home," he concluded.[12]

Federal commissaries of subsistence, charged with feeding Union forces, were attuned to the tastes of their men and tried whenever possible to give them what

FIG. 8.1. Providing Meat for Soldiers. Providing fresh beef for soldiers was the most complex and difficult part of an army commissary's job. This image vividly illustrates that the killing of cattle, and the processing and distributing of beef, was big business within the military system. Most of this took place outdoors in close proximity to army camps in all sorts of weather and during all seasons. While many soldiers craved fresh beef and pork, many others could not digest these meats properly and hungered for more fruits and vegetables, which the army ration failed to provide in proper quantities for a balanced diet. *Frank Leslie's Scenes and Portraits of the Civil War* (New York: Mrs. Frank Leslie, 1894), 331b.

they wanted. They knew that beef was the top choice of meat for most, but they recognized that it was the "costliest meat ration" as well. Capt. S. S. Patterson reported that the soldiers preferred beef when in camp but found it too "heavy and bulky" when on the march. It had to be cooked and eaten on the spot where issued, and the troops tended to throw it away when their units were on the move. Commissary John L. Hathaway, in contrast, thought soldiers preferred salt pork as a rule. "The quantity goes further, is easier kept, and can be used in a greater variety of ways than any other, and has the advantage of being used raw." The men really liked good bacon, but it too easily spoiled. When it came to beef, Hathaway argued that soldiers disliked salt beef but enjoyed fresh beef for at least three days out of five.[13]

Providing meat to the army consumed more time, effort, and funds than did any other item on the army ration. A slaughter yard near Nashville employed

182 butchers who managed to kill and cut up fifty-four cattle each morning. "An animal would be knocked down and nearly skinned before he was dead," observed one soldier, "it being weighted out as fast as killed." The Nashville yard issued 100,000 rations per day. Commissaries at the National Monument Yard in Washington, DC, slaughtered 13,741 cattle from March 1864 to July 1865, issuing 8,315,550 pounds of fresh beef. In addition to that amount, they had to condemn 9,785 pounds of it for various reasons and sold 271,900 pounds of fresh beef to officers, who were responsible for purchasing their own food.[14]

"Fresh beef bothers me more to issue than all the rest," complained an officer who filled in for the regimental commissary of the 1st Alabama Cavalry (US) for a few days. Still, most commissaries worked hard to satisfy the demand. To prepare for the Overland Campaign, Lieutenant Colonel Thomas Wilson, chief commissary of the Army of the Potomac, needed 6,000 cattle shipped fifty miles from Alexandria, Virginia, to the army in the field. The Orange and Alexandria Railroad had cattle cars only for 300 head per day, but Wilson needed 1,200 head per day for five days. So, railroad workers put fences on flatcars and broke open holes in the side of boxcars to provide some ventilation and accommodate more cattle. The railroad thus managed to transport 1,800 head per day to Wilson, who used three hundred men to unload and take care of the cattle.[15]

Wilson did not mention beef when compiling a list of food items he provided the Army of the Potomac during the Overland Campaign, but pork certainly ranked high on that list. From May 1 to June 3, 1864, he supplied 1,003,400 rations of pork to the men, who numbered about 100,000 at the start of the drive. In contrast, he supplied them with very little in the way of vegetables. Dried apples amounted to 535,840 rations, pickles to the amount of 139,200 rations, and pickled cabbage at 416,533 rations. The troops received about as much whiskey (410,787 rations) as they did vegetables. Only coffee, sugar, and salt exceeded the number of meat rations issued by Wilson.[16]

With so much experience issuing fresh beef, commissaries became expert at the process. Based on three years of dealing with cattle herds, Captain W. R. Murphy recommended choosing fleshy rather than fat cattle so they would not lose so much weight on the road. He found that soldiers usually rejected fat beef and preferred to boil their beef rations. He thought cattle reached maturity at four years and began to age at seven years, after which the meat became "coarser and tougher." Murphy estimated that a head of cattle weighing from 1,100 to 1,400 gross pounds was optimal.[17]

The problem with fresh beef was that it tended to go bad quickly. Samuel H. Stevenson of the 48th Ohio thought it "invariably spoils before the second week." Union and Confederate soldiers observed maggots crawling around on fresh meat and piles of rotting beef in army camps. That is why Lieutenant Colonel G. Bell told John L. Hathaway to conduct an experiment at the National Monument Yard in November 1864. He wanted to establish some data on how quickly the flesh of slaughtered cattle would spoil. Hathaway weighed two cattle before killing them and then weighed each quarter separately after the slaughtering. Bell told him to weigh the carcass every hour "until the meat ceases to lose weight or you are compelled to issue it in consequence of not being able to keep it from spoiling." Bell also instructed Hathaway to regularly check the temperature of the carcass, as well as the air both outside and inside the building, to measure the "time required for all the animal heat to leave the meat." Hathaway was to note how long it took for it "to become fixed, rigid, and firm." The results presumably were useful to the army in its large-scale issue of fresh beef to thousands of soldiers.[18]

Bell's concern about body temperature leaving the meat relates to a common idea that this heat was unhealthy for the consumer. Captain Murphy recommended that, when butchered during the summer months, cattle carcasses should be hung up overnight so "all the blood heat will have departed, and many cases of diarrhea prevented among the troops, caused in a majority of instances by the cooking of fresh beef just slaughtered and the blood heat remaining therein."[19]

It is apparent that widespread desire for meat led to large administrative structures to supply it both within the army and within American civil life. In fact, American and British societies have always ranked very high among international meat eaters both in terms of demand and supply. Writing in 1859, two years before Fort Sumter, Peter Lund Simmonds commented on this subject in his *The Curiosities of Food*. He noted the link in most people's minds between extensive meat eating and affluence. "A poor nation could not indulge in the luxury," Simmonds commented of the English. In France the average man consumed as little as one-sixth of a pound of meat per day. "An Englishman or an American would starve upon such fare," Simmonds asserted. He noted that in New York and London, half a pound of meat a day per person was consumed, with more beef and less sheep in New York compared to the English capital.[20]

Although the most advanced nations in the West were slowly creating a massive international system of growing, shipping, and slaughtering animals to meet this demand, the turning point in the meat industry was reached in 1945. Animal historians refer to the "Great Acceleration" that took place after World War II, as the link between food culture and global industry provided ever increasing numbers of food animals until today something like 50 billion of them are slaughtered worldwide every year. The per-capita consumption of meat in the United States rose from 183.9 pounds annually in the 1850s to 274.4 pounds by 2002. The inhumane conditions imposed on most of these sentient creatures in what have amounted to animal factories have justly raised criticism from concerned observers.[21]

By the time of the Civil War, Europe was experiencing a decided increase in the demand for meat that suppliers there could not satisfy. Population was increasing along with average wealth; people were switching from cereal-based diets to ones based on meat. The United States, and to a lesser degree Canada, Australia, New Zealand, Argentina, and Uruguay, began to supply that demand as the international meat industry grew rapidly.[22]

The Ohio Valley was the center of the livestock industry in America before the Civil War, with Cincinnati the acknowledged pork capital of the country. But Chicago was poised as its major competitor before 1861. In fact, the demand for meat by Union soldiers greatly increased Chicago's share of the market. It "had virtually supplanted Cincinnati as the livestock capital of the United States" by 1865. Then, with British consumers as its best customers, the US meat industry boomed by the 1880s.[23]

Even as the international meat industry began to form, a vibrant vegetarian movement developed in Britain and the United States. It began simultaneously in both countries during the 1830s, an age of social reform in many interconnected ways. Promotion of a plant-based diet became prominent enough to enlist the sympathies of many and draw attention from the meat eaters. The Alcott House community in England coined the term "vegetarian" by 1838, and nine years later a Vegetarian Society appeared. Adherents stressed the immorality of killing animals for human taste and noted that many people had health problems exacerbated by a meat-heavy diet.[24]

The roots of vegetarianism are deep, extending to ancient Greece. In North America Benjamin Franklin had practiced its philosophy, while small groups in colonial America had refused to eat meat. A biblical injunction from Genesis, chapter 1, verses 29–30 enjoins humans to consume only vegetables and herbs. When the modern movement began in the United States during the 1830s, Sylvester Graham emerged as a major figure, becoming a temperance advocate at the same time. He gave lectures urging a plant-based diet mainly for health reasons. A vegetarian community called Fruitlands was created by A. Bronson Alcott, father of Louisa May Alcott, in Massachusetts in 1843.[25]

The American Vegetarian Society appeared following a major convention of advocates in New York City in 1850. Members typically were involved in many other social-reform movements, too, such as abolitionism, temperance, and feminism. They saw connections between meat eating and war, urging listeners to stop violence to animals and thereby reduce the culture of violence toward people. Their provocative messages more often fell on indifferent than receptive ears. Worse yet, they often drew overheated criticisms from meat eaters who denounced them as heretics. Vegetarians had to endure a good deal of prejudice, ignorance, misunderstanding, and scorn.[26]

In both the United States and Britain, the vegetarian movement began to wane by the time the Civil War broke out. The only bona-fide vegetarian I have found in either army was Henry Stephen Clubb. Born in England, he migrated to the United States in 1853 and became an abolitionist. Working as a journalist for the *New York Tribune,* Clubb moved to Michigan by 1857. He became a captain and assistant quartermaster in the Union army. As an officer, Clubb was responsible for procuring his own food and asked his wife, Anne, to send him a large quantity of dried blackberries. After the Battle of Iuka on September 19, 1862, Clubb also acted as commissary of subsistence for Col. William W. Sanford's brigade in the Union Army of the Mississippi. Now responsible for feeding several thousand soldiers, he utilized local mills to grind corn for the brigade after Confederate cavalry cut their railroad supply line during Grant's operations in North Mississippi. Clubb was sure the cornmeal would be healthier for the men than flour.[27]

In 1862, when Clubb was feeding his men, physician Reuben Mussey published a strong argument in favor of vegetarianism in his book *Health: Its Friends and Its Foes.* As a professor of anatomy and surgery at Dartmouth College, Mussey argued that humans, like the great apes, were designed by nature for a plant-based diet. He cited the economy of such a diet, believing that the land devoted to feeding pigs and cattle for human consumption could support a far larger human population if devoted to fruits and vegetables. He argued that fruits and vegetables contained all the nutrients man's constitution required, and a vegetarian diet would make people less aggressive. Mussey himself had been a practicing vegetarian for thirty years.[28]

Given the lack of identifiable vegetarians in the armies of the Civil War, it is impossible to argue that the philosophical and moral arguments of the plant-based-diet advocates had any effect on soldiers. But their argument concerning health definitely can be proven among those men in uniform. Mussey was right to argue that the human constitution was not uniformly capable of absorbing large amounts of meat.

"I had a severe cholic and diarrhea this morning from eating fresh beef," wrote William H. Bradbury of the 129th Illinois to his wife. Confederate William T. McGlothlin of the 30th Tennessee complained during the Vicksburg Campaign that many of his comrades were "sickening from the use of *bad* water, fresh beef, & marching in the dust." Some men identified pork rather than beef as their dietary culprit. Onley Andrus of the 95th Illinois told his Molly that he could not stomach pork unless "forced right down to it." He marveled that some of his comrades could "live on it if they can get it." Paymaster John Oscar Culver allied with Andrus in his low tolerance level. "I feel kind of peculiar, from eating so much *pork* I suppose," he told his wife. William B. Baker of the 1st Maine Cavalry knew that vegetables were "essential to our health," yet the army did not provide nearly enough of them.[29]

Many soldiers experienced what Henry S. Nourse of the 55th Illinois called an "irrepressible craving . . . for fresh vegetables, fruit and other savory additions to the unvarying army rations." These men foraged for wild blackberries, domestic peaches, apples, green corn, tomatoes, potatoes, and turnips with the same intensity as Elisha Stockwell foraged for pork.[30]

Hunger for fruits and vegetables increased on active campaign because the marching ration of both armies restricted commissaries to the basics only—hardtack, salt pork, and small rations such as sugar and salt—to lessen the burden on strained logistical systems. Only when stationary in camp could soldiers receive the full army ration. Even that full ration, however, contained minimal fruits and vegetables. Commissaries had options within the standard army ration, but they usually privileged meat over fruits and vegetables. Desiccated vegetables were widely issued in the Union army, but soldiers did not take to them. "The men give no reason," reported Commissary W. P. Martin "except that they don't like them." Desiccated food "will hardly be taken by the troops as a gift," frankly wrote another commissary.[31]

At its best, the Union's army ration was unbalanced in favor of meat and shortchanged fresh fruits and vegetables, despite its reputation as the most generous in the world. At its worst, when on active campaign, the military ration caused serious health problems. Robert Bruce Hoadley of the 26th Iowa was among 30,000 Federals who lived almost continuously on Mississippi River steamers during the Chickasaw Bayou and Arkansas Post campaigns. The men were not allowed to start fires on board and thus existed on hardtack and raw pork. Once deposited on dry land again, "we lived better[,] had vegetables," and "the mens health began to improve." As the Atlanta Campaign stretched into four months of continuous contact with the enemy, Federal soldiers lived for a long time on the marching ration. "I never before so felt the lack of vegetables, as I have on this campaign," wrote Mendal C. Churchill to his wife.[32]

Union soldiers relied on their own resources to satisfy cravings for fruits and vegetables during and after the Siege of Vicksburg. Fruit was "stripped off [the trees] so fast as it shows the least appearance of ripeness by the negroes & sold to the soldiers," wrote Samuel H. Stevenson of the 48th Ohio. Sick of eating pork, Charles Willison of the 76th Ohio "bought me a can of plums, holding about a pint, which only cost me a dollar. Golly! But they were good, I only wish dollars or fruit were plenty." Whenever the season for any kind of fruit or vegetable arrived, soldiers foraged from the countryside. "We draw flour and make blackberry puding and peach pies and live like kings," wrote Samuel Styre of the 42nd Ohio. "If I should live to get home I promise myself a luxurious time living on fruits that I am almost totally denied here," declared Quartermaster George Thomas of the 53rd Indiana after the fall of Vicksburg.[33]

We must keep in mind that cravings for fruits and vegetables involved much more than taste. They were related to the overemphasis on meat in the army ration, which was the result of actions by commissaries and the politicians in Congress who were responsible for approving every item in that ration.

For many volunteers, their initial exposure to army rations was a shock. "For the first time in our lives we were fed on salt meat and tack bread," recalled Frank L. Richardson of the 13th Louisiana. Farm boys in the regiment, "accustomed to regular habits and vegetable food at home, were attacked by diarrhoea, and became generally debilitated." City boys fared better. Richardson's observation that volunteers who lived in the countryside were hit harder by the army ration is borne out by statistical evidence coming from the Early Indicators project, an analysis of massive datasets on the military service and postwar health of Union soldiers.[34]

Officers purchased their own food but often had to subsist on the same fare as enlisted men during active campaigns. During the Atlanta drive, there was very little to be purchased from local markets, and most Union officers bought food from army commissaries who had only the marching ration to sell them. Lieutenant Colonel Charles F. Morse of the 2nd Massachusetts complained of a "never changing diet of pork, hard bread and coffee with occasional fresh beef." He was disgusted by the fare. "I feel almost a loathing at the sight [of] what is spread on the table I never eat more than enough to just satisfy my appetite and then get out of sight and smell of the dinner or other meal as soon as possible and take a pipe."[35]

The most serious health consequence of the shortage of fruits and vegetables in the army ration was the widespread occurrence of scurvy. It was far more thoroughly documented among Union forces than among the Confederates, but one can safely assume it was a problem for both North and South. Two to three months without significant intake of vitamin C usually was enough to bring on the condition. The body does not store more than a six-month supply of vitamin C, but mid-nineteenth-century people did not have access to the extensive fruit and vegetable storage facilities available in the twenty-first century and had to eat them on a seasonable basis. Their bodies typically stored much less than a six-month supply of the needed vitamin. The almost universal occurrence of scurvy among army populations arose from the restrictions inherent in the army ration and the limited opportunities for soldiers to procure fruits and vegetables on their own.[36]

Scurvy was on the rise in the Union army by the latter part of the war due to persistent malnutrition caused by the lack of fruits and vegetables. The onset of almost continuous campaigning by the major armies meant that soldiers existed on the marching ration for months on end. This rise in scurvy was linked to a dramatic increase in the percentage of wounded men who died of their battlefield injuries. The condition weakened their constitutions enough to limit their ability to recover from combat wounds. During Sherman's operations in the last year of the war, the death rate of wounded Federals "mimicked the incidence of diagnosed scurvy" in his army group, according to a medical historian.[37]

Contemporary physicians saw the connection between scurvy and the lack of fruits and vegetables. The best antidote was "a liberal supply of fresh vegetable food." Joseph Janvier Woodward criticized the government for paying so little attention to the need for fruits and vegetables in the ration and was not surprised that some degree of scurvy would be present virtually throughout the army.[38]

Because scurvy produced a severe drain on army effectiveness, commanders reacted when alerted to its presence. Army of the Potomac headquarters issued special orders for antiscorbutics to be shipped and issued to the men at the end of the Overland Campaign as operations continued around Petersburg.[39]

Still, many soldiers in that army suffered for want of proper food to combat this plague. Meat-eater John Haley of the 17th Maine heard of a sour-apple tree near his regiment's position and made his way to it. He found it was exposed to Confederate fire but decided that "it was less disagreeable to die by the bullet than by scurvy," which he noted was "making such inroads into my health." A month later, in mid-July 1864, Haley's situation had not improved. "Hundreds of men, myself included, amble around on legs as raw as a piece of meat. This condition is the result of having little or no vegetable food. We exhausted all the local gardens weeks before. Even then, but one man in ten managed to get a mouthful of vegetable sustenance."[40]

Charles O. Musser of the 29th Iowa suffered from scurvy during the Mobile Campaign of March–April 1865. "Most all of us had a touch" of it, he reported home, "from liveing on nothing but Bacon, Hardbread, and Coffee—No vegetables at all." Musser reduced in weight from 146 to 118 pounds by the end of this relatively short campaign.[41]

As bad as scurvy was for Union soldiers in the field, it was far worse for those penned up in military prisons by a government that failed to provide them basic living conditions. Orderly Sergeant Edwin R. Mason of the 13th Iowa recalled the horrid effect of scurvy on the prison population at Andersonville. "I have seen men walking around with the flesh falling off their legs and arms, their sores filled with maggots, and no way of getting rid of them—literally eaten alive" by the effect of advanced stages of scurvy.[42]

Night blindness was a somewhat less severe condition brought on by a deficiency of fruits and vegetables. Although not as widespread as scurvy, it affected thousands of soldiers. The body can store vitamin A longer than vitamin C, and thus evidence of night blindness took longer to manifest. The army ration was just as deficient in both vitamins, especially the marching ration. Foods such as sweet potatoes, eggs, cheese, and liver are rich in vitamin A, but the only item in the army ration that could supply the essential vitamin was Irish potatoes.[43]

Vegetarians were right to urge everyone to switch from an animal-based diet to a plant-based diet for health reasons. Even if one did not want to go that far, most Americans could have lived a healthier life if they had balanced their diet with more fruits and vegetables compared to meat. Many Civil War soldiers reflected general dietary preferences and placed meat at the head of their list of preferred foods, while an equal number of other soldiers desperately wanted more fruits and vegetables than the army gave them. Because the military and the politicians who regulated its ration ignored the vegetarian perspective, literally thousands of soldiers suffered unnecessary health problems in the form of scurvy and night blindness that sapped the field effectiveness of army units.

As noted earlier, the postwar era saw a dramatic increase in the demand for meat in the Western world, but it also saw a rejuvenation of the vegetarian movement. Henry Stephen Clubb survived his army service to play a major role in this revival. He created the Vegetarian Society of America in Philadelphia in 1866 and started a magazine, *Food, Home and Garden,* in 1889. Clubb wrote *Thirty-nine Reasons Why I Am a Vegetarian,* which was published as a pamphlet by his society in 1903. He noted that the slaughtering process created anxiety and fear in animals, filling their flesh and blood with toxins that humans then consumed. He also argued that grains, fruits, and vegetables provided enough nutrition for people without resorting to the fast-decaying flesh of other animals. Nurse Clara Barton converted to this food philosophy in 1873 for health reasons. Physician John Harvey Kellogg took the movement to new heights of awareness toward the turn of the twentieth century. A corresponding rebirth of the vegetarian movement took place in Britain at the same time.[44]

"Man debases himself by his use of animal food," A. Bronson Alcott once wrote, "there was no butcher in Paradise." Clubb cited another moral reason why he practiced vegetarianism. "A spiritual-minded man cannot partake of that which requires him to destroy the lives of inoffensive creatures in order to partake of their bodies." He also pointed out that strong animals, such as horses, elephants, camels, and oxen, were all vegetarians and needed no meat in their diet to perform hard physical work for humans.[45] But neither the moral argument nor the rational one attained mainstream support in the Civil War era, at least within the army. Also ignored was the widespread evidence that a meat-based diet was inadequate to sustain soldier health. Much suffering could have been averted if carnism had not held sway so vigorously in mainstream American culture.

## NOTES

1. Margo DeMello, *Animals and Society: An Introduction to Human-Animal Studies* (New York: Columbia University Press, 2012), 38–139.

2. Byron R. Abernethy, ed., *Private Elisha Stockwell, Jr., Sees the Civil War* (Norman: University of Oklahoma Press, 1958), ix, 61, 98–100, 109–11, 136–39.

3. Ibid., 52–53, 55.

4. Ibid., 57–58.

5. Bush to wife Mary, January 17, 1863, Andrew Bush Letters, Old Court House Museum, Vicksburg, MS; December 23, 1862, William E. Carpenter Army Record, Huntington Library, San Marino, CA; July 3, 1863, True Morrill Diary, State Historical Society of Iowa, Des Moines.

6. C. W. Gerard, *A Diary: The Eighty-Third Ohio Vol. Inf. in the War, 1862–1865* (Cincinnati, OH: N.p., 1889), 13; Sherman to Ellen, June 27, 1863, *Sherman's Civil War: Selected Correspondence of William T. Sherman, 1860–1865*, ed. Brooks D. Simpson and Jean V. Berlin (Chapel Hill: University of North Carolina Press, 1999), 493.

7. John Haley Journal, *The Rebel Yell and the Yankee Hurrah: The Civil War Journal of a Maine Volunteer*, ed. Ruth L. Silliker (Camden, ME: Down East Books, 1985), 71, 159, 204, 276, 282.

8. Eugene Mack to David D. Porter, June 10, 1863, *Official Records of the Union and Confederate Navies in the War of the Rebellion*, vol. 25 (Washington, DC: Government Printing Office, 1912), 67; Edwin Rennolds Diary, June 7, 1864, Edwin Hansford Rennolds Sr. Papers, Special Collections, University of Tennessee, Knoxville.

9. James B. Legg and Steven D. Smith, *"The Best Ever Occupied . . .": Archaeological Investigations of a Civil War Encampment on Folly Island, South Carolina* (Columbia: South Carolina Institute of Archaeology and Anthropology, 1989), ii, B-1, B-16.

10. Charles O. Musser to father and mother, February 17, 1863, *Soldier Boy: The Civil War Letters of Charles O. Musser, 29th Iowa*, ed. Barry Popchock (Iowa City: University of Iowa Press, 1995), 28; Haley Journal, in Silliker, *Rebel Yell*, 228–29.

11. Henry W. Halleck to Edwin M. Stanton, November 25, 1862, *The War of the Rebellion: A Compilation of the Official Records of the Union and Confederate Armies*, 70 vols. in 128 parts (Washington, DC: Government Printing Office, 1880–1901), ser. 1, 19(1):6 (hereafter *OR*, all citations to series 1 unless otherwise stated); Edgar Winfield Martin, *The Standard of Living in 1860* (Chicago: University of Chicago Press, 1942), 72, 400; Richard Delafield, *Report on the Art of War in Europe in 1854, 1855, and 1856* (Washington, DC: George W. Bowman, 1860), 89.

12. Brett to wife, March 22, 1863, *"My Dear Wife . . .": The Civil War Letters of David Brett, 9th Massachusetts Battery, Union Cannoneer*, ed. Frank Putnam Deane II (Little Rock: Pioneer, 1964), 41.

13. John L. Hathaway to A. B. Eaton, June 28, 1865, *How to Feed an Army* (Washington, DC: Government Printing Office, 1901), 62; S. S. Patterson to A. B. Eaton, August 25, 1865, ibid., 149.

14. Jenkin Lloyd Jones, *An Artilleryman's Diary* ([Madison, WI]: Democrat Printing, 1914), 275; *How to Feed an Army,* 38–40.

15. Federal officer quoted in Glenda McWhirter Todd, *First Alabama Cavalry, U.S.A.: Homage to Patriotism* (Bowie, MD: Heritage Books, 1999), 135; Thomas Wilson, "Feeding a Great Army," *United Service* 2, no. 2 (February 1880): 149.

16. E. R. Goodrich to Thomas Wilson, May 25, 1864, *OR,* 36(3):197; Wilson, "Feeding a Great Army," 158.

17. W. R. Murphy to A. B. Eaton, n.d., *How to Feed an Army,* 127.

18. Samuel H. Stevenson to parents, brothers, and sisters, June 12, 1863, 48th Ohio Folder, Vicksburg National Military Park, Vicksburg, MS; Haley Journal, in Silliker, *Rebel Yell,* 177; Flavel C. Barber Diary, *Holding the Line: The Third Tennessee Infantry, 1861–1864,* ed. Robert H. Ferrell (Kent, OH: Kent State University Press, 1994), 128; *How to Feed an Army,* 44, 46.

19. W. R. Murphy to A. B. Eaton, n.d., *How to Feed an Army,* 129.

20. Peter Lund Simmonds, *The Curiosities of Food: Or the Dainties and Delicacies of Different Nations Obtained from the Animal Kingdom* (Berkeley, CA: Ten Speed, 2001), 2–3, 5.

21. DeMello, *Animals and Society,* 144; "List of Countries by Meat Consumption," Wikipedia, last edited March 26, 2021, https://en.wikipedia.org/wiki/List_of_countries_by_meat_consumption; Chris Otter, "Eating Animals," *The Routledge Companion to Animal-Human History,* ed. Hilda Kean and Philip Howell (London: Routledge, 2019), 474, 476.

22. Richard Perren, *Taste, Trade, and Technology: The Development of the International Meat Industry since 1840* (Aldershot, UK: Ashgate, 2006), 7–9.

23. Jimmy M. Skaggs, *Prime Cut: Livestock Raising and Meatpacking in the United States, 1607–1983* (College Station: Texas A&M University Press, 1986), 18, 44–45, 90, 108; Perren, *Taste, Trade, and Technology,* 79.

24. James Gregory, *Of Victorians and Vegetarians: The Vegetarian Movement in Nineteenth-Century Britain* (London: Tauris Academic Studies, 2007), 1–5, 22, 31, 34, 36–38, 188.

25. Karen Iacobbo and Michael Iacobbo, *Vegetarian America: A History* (Westport, CT: Praeger, 2010), ix–x, xv, 1, 9, 17, 20, 60–61.

26. Ibid., 71, 73, 75–76, 113.

27. Gregory, *Of Victorians and Vegetarians,* 51; Iacobbo and Iacobbo, *Vegetarian America,* 89, 91; Clubb to Anne, August 23, 31, September 30, December 21, 1862, Henry Clubb Collection, Special Collections, University of Mississippi, Oxford.

28. R. D. Mussey, *Health: Its Friends and Its Foes* (Boston: Gould and Lincoln, 1862), 172, 219, 224, 232; Iacobbo and Iacobbo, *Vegetarian America,* 44–45.

29. Bradbury to wife, May 30 1864, *While Father Is Away: The Civil War Letters of William H Bradbury,* ed. Jennifer Cain Bohrnstedt (Lexington: University Press of Kentucky, 2003), 162; William T. McGlothlin Diary, June 3, 1863, Huntington Library, San Marino, CA; Onley Andrus to Molly, December 25, 1862, *The Civil War Letters of Sergeant Onley Andrus,* ed. Fred Albert Shannon (Urbana: University of Illinois Press, 1947), 44; John Oscar Culver to Minnie, February 7, 1863, Folder 7, Box 1, Culver Family Papers, Special Collections, Stanford University, Palo Alto, CA; Baker to sister, February 12, 1863,

William B. Baker Papers, Southern History Collection, University of North Carolina, Chapel Hill.

30. Henry S. Nourse quoted in *The Story of the Fifty-Fifth Regiment Illinois Volunteer Infantry in the Civil War, 1861–1865* (Clinton, MA: W. J. Coulter, 1887), 265; Force to father, [September] 4, 1863, M. F. Force Papers, Special Collections, University of Washington, Seattle; England to Deed, July 2, 1863, Orin England Letters, Rutherford B. Hayes Presidential Center, Fremont, OH.

31. Daniel Wait Howe, *Civil War Times, 1861–1865* (Indianapolis: Bowen-Merrill, 1902), 58–59; H. V. Redfield, "Characteristics of the Armies," in *Annals of the War Written by Leading Participants North and South Originally Published in the Philadelphia Weekly Times* (Edison, NJ: Blue and Gray, 1996), 366; Joseph Janvier Woodward, *Outlines of the Chief Camp Diseases of the United States Armies as Observed during the Present War: A Critical Contribution to Military Medicine* (Philadelphia: J. B. Lippincott, 1863), 65–66; C. L. Kilburn to A. B. Eaton, June 19, 1865, *How to Feed an Army,* 8–9; N. J. Sappington to A. B. Eaton, June 28, 1865, ibid., 62–63; W. P. Martin to M. R. Morgan, n.d., ibid., 108.

32. Hoadley to cousin, May 27, 1863, Robert Bruce Hoadley Papers, Rubenstein Rare Book and Manuscript Library, Duke University, Durham, NC; Churchill to wife, August 1, 1864, Mendal C. Churchill Papers, American Heritage Center, University of Wyoming, Laramie.

33. Samuel H. Stevenson to parents, July 2, 1863, 48th Ohio Folder, Vicksburg National Military Park, Vicksburg, MS; Charles Willison to sister, July 1 1863, 76th Ohio Folder, ibid.; Styre to parents, July 1, 1863, Samuel Styre Papers, Rubenstein Rare Book and Manuscript Library, Duke University, Durham, NC; George Thomas to Minerva, July 14, 1863, Thomas Family Correspondence, Special Collections, University of Notre Dame, South Bend, IN.

34. Frank L. Richardson, "War as I Saw It, 1861–1865," *Louisiana Historical Quarterly* 6 (January 1923): 91–92; Earl J. Hess, "The Early Indicators Project: Using Massive Data and Statistical Analysis to Understand the Life Cycle of Civil War Soldiers," *Civil War History* 63, no. 4 (December 2017): 390–91.

35. Morse to Ellen, August 9, 1864, Charles F. Morse Papers, Massachusetts Historical Society, Boston.

36. Alfred Jay Bollet, *Civil War Medicine: Challenges and Triumphs* (Tucson, AZ: Galen, 2002), 344, 346, 349; Mary C. Gillett, *The Army Medical Department, 1818–1865* (Washington, DC: Center of Military History, 1987), 159.

37. Bollet, *Civil War Medicine,* 189–90.

38. Woodward, *Outlines,* 62–64, 66.

39. Special Orders No. 158, Headquarters, Army of the Potomac, June 10, 1864, *OR,* 36(3):729.

40. Haley Journal, in Silliker, *Rebel Yell,* 167, 173, 182.

41. Charles O. Musser to father, May 22, 1865, Popchock, *Soldier Boy,* 207.

42. Edwin R. Mason quoted in [Henry H. Rood], *History of Company "A," Thirteenth Iowa Veteran Infantry, from September 12th, 1861, to July 21st, 1865* (Cedar Rapids, IA: Daily Republican, 1889), 18.

43. Gillett, *Army Medical Department,* 228; Douglas J. Lanska, "Seasonal Variation in

Night Blindness Incidence among Union Soldiers in the U.S. Civil War," *Neurology*, 83, no. 11 (2014): 1025–27; Bollet *Civil War Medicine*, 356.

44. Iacobbo and Iacobbo, *Vegetarian America*, 99, 111; Henry S. Clubb, *Thirty-Nine Reasons Why I Am a Vegetarian* (Philadelphia: Vegetarian Society of America, 1903), n.p.; Gregory, *Of Victorians and Vegetarians*, 53–56.

45. Iacobbo and Iacobbo, *Vegetarian America*, 61; Clubb, *Thirty-Nine Reasons*, n.p.

# V

# Dogs during and after THE Civil War

# The Dogs of War

## *Canine Exploitation in the American Civil War*

JOAN E. CASHIN

THE RELATIONSHIP between human beings and dogs has always been fraught with contradictions. People domesticated canines around thirty thousand years ago in multiple locations, as humans transitioned from nomadic to agricultural societies. Most dogs accepted human dominance, probably because wolves, their progenitors, accepted hierarchies within their packs; after dogs became domesticated, human society absorbed them as constituents. Canines became acutely sensitive to human behavior, and they often resided with people in their homes. In much of the Western world, canines have held an intermediate status as liminal creatures between humans and other animals because they had sustained intimate contact with people. Dogs express their feelings openly and freely, and they are capable of rich emotional exchanges with human beings. They can evoke strong reactions in people, elevating oxytocin levels in the brain by their very presence. Whether dogs have any self-awareness or capacity for cognition is hotly debated. But the old cliché, that *canis familiaris* is humanity's best friend, has much truth to it. Dogs have been what I wish to call charismatic minifauna, smaller than megafauna such as whales and pandas beloved by humans, but presenting the same emotional appeal.[1]

Yet that status did not protect them from exploitation in the nineteenth century, before or during the Civil War. Historians of the time period have neglected dogs as historical actors, except for passing references to wartime mascots, but scholars in other fields have addressed canine-human relations in some depth. They differ sharply over issues of power, with some writers emphasizing the dominance of humans over dogs and all animals, while others counter that co-production defines these relationships, with dogs and humans shaping each other as roughly equitable partners. In this essay I take a different approach. I argue that the relationship was flexible but nonetheless profoundly inequitable before the conflict in both the North and the South. Those inequities grew dramatically after the Civil War broke out in 1861. In fact, both armies weaponized canines in their all-out effort to win the contest.[2]

In the antebellum North and South, the economies were much the same—rural, agricultural, with many small towns and a few big cities—and the human-canine relationship was similar in both regions, with a strong emphasis on flexibility. People of all races and ethnic groups appreciated their dogs, which were known to save human beings in danger and show lasting fidelity to their owners. Many humans loved their dogs in return. They gave canines as gifts to family members and praised the animals for their physical beauty. But they also put them to work and worked them hard. In a society without electricity or other modern conveniences, canine labor mattered. Inside the city dogs served as guards, rat killers, and messengers; in one nail factory in New York, they pulled a wheel that operated the bellows. Out in the country, dogs herded animals, patrolled houses, guarded property, and went hunting for food and for sport with their owners. Many people viewed dogs as boon companions, yes, but as valuable workers, too.[3]

The human-dog relationship featured a cold indifference toward canines as well, for some people took a ruthless view of them. One yeoman farmer's wife in Virginia nursed an injured dog back to health, but when she realized it could no longer work, she tried to give it away. Humans saw canines as expendables if the animals threatened their own health, as people in all regions killed dogs on the mere suspicion that they might be rabid. Many people wanted to get living dogs under control by any means, including through behavior that is now deemed reprehensible. A pack of dogs with no "acknowledged masters" roamed through rural Pennsylvania, so a white man, Elias Fisher, captured and trained them by alternatively soothing them and beating them with a whip; he then set the dogs to work pulling a small wagon. The sanctioned murder of hundreds of canines sometimes occurred in American cities, as it did in New York City, where the public debate over how to cope with rabies had hung fire since the 1830s. Mayor William Havemeyer, anxious about a summertime increase in cases in 1848, authorized a bounty of fifty cents for each canine corpse brought to the police departments. Although some New Yorkers harshly criticized the measure, boys with clubs roamed through the streets murdering every dog they saw. Even people who did not abandon, mistreat, or kill dogs saw them as inferior beings that had to do as they were told. As ethologist Marc Bekoff observes about humans and dogs in today's society, the relationship is asymmetrical.[4]

Many hierarchies existed inside the human population, of course, and one of the most significant in nineteenth-century America was that of race. Little research has been done on slaves and canines in either the North or South, but some generalizations can be ventured. Bondage was disappearing from the North, although it lasted in Delaware and New Jersey up to 1860; the institution thrived in the South, of course, as the cotton economy boomed for most of the last generation before the war. Scattered references to slaves and their dogs appear in the historical record for these years. Some states tried to ban or discourage dog ownership by slaves, but bondsmen in Dixie nonetheless had their own canines, and with the master's permission, they hunted together for wild animals. Individual slaves clearly loved their dogs, as did Samuel, a Kentuckian who had the "greatest faith" in his canines, and their dogs loved them back. Runaway slaves sometimes outwitted masters by taking their own canines along to protect them. Most slaves despised the bloodhound, however, many of which were trained from the time they were puppies to chase down slaves. African Americans knew well this dog's alertness and stamina, the leader's role in a pack, and the pack's fealty to its leader.[5]

Americans white and Black sometimes referred to breeds aside from bloodhounds, such as the Newfoundland or the setter, but most people used the word "dog" as a generic term for canines of many sorts. A Virginia planter commented in half-hearted fashion that he might breed some pointers, although he called it a lot of "trouble." Many people evidently agreed with him that canine breeding was too much trouble. The modern practice of the careful, systematic breeding of dogs did not develop until the late nineteenth century, and before then, even the bloodhound, the premiere hunting dog, sometimes had mixed ancestry. In antebellum America most people knew nothing of pedigrees or were indifferent to them. Instead, they valued dogs for their miscellaneous qualities of size, color, speed, hunting capacity, loyalty, and bravery.[6]

Dogs of all types inhabited a world that humans have never been able to enter fully or understand. Canines did not have the same agency as people, scholar Chris Pearson believes, and they had no political views as we understand them. They had limited choices, but they did show intention, and they exercised their own wills on occasion. For reasons only they knew, dogs ignored their owners and explored the neighborhood, ran off to live in the woods, or attacked sheep on farms. These independent actions amused, perplexed, and infuriated people, but humans still had the advantage, being for the most part bigger than dogs and having access to weapons. In antebellum America overlapping elements of love, dependency, hostility, and incomprehension coexisted within the rubric of human domination.[7]

When the war commenced in 1861, soldiers perceived dogs as valuable assets. As the conflict soon transformed into a total war, the human-canine relationship shifted toward the starkly utilitarian, with some lingering manifestations of antebellum-style affection. White troops from both regions treated dogs in very similar ways, as did Black soldiers, who are discussed below. Neither army had an official policy on canines. When Lieutenant Colonel Henry Lee Scott published his all-purpose almanac, *Military Dictionary,* the year the war started, he observed that dogs could work as messengers, and that was it. With no guidance then or afterward from officers or civilian policymakers, troops were left to their own devices. They brought their personal canines from home, kidnapped others from civilians, or confiscated those that trotted around unattended. The men had their favorite pets, as did Confederate colonel Barnard Bee, who was "devoted" to his pointer, and David Dixon Porter, the Union naval commander, who kept eight dogs on board his ship and fed them a fancy diet. Some dogs functioned as mascots for military units, while others served as companions for wounded men at convalescent camps. These services were an extension of their antebellum role of providing comfort for human beings.[8]

Many soldiers in the two armies put their dogs to work at practical tasks, as armies have done throughout history. They were "muster[ed]" into service, according to the Tennessee Unionist Parson Brownlow, conscripted at the behest of human beings. From the war's first year, canines working singly or in packs guarded camps, forts, military hospitals, and prisons for both armies, in the Union in such places as Kentucky and Maryland, and in the Confederacy in such places

FIG. 9.1. Dogs in Camp. A dog lies peacefully in company with two Union generals and their staff members on a quiet day during the Peninsula Campaign in June 1862. In this photograph by James F. Gibson, Brigadier General George Stoneman (seated far right), chief of cavalry, Army of the Potomac, receives a visit from Brigadier General Henry M. Naglee (seated second from right), commander of the First Brigade, Third Division, Fourth Corps. Dogs were ever present in army camps not only as unit mascots but as personal pets of generals and enlisted men alike. Library of Congress, LC-DIG-ds-05132.

as Georgia. At Andersonville prison, a pack of dogs circled the perimeter every day, and outside the hospital, dogs were "always on hand," observed one Confederate. Here they performed the guard functions they had done in peacetime, although in a far more dangerous environment.[9]

The armies went further and deployed canines as soldier substitutes. More than any wartime development, this practice underscores the plasticity of human-canine relations within the framework of domination. People sent dogs into combat, although canines did not wear armor as animals did in the ancient world, and they had no procedural protections as humans did if they were captured. During the Peninsular Campaign in 1862, Federal soldiers used Newfoundlands as "advance pickets" by sending them out ahead of troops; when rebel soldiers encountered these pickets, they did not hesitate to shoot what Confederate Benjamin Cathey termed "quadruped Yanks." Troops on both sides relied on canine courage. They expected dogs to clear the way, as cavalry units commanded them to run ahead of horses in the field. Soldiers took canines into battle, where they died, shot alongside their owners. Men saw dogs in the other army as their foes, and they angrily shot or stabbed canines that attacked them on the battlefield or in front of civilian homes.[10]

Dogs did not change the outcome of any of the significant battles, but they could make the difference in small-scale engagements. As rebel soldiers tried to capture a northern schooner on the James River early one morning in 1862, a dog on board began barking furiously. The Confederates tried to drown him, but the racket woke up the Union captain, which saved the officer, the canine, and the schooner. Barking dogs on land could alert people fleeing the Yankees, permitting one rebel major to escape from enemy troops closing in on him in Virginia. Canines often did what humans could not do, tracking down such persons as the Unionist James J. Andrews after his failed attempt to steal a Confederate train in Georgia. Before he was executed in 1862, Andrews remarked that he had been able to escape the men pursuing him but not the dogs.[11]

Humans of all backgrounds feared and admired one dog above all, the bloodhound. Ironically, the war's demands elevated this animal above other canines. Dogs track people by following traces of dissolved salts and butyric acid left in their footprints, and bloodhounds have an extremely powerful sense of smell, more powerful than other dogs or any human being. Their superior ability comes from a mass of neural tissue under the brain, which decodes smell, plus approximately 300 million scent receptors in the nose. Renowned for their capacity to discriminate among many odors and fixate on a single scent, bloodhounds sold for steep prices during the war, as high as $150 per dog. When soldiers captured enemy cavalrymen, they took their bloodhounds, too. A few men claimed they could identify a bloodhound who would "tree," meaning hunt effectively, but unfortunately did not describe what those traits might be.[12]

The bloodhound's distinct vocalization could make human blood freeze in terror. One Yankee prisoner felt horrified by its "deep ominous bay" echoing across the landscape, its persistence, and its lack of mercy. Many troops had a visceral fear of these dogs, comparing them to "monsters," and dreaded what Federal soldier John Geer described as their "powerful jaws" bearing "large, terrible teeth." Taking advantage of the animal's phenomenal abilities, humans set bloodhounds to work chasing down people in flight, including prisoners of war from both armies, deserters from both armies, runaway slaves, white Unionist civilians, and Confederate draft dodgers. These dogs frequently caught their prey, and sometimes they sank their large teeth into them. Bloodhounds were known to kill Yankee prisoners of war when they caught them, and in return, those men sometimes killed bloodhounds on sight.[13]

Troops in both armies treated many types of dogs badly, not just bloodhounds. The war devalued animal life, just as it devalued human life, and it seems to have unleashed greater aggression in many people, resulting in a swift increase in what we could call animal cruelty. Despite the dog's liminal status before 1861, troops sometimes used canines as the equivalent of test dummies. Rebel troops at Yorktown in May 1862 crouched behind their works and held up a dog as a mark to draw enemy fire. Federal soldiers experimented on dogs to protect themselves, as did an officer who forced a dog to drink some water to see if it was poisoned. Sometimes they executed canines because of fear of what the creatures *might* do. A "big yellow cur" was killed in Kentucky after it snapped at rebel troops in somebody's yard.[14]

It is indeed striking how easily soldiers disposed of canines that threatened their military goals. In peacetime humans killed those that might be rabid, but now they killed healthy dogs that simply got in the way. Rebel troops cut the throat of one animal following them to silence its barking as they approached US forces near Richmond. Edgar Warfield, a Confederate soldier, voiced the antebellum love of dogs by expressing genuine pity for this "poor" creature, whom the company had named Sadler, but added that the killing was done under orders. Dogs could become collateral damage, murdered because they were in the wrong place at the wrong time. Northern troops seeking rebel guerillas shot "all the dogs" in one Alabama neighborhood because they feared the barking would allow the enemy to escape, as one Federal officer reported in a casual tone. Men could kill dogs for the most self-indulgent reasons. In Virginia a Yankee sergeant made a company butcher destroy a Newfoundland because he wanted to use its hide for a saddle.[15]

Soldiers exploited dogs in another, elementary way, by eating them. Neither army was very efficient at supplying its troops with rations, so men in blue and gray had to consume proteins they had never eaten before. Compelled by necessity, they now ate what had been considered taboo or unacceptable foods before the war, as did the southern troops who ate dogs during the Yankee siege to capture Vicksburg in 1863. Yet this was not just an issue during lengthy sieges, nor did it occur in only one army. Union soldiers were known to trick their comrades into eating dogs as a practical joke by telling them it was mutton. Other men, no matter how hungry they might be, could not bring themselves to eat dogs. They believed that it violated what Union soldier Wiley Britton called an unwritten taboo, reflecting, at least in this particular sense, the animal's special status in antebellum society.[16]

Little historical evidence exists on how southern slaves viewed or treated dogs during the war, but we do know that they used their knowledge of bloodhounds to assist Union forces when they could. They advised escaped Federal prisoners of the folk belief that traveling through water or sprinkling the ground with pepper would throw off the hounds. Many newly freed Black men hated these dogs precisely because they had been used to track runaway slaves before the war. Those who worked as pioneers, or woodcutters, in the Union army killed bloodhounds whenever they encountered them on plantations. Black men serving in uniform felt deep affection for their own dogs, however, and followed the same customs white troops did. After the northern army permitted Blacks to join in 1863, they had their own canine mascots, and their dogs were sometimes wounded in combat. They, too, admired the animals for their hardiness and their courage. Further research should uncover more evidence of this aspect of African American history.[17]

When we turn to white southern civilians, we can see that they still cared for their dogs. Many held to their antebellum affection for the animals, trying to sustain them in the face of war's upheavals. The Spencer family refused to give food to some Federal soldiers because, they said, their dogs needed it more. Other civilians got into disputes with their neighbors over the deaths of their dogs, suing in court. But noncombatants still put their canines to work as the war required, utilizing them as watchdogs in this new, more dangerous environment, both outside and inside private homes. Mrs. Calvin Newsome, a plantation mistress, kept a large bulldog in her bedroom at night for security. Planters also used dogs in new ways to protect their cotton harvests, which increased in value as the southern economy crumbled. They set up what planter Thomas B. Lenoir called "biting" dogs—no breed specified—to guard their bales in Bolivar County, Mississippi, tying the dogs to the bales and placing both cotton and canine on the front porch.[18]

White civilians in the South discovered that the military could hurt or even destroy their dogs. In daily life they witnessed many sudden, deadly attacks on their animals by troops from both armies. In Richmond a member of the

Confederate Quartermaster Department shot a dog on the street because the animal charged his horse; the owner, a white man, then got into a fistfight with the soldier. Troops passing through a community murdered dogs and then disappeared before their civilian owners could react; Federal soldiers killed what Samuel Nichols called a "troublesome" canine on a farm during an illicit foraging expedition in Virginia. Gender did not protect a dog owner from loss. One white woman pleaded with Yankee troops not to kill her canines during Sherman's March to the Sea in 1864, but they killed the grown dogs and their pups. Hundreds of dogs may have died at the hands of Sherman's men during the march.[19]

One white southern civilian went beyond all his peers, both soldiers and noncombatants, to advocate the mass slaughter of dogs to aid the rebel war effort. His ideas, which are horrifying to most modern readers, are worth discussing for what they reveal about the conflict. In 1863 Virginia legislator J. Marshall McCue introduced a bill requiring all the dogs in the state to be murdered because they killed sheep, which provided wool to clothe rebel troops. Just as important, he argued that the canine corpses could make millions for the Confederacy: oil could be extracted from their bodies to treat leather, and their hides could be used to make gloves and boots. What was left of the carcasses, he suggested, could be dumped into niter beds to produce saltpeter for gunpowder. McCue's biography reads like that of many affluent white male Virginians of his generation. He was a successful farmer and attorney, well-read and well-traveled. Born in Augusta County in 1816, he graduated from Washington College and practiced law before joining the Old Dominion's House of Delegates in 1857. In 1860 he owned seven slaves and almost $48,000 worth of land. He knew something about sheep husbandry, although other agricultural experts did not agree with his view that dogs posed a dire threat to the sheep population.[20]

McCue nevertheless became obsessed with dogs who killed sheep and thereby hurt the Confederacy's struggle to clothe its army. The explanation for his obsession seems to lie in his ardent—indeed fanatical—support for the rebel cause. In the fall of 1863, he launched a political campaign to achieve the mass killing of canines. He wrote to a leather merchant in Richmond asking about possible markets for dog oil and dog skins, and when the man replied that they were marketable, a Richmond journal published the correspondence. Next, he asked Augusta County citizens to send him their estimates of the number of their sheep killed by dogs. In September he introduced his bill into the House of Delegates, and over two days in October, he made a lengthy speech advocating the measure. McCue published the speech as a pamphlet and sent copies to regional newspapers, even as he wrote to several Confederate governors about it. As his hometown paper noted with some bafflement, he pursued the measure with "much zeal."[21]

In his speech McCue grudgingly admitted that canines were faithful to humans, even though people sometimes mistreated them. He further admitted that other white male politicians opposed the bill because of the useful work that dogs did on farms: hounds killed foxes that hunted lambs and pigs, while terriers killed rats. He acknowledged with some impatience that other people felt an "*indissoluble*" emotional bond with their canines. But McCue insisted that Confederates, who were in his opinion upholding the legacy of the Founders, had to sacrifice everything to win the war. Most people had too many dogs anyway, he argued, but he could not settle on a figure for Virginia's total canine population, first gauging it at one million and then at six hundred thousand; both figures were probably wrong since a contemporary estimated the dog population in the entire Southeast at approximately one million in 1861. Whatever the true number, McCue asserted that they all had to die for the Confederacy. He blithely remarked that he had already had some medium-sized "worthless *curs*" killed so he could experiment with their body oil. These unfortunates yielded about two gallons of oil per dog, he was eager to report, and he found the oil could indeed be used to treat leather. He did not disclose exactly how the animals were killed or who killed them, much less how humans were supposed to kill thousands of canines if his bill passed. But eradication, not coproduction, was McCue's purpose.[22]

When the Virginia House of Delegates voted on the measure in February 1864, the debate was raucous, illuminating the complex wartime relations between dogs and people. One delegate defended canines, exclaiming that humans killed sheep, too, so dogs should not take all the blame, and he reminded listeners that almost every rural household had a farm dog and a house dog. Another delegate denounced the bill as simply "monstrous." The measure would harm his constituents, he added, and some of them had already protested against it. Others spoke in favor, one of them proclaiming that "the good of the country and the cause" required this measure. The bill passed, barely, by a vote of 50 to 46, and it was sent to the Virginia Senate. But that body drastically watered it down, so the final version stipulated merely that the owner of a canine who killed sheep had to compensate the sheep owner, with no dog deaths required. The senate left no record on how its members reached this decision, but they obviously shrank from killing thousands of canines.[23]

McCue's attempt to persuade other Confederate states to pass sweeping dog-murder bills also failed. A diligent search of regional newspapers and rebel law codes turned up only two references to the issue. The Georgia legislature debated a measure to slaughter one hundred thousand "superfluous" canines in 1863 to stop them from killing sheep, but members voted it down. In North Carolina one writer called for the death of "thousands of worthless dogs" to protect sheep, but the legislature passed a bill requiring the owners of sheep-killing canines to pay fifty dollars if they did not either exterminate the dogs or pen them up. Thus, the law gave dog owners a choice, with no reference to slaughtering every canine in the state. Once again, the historical record is silent on how legislators in the two states came to these decisions. McCue's reaction to these political defeats is unknown.[24]

Lest this be categorized as a purely regional issue, states inside the Union also grappled with the issue of sheep-killing dogs during the war. The Ohio legislature debated a petition to tax dog owners whose animals killed sheep in 1863 but did not consider dog execution. By that year, several other northern states allowed farmers to murder sheep-killing dogs, while others did not, but none allowed the statewide mass murder of canines. Yet New York City's dog-slaughter ordinances, enacted to halt the spread of rabies, continued on a seasonal basis throughout the nineteenth century. McCue's bill, which would have required many more deaths, is best interpreted as a feature of war rather than region. His project failed, but the fact that he proposed his bill in the first place, that one legislative house approved it, and that others publicly debated it serve to underscore the war's all-consuming nature. Beyond that, it illustrates the ultimate outcome if assumptions about human superiority over dogs had been pushed to their logical conclusion.[25]

We can only wonder at how dogs experienced the war. Human-authored documents suggest that canines usually conformed to people's expectations, but dogs did exercise their wills, just as they did in the antebellum era. Sometimes they ran into the hills, hunting wild animals without human supervision. In their interactions with people, dogs chose which soldiers they would follow and who they would shun; packs were just as unpredictable and would follow some humans but not others. Canines decided who they would protect, such as the dog who fought off a marauding Confederate soldier to protect its owner's belongings. They had meaningful, lasting loyalties to some people, which humans could find touching. One dog refused to leave the body of Union sergeant W. H. Brown after he died at Fredericksburg and then followed the corpse to the graveyard. But most canines remained at the mercy of humans and vulnerable to the violence they unleashed. Dogs, along with people, were literally blown up by explosions during the Vicksburg siege. Canines are social animals who watch human beings closely, scanning their faces and body language for information, and they must have been stunned by the unprecedented scale of violence even as they continued to love particular human beings.[26]

Into the war's last months, dogs figured in military affairs, both as soldier substitutes and as powerful symbols. A big white dog—no other description given—patrolled a Confederate camp in Virginia in January 1865 with one Captain Young to stop rebel troops from deserting to the Federal army. The canine was so effective that Union major general George Meade offered a reward for its capture, but a posse of Union soldiers failed to track it down. By the time Robert E. Lee surrendered to U. S. Grant at Appomattox Court House in April 1865, thousands of feral and stray dogs wandered through the region. Departing Yankees took canines home as souvenirs, including one special prize, a bulldog-bloodhound mix from Richmond. This dog, unnamed, once belonged to Mayor Joseph Mayo and served under several commanders at the city's military prisons, where it was used to hunt Yankee prisoners of war. The newspapers covered its travels closely as it headed north, describing it as big, dark, and fierce. The northern public seemed fascinated by the animal, perhaps because its capture seemed to embody the Union victory.[27]

We must conclude, then, that dogs became weaponized during the war, as humans exploited canine abilities to the limit. The prewar dominion over canines expanded to include new demands, although some humans remained emotionally attached to some dogs, who returned the feeling. The dog's antebellum status as charismatic minifauna did not protect it during the war; the conflict only intensified its exploitation. For historians of the Civil War, the canine narrative underscores the way that armies, those mighty instruments of human beings, deployed almost every resource in a total war. Dogs were in the thick of the endeavor from the beginning to the end, their liminal standing before 1861 put aside or rejected. They have good memories, and like human beings they can develop post–traumatic stress disorder. After 1865, many canine veterans must have suffered from what they had witnessed and experienced during their service.[28]

## NOTES

1. Abraham Gibson, *Feral Animals in the American South: An Evolutionary History* (New York: Cambridge University Press, 2016), 16; Juliet Clutton-Brock, *Animals as Domesticates: A World View through History* (East Lansing: Michigan State University Press, 2012), 3, 8; Marion Schwartz, *A History of Dogs in the Early Americas, with Selected Drawings by Susan Hockgraf* (New Haven, CT: Yale University Press, 1997), 2; Marc Bekoff, *Canine Confidential: Why Dogs Do What They Do* (Chicago: University of Chicago Press, 2018), 129; Louis Bromfield, *Animals and Other People, Drawings by Paul Laune* (New York: Harper & Brothers, 1955), 168; Miho Nagasawa et al., "Oxytocin-Gaze Positive Loop and the Coevolution of Human-Dog Bonds," *Science* 348 (17 April 2015): 333–36; Clinton Sanders, *Understanding Dogs: Living and Working with Canine Companions* (Philadelphia: Temple University Press, 1999), 5, 121–40; Leslie Irvine, *If You Tame Me: Understanding Our Connection with Animals*, foreword by Marc Bekoff (Philadelphia: Temple University Press, 2004), 46–47, 76–77. On animals who inhabited a liminal status in urban Europe, see Clemens Wischermann, Aline Steinbrecher, and Philip Howell, eds., *Animal History in the Modern City: Exploring Liminality* (London: Bloomsbury Academic, 2019).

2. Brian Steele Wills, *Inglorious Passages: Noncombat Deaths in the American Civil War* (Lawrence: University Press of Kansas, 2017), 132–33. Harriet Ritvo emphasizes that humans dominated animals, including dogs, while Donna Haraway posits that the human-canine relationship is best characterized as coproduction. See Ritvo, *The Animal Estate: The English and Other Creatures in the Victorian Age* (Cambridge, MA: Harvard University Press, 1987), 2–3, 6, 20, 41–42, 125, 176; and Haraway, *The Companion Species Manifesto: Dogs, People, and Significant Otherness* (Chicago: Prickly Paradigm Press, 2003), 2, 29. Most scholars agree with the basics of Haraway's argument, including Edmund Russell, *Greyhound Nation: A Coevolutionary History of England, 1200–1900* (Cambridge: Cambridge University Press, 2018), 1–20, 185–93; Gibson, *Feral Animals*, 1–4, 25; and Michael Worboys, Julie-Marie Strange, and Neil Pemberton, *Invention of the Modern Dog: Breed and Blood in Victorian Britain* (Baltimore: Johns Hopkins University Press, 2018), 14, 16.

3. R. Douglas Hurt, *American Agriculture: A Short History*, rev. ed. (West Lafayette, IN.: Purdue University Press, 2002), 117–20, 127–28, 133, 149–55; Steven Stoll, *Larding the Lean Earth: Soil and Society in Nineteenth-Century America* (New York: Hill and Wang, 2002), 7–8, 19–24, 33–34; Gibson, *Feral Animals*, 43, 56–57; "Noble Conduct of a Newfoundland Dog," *Natchez Courier*, August 20, 1852; "A Chapter on My Good Old Dog," *New England Weekly Review* (Hartford, CT), January 18, 1840; Thomas Hart Shelby to Mary Shelby, April 19, 1850, Mary Cosby Shelby Correspondence, University of Kentucky, Lexington; Erica Fudge, *Pets: The Art of Living* (New York: Routledge, 2008), 4, 7–8; Catherine McNeur, *Taming Manhattan: Environmental Battles in the Antebellum City* (Cambridge, MA: Harvard University Press, 2014), 1–8; Mrs. Roger A. Pryor, *Reminiscences of Peace and War* (New York: Macmillan, 1904), 4; "A New Idea," *Daily Morning News* (Savannah), February 27, 1850; Elizabeth W. Allston Pringle, *Chronicles of Chicora Wood, Illustrated* (New York: Charles Scribner's Sons, 1922), 98; John Palmer, *Journal of Travels in the United States of North America and in Lower Canada, Performed in the Year 1817* (London:

Sherwood, Neely, and Jones. 1818), 115, 128; Jon T. Coleman, *Vicious: Wolves and Men in America* (New Haven, CT: Yale University Press, 2004), 95–97; Champ Clark, *My Quarter Century of American Politics,* 2 vols. (New York: Harper & Brothers, 1920), 1:23.

4. Katherine C. Grier, *Pets in America: A History* (Chapel Hill: University of North Carolina Press, 2006), 64, 150–52; Martha L. Roadcap to Charles McGuffin, January 26, 1861, McGuffin and Baylor Families, 1861–1865, Augusta Co., VA, Letters & Diaries, The War Years, *Valley of the Shadow,* https://valley.lib.virginia.edu; "Died, of Hydrophobia," *Globe* (Washington, DC), 16 July 1833; "Miscellany," *Vermont Patriot* (Montpelier), May 27, 1847; Jessica Wang, *Mad Dogs and Other New Yorkers: Rabies, Medicine, and Society in an American Metropolis, 1840–1920* (Baltimore: Johns Hopkins University Press, 2019), 11–16, 50–51, 86–88; US House, *Report of the Commissioner of Agriculture for the Year 1863,* 38th Cong., 1st Sess., H. Exec. Doc. 91 (Washington, DC: Government Printing Office, 1863), 450; McNeur, *Taming Manhattan,* 19–23; "Proclamation," *New York Herald,* July 13, 1848; "Dog Laws," *New York Herald,* August 10, 1848; "The Great Dog War of 1848," *New York Herald,* July 16, 1848; Bekoff, *Canine Confidential,* 167. Several southern cities also debated measures against rabid dogs or killed them. See Gibson, *Feral Animals,* 58–59.

5. Gibson, *Feral Animals,* 55–56; Mark Fiege, *The Republic of Nature: An Environmental History of the United States* (Seattle: University of Washington Press, 2012), 127; Thomas W. Bullitt, *My Life at Oxmoor: Life on a Farm in Kentucky before the War* (N.p.: privately printed, 1995), 40–41; Interview with George Henderson, 7:5, Kentucky, Born in Slavery: Slave Narratives for the Federal Writers' Project, 1936–38, Library of Congress, https://www.loc.gov/collections; Jacob Stroyer, *My Life in the South: New and Enlarged Edition* (Salem, MA: Newcomb & Gauss, Printers, 1898), 69–70; Frederick Law Olmsted, *The Cotton Kingdom,* ed. Arthur M. Schlesinger Sr., introduction by Lawrence N. Powell (New York: Modern Library, 1984), 122, 387. I found no documents on slave women and their relationships with dogs.

6. "A Valuable Dog," *Caledonian* (St. Johnsbury, VT), July 18, 1843; "Personal Property, Viz.," *West-Jersey Pioneer* (Bridgeton, NJ), January 13, 1855; Interview with George Henderson, 7:5; "Pointer Dogs," *American Turf Register and Sporting Magazine* 4 (December 1832): 187–88; Gibson, *Feral Animals,* 57; Worboys, Strange, and Pemberton, *Invention of the Modern Dog,* 1–20; Olmsted, *Cotton Kingdom,* 387; Thomas Hart Shelby to Mary Shelby, April 19, 1850, Shelby Correspondence; Hyde [*sic*] to Sarah D. Grimke, (no month or day), 1838, Grimke Family Papers, College of Charleston, Lowcountry Digital Library, https://lcdl.library.cofc.edu/content/grimke-family-papers-1678-1977/; "The Old Man's Ghost Story," *Sunbury (PA) American and Shamokin Journal,* August 14, 1841.

7. Robert Burton, *The Language of Smell* (London: Routledge & Kegan Paul, 1976), 86; Anna L. Peterson, *Being Animal: Beasts and Boundaries in Nature Ethics* (New York: Columbia University Press, 2013), 18; Chris Pearson, "History and Animal Agencies," in *The Oxford Handbook of Animal Studies,* ed. Linda Kalof (New York: Oxford University Press, 2017), 249–53; "An Orthodox Dog," *Daily Register* (Raleigh), September 28, 1853; "Wild Dog," *Daily Ohio Statesman* (Columbus), September 14, 1852; "Sheep Killing Dogs," *Newark (OH) Advocate,* August 4, 1858.

8. Henry Lee Scott, *Military Dictionary* (New York: D. Van Nostrand 1861), 560; "Letter from Frank A. Haskell," *Wisconsin State Register* (Portage), October 4, 1862; Lizzie Jackson Mann, "Recollections of the Civil War, 1861 to '65," 5, Virginia Historical Society, Richmond; *Far, Far from Home: The Wartime Letters of Dick and Tally Simpson, 3rd South Carolina Volunteers,* ed. Guy R. Everson and Edward H. Simpson Jr. (New York: Oxford University Press, 1989), 89, 108; Gilbert E. Govan and James W. Livingood, eds., *The Haskell Memoirs: John Cheves Haskell* (New York: G. P. Putnam's Sons, 1960), 5; *Official Records of the Union and Confederate Navies in the War of the Rebellion,* 30 vols. (Washington, DC: Government Printing Office, 1894–1922), ser. 1, 20:28; Samuel W. North to his brother, November 1, 1862, Samuel W. North, 1862–64, Franklin Co., PA, Letters & Diaries, The War Years, *Valley of the Shadow,* https://valley.lib.virginia.edu. Gibson, *Feral Animals,* concentrates on dogs in the antebellum era.

9. Jilly Cooper, *Animals in War* (London: Corgi Books, 2010), 83, 92–93; John Sorenson, "Animals as Vehicles of War," in *Animals and War: Confronting the Military-Animal Industrial Complex,* ed. Colin Salter, Anthony J. Nocella II, and Judy K. C. Bentley (Lanham, MD: Lexington Books, 2014), 23; Gibson, *Feral Animals,* 54; W. G. Brownlow, *Sketches of the Rise, Progress, and Decline of Secession, with a Narrative of Personal Adventures among the Rebels* (Philadelphia: George W. Childs, 1862), 349; "Trials and Triumphs," *Daily Southern Crisis* (Jackson, MS), January 10, 1863; *The War of the Rebellion: A Compilation of the Official Records of the Union and Confederate Armies,* 70 vols. in 128 parts (Washington, DC: Government Printing Office, 1880–1901), ser. 2, 2:385, 7:121 (hereafter *OR,* all citations to series 1 unless otherwise stated); Peterson H. Cherry, *Prisoner in Blue: Memories of the Civil War after 70 Years* (Los Angeles: Wetzel, 1931), 34.

10. Edwin H. Richardson, *British War Dogs: Their Training and Psychology* (London: Skeffington & Son, 1920), 23; *Histories of the Several Regiments and Battalions from North Carolina in the Great War, 1861–1865,* ed. Walter Clark, 5 vols. (Goldsboro, NC: Nash Brothers, 1901), 1:754; Robert Stiles, *Four Years under Marse Robert* (New York: Neale, 1903), 83; *OR,* 28(1):745–46; "Letter from Frank A. Haskell," *Wisconsin State Register* (Portage), October 4, 1862; W. W. Blackford, *War Years with Jeb Stuart* (Baton Rouge: Louisiana State University Press, 1993), 174.

11. "Daring Feat—Burning a Federal Vessel," *Fayetteville (NC) Observer,* August 4, 1862; *Official Records of the Union and Confederate Navies,* ser. 1, 5:403; *OR,* ser. 2, 5:417.

12. Burton, *Language of Smell,* 86; Stanley Coren, *How Dogs Think: Understanding the Canine Mind* (New York: Free Press, 2004), 51, 55–56, 73–74; Edmund Kirke, *Among the Pines; or, South in Secession-Time,* 3rd ed. (New York: J. R. Gilmore, 1862), 171; "The Eastern News," *Daily Evening Bulletin* (San Francisco), March 22, 1864; Everson and Simpson, *Far, Far from Home,* 89.

13. F. W. Swift, *My Experiences as a Prisoner of War* (Detroit: William S. Ostler, Printer, 1888), 8; J. J. Geer, *Beyond the Lines; or, A Yankee Prisoner Loose in Dixie* (Philadelphia: J. W. Daughaday, 1863), 127, 139; M. A. DeWolfe Howe, ed., *Marching with Sherman: Passages from the Letters and Campaign Diaries of Henry Hitchcock, Major and Assistant Adjutant General of Volunteers, November 1864-May 1865* (1927; reprint, with an introduction by Brooks Simpson, Lincoln: University of Nebraska Press, 1995), 78, 143, 178, 288–89; Wiley

Britton, *Memoirs of the Rebellion on the Border, 1863* (Chicago: Cushing Thomas, 1882), 196; "The Eastern News," *Daily Evening Bulletin* (San Francisco), March 22, 1864.

14. "Incidents of the War," *Frank Leslie's Illustrated Newspaper*, May 17, 1862, 75; "The Latest from Galveston," *New York Herald*, February 2, 1863; Sam Watkins, *Company Aytch; or, A Side Show of the Big Show*, ed. M. Thomas Inge (New York: Plume, 1999), 46. On the moral issues raised by mistreating animals, see Christine M. Korsgaad, *Fellow Creatures: Our Obligations to the Other Animals* (New York: Oxford University Press, 2018), 3–15, 60–67.

15. Edgar Warfield, *A Confederate Soldier's Memoirs* (Richmond: Masonic Home, 1936), 172; *OR*, 52(1):113; Jeffrey D. Marshall, ed., *A War of the People: Vermont Civil War Letters* (Hanover, NH: University Press of New England 1999), 137.

16. Joan E. Cashin, *War Stuff: The Struggle for Human and Environmental Resources in the American Civil War* (Cambridge: Cambridge University Press, 2018), 54–81; "The Surrender of Vicksburg," *New York Times*, July 19, 1863; Marshall, *War of the People*, 137; Britton, *Memoirs*, 308.

17. Geer, *Beyond the Lines*, 127–28; *Autobiography of James L. Smith*, 2nd ed. (Norwich, CT: Press of the Bulletin Company, 1882), 126; Edwin S. Redkey, ed., *A Grand Army of the Black Men: Letters from African-American Soldiers in the Union Army, 1861–1865* (Cambridge: Cambridge University Press, 1993), 51–52.

18. *OR*, 34(1):1058; ibid., ser. 2, 2:1447; Diary of Sylvanus Crossly, February 17, 1865, Library of Congress; "An Atrocious Incident," *Fayetteville (NC) Observer*, July 28, 1864; Andrew Ward, *The Slaves' War: The Civil War in the Words of Former Slaves* (Boston: Mariner Books, 2009), 78; "More Southern News," *Daily National Intelligencer* (Washington, DC), October 22, 1863.

19. "Mayor's Court," *Daily Richmond Examiner*, October 15, 1863; *"Your Soldier Boy Samuel": Civil War Letters of Lieutenant Samuel Edmund Nichols, Amherst '65 [sic] of the 37th Regiment Massachusetts Volunteers*, arranged by Charles Sterling Underhill (N.p.: privately printed, 1929), 43–44; Howe, *Marching with Sherman*, 143; Gibson, *Feral Animals*, 105.

20. "Sheep and Dogs," *Fayetteville (NC) Observer*, November 9, 1863; David Cressy, *Saltpeter: The Mother of Gunpowder* (New York: Oxford University Press, 2013), 1–5; *Journal of the House of Delegates of the State of Virginia, for the Session of 1857–1858* (Richmond: William F. Ritchie, 1857), 343–44; J. M. McCue, 1860 Census, Augusta Co., Va., 1860 Slaveowner Census, Census & Tax Records, The Eve of the War, *Valley of the Shadow*, https://valley.lib.virginia.edu; John N. McCue, *The McCues of the Old Dominion, Supplemented with Brief Charts of the Steele, Arbuckle, and Cunningham Families* (Mexico: Missouri Printing & Publishing, 1912), 38–41; *Speech of Mr. McCue, of Augusta, Delivered in the House of Delegates, on the 16th and 17th October 1863, on the Bill to Protect Sheep and Increase the Production of Wool* (Richmond: George P. Evans, 1863), 13–16, and appendix; Henry S. Randall, *Sheep Husbandry in the South: Comprising a Treatise on the Acclimation of Sheep in the Southern States and an Account of the Different Breeds* (Philadelphia: J. S. Skinner, 1848), 65.

21. *Speech of Mr. McCue*, 3–5, 17, and appendix; "The Value of Dead Dogs," *Richmond Whig*, September 22, 1863; "For the Spectator," *Staunton (VA) Spectator*, September 22, 1863; "General Assembly," ibid.; "Anti-Dog Speech," *Richmond Examiner*, November 18, 1863; "The Wool Interest of Virginia," *Staunton (VA) Spectator*, February 16, 1864.

22. *Speech of Mr. McCue*, 3–4, 6–7, 9 11, 13; "Sheep and Dogs," *Fayetteville (NC) Observer*, November 9, 1863; "Anti-Dog, Speech," *Richmond Examiner*, November 18, 1863; Gibson, *Feral Animals*, 57.

23. "House of Delegates: The Sheep Bill and its 'Ryders,'" *Richmond Examiner*, February 2, 1864; "The Wool Interest of Virginia," *Staunton (VA) Spectator*, February 16, 1864.

24. "Down on the Dogs," *National Intelligencer* (Washington, DC), June 12, 1863; "Killing Sheep," *Western Democrat* (Charlotte, NC), December 1, 1863; *Public Laws of the State of North Carolina, Passed by the General Assembly at the Called Session of 1863* (Raleigh: W. W. Holden, 1863), 17.

25. "Columbus Correspondence," *Cleveland Daily Herald*, February 12, 1863; *Report of the Commissioner on Agriculture for the Year 1863*, 457–62; Wang, *Mad Dogs*, 302n14. Soldiers in other wars have slaughtered large numbers of dogs. For US troops in Vietnam, see Sorenson, "Animals as Vehicles of War," 23. Civilians engaged in the mass killing of dogs and cats in wartime England in 1939. See Hilda Kean, *The Great Cat and Dog Massacre: The Real Story of World War Two's Unknown Tragedy* (Chicago: University of Chicago Press, 2017), 4–21, 48–68.

26. Diary of Augustus L. Yenner, October 9, 1863, Civil War Collection, Western Michigan University, Kalamazoo; Govan and Livingood, *Haskell Memoirs*, 15; *OR*, 34(2):977; Blackford, *War Years*, 106–7; "Fidelity of a Dog," *Charleston (SC) Courier Tri-Weekly*, January 29, 1863; Jenkin Lloyd Jones, *An Artilleryman's Diary* (N.p.: Wisconsin History Commission, 1914), 90; Alexandra Horowtiz, "Preface," in *Domestic Dog Cognition and Behavior: The Scientific Study of* Canis Familiaris, ed. Alexandra Horowitz (Berlin: Springer, 2014), v–vi; Coren, *How Dogs Think*, 7, 61, 66–67, 109; Gregory Berns, *What It's like to Be a Dog, and Other Adventures in Animal Neuroscience* (New York: Basic Books, 2017), 157–58, 170–71, 245–46.

27. Mason Whiting Tyler, *Recollections of the Civil War*, ed. William S. Tyler (New York: G. P. Putnam's Sons, 1912), 319, 321–22; Gibson, *Feral Animals*, 106; "Telegraphic," *Daily Cleveland Herald*, May 16, 1865; "The Guard of Castle Thunder," *Boston Daily Advertiser*, May 25, 1865; "That Big Black Dog Again," *Milwaukee Daily Sentinel*, May 27, 1865.

28. Coren, *How Dogs Think*, 7, 303–4; Margo DeMello, *Animals and Society: An Introduction to Human-Animal Studies* (New York: Columbia University Press, 2012), 199. The wartime mistreatment of animals helped inspire the founding of the American Society for the Prevention of Cruelty to Animals. See Janet M. Davis, *The Gospel of Kindness: Animal Welfare and the Making of Modern America* (New York: Oxford University Press, 2016), 8, 14–15, 21.

# "The Dogs Ought to Be Exterminated"

## *Dogs, Slavery, and the Consequences of Emancipation*

**LORIEN FOOTE**

ON JUNE 2, 1863, a detachment of three hundred Black soldiers from the 2nd South Carolina, a regiment in the Union army, ascended twenty-five miles up the Combahee River on three armed transports. The soldiers were former slaves recruited from Key West, Florida, and Port Royal, South Carolina. Their purpose on this raid was to liberate enslaved men, women, and children and to destroy the rice fields and mansions that lined the river. Confederate pickets at Williams Middleton's plantation spotted the vessels at 6:20 A.M. Rather than fire their weapons and contest the landing, the members of the Combahee Rangers on the scene left to get the "negro dogs," the military dogs of the 4th South Carolina Cavalry that Confederates guarding the river used to police the slaves who lived and worked there. The slaves in the rice fields saw the small flotilla at the same time. They dropped their equipment, ran to gather family members, and headed toward the river. "We saw some of Blake's negroes endeavoring to get to the ferry," John D. Sanders, one of the pickets, reported to his superiors. "We went back to the road to get the dogs and cut them off; some of the negroes turned back. The enemy had burned all the buildings at Mr. Middleton's and taken off the negroes." The Union soldiers made several landings along the Combahee, and at each of them, the pickets sought the assistance of dogs. Although Confederate cavalry and infantry attacked the Federals and were repulsed, many of the rebel soldiers on the scene did not fire their rifles at the soldiers. Instead, they tried to prevent the escape of slaves with the dogs, their favorite weapon for that purpose. The raiders from the 2nd South Carolina flooded the rice fields for fifteen miles along the river; burned four houses, six mills, and thirty-four barns; and liberated 725 slaves. Hundreds more were left behind because there was not enough room for them on the transports.[1]

During the American Civil War, dogs served as essential members of the military force maintaining a tenuous control over the slave population in South Carolina. Corporal Robert Sutton, an escaped slave serving in the Union army's 1st South Carolina Infantry Regiment, aptly told his commander, "dogs are the detective officers of Slavery's police."[2] Confederates used them as a weapon to maintain white supremacy and to fight the Black soldiers that Union commands sent into the state. Primary-source records suggest that South Carolina would not have been able to mobilize its white male population for service in the Confederate army without the deployment of canines to maintain order inside the state.

The high number of dogs living in South Carolina and the way that humans in a slave state controlled and managed this animal population during the Civil War and Reconstruction was controversial, however. Agricultural reformers, who viewed dogs as worthless and destructive, wanted to reduce the canine population of the state. They launched a campaign in the public press to paint the animals as sheep killers that held back the economic progress of the South and to place a tax on them designed to eliminate dog ownership among Black people. Powerful interests fought against state control over the dog population and eventually won, however, because these animals supported subsistence hunting and white supremacy.

In order to understand why the controversy over dogs escalated in the aftermath of the Civil War, one must consider how these domesticated animals were a marker of race and social class in the South. Joan Cashin's essay in this volume presents a broad overview of the human-dog power relationship in the antebellum period and the Civil War. This chapter uses South Carolina as a case study, supplemented with some evidence from other southern states, to consider in depth how the issue of dog control intertwined with slavery, emancipation, the maintenance of white supremacy, and resistance to Reconstruction. In addition, it helps us consider for the first time the consequences of emancipation for the canine population in the South.[3]

Dogs were omnipresent in the fields, farms, plantations, villages, and cities of South Carolina. Ordinary farm dogs guarded territory and alerted their keepers to movement along the roads and through the byways of the rural countryside. Anyone who traveled a path or approached a house in South Carolina encountered at least one, whose barking brought an armed landowner to the scene. Union soldiers who escaped from Confederate military prisons in the state were shocked at the number and effectiveness of local farm dogs. "Almost every house had a dog or two, and they ever seemed on the alert for tramps," Alonzo Cooper wrote of his escape journey, "and it was quite a risk to attempt to dig for sweet potatoes with those dogs making such a racket. . . . How those dogs would bark! It seemed as though they would arouse the whole neighborhood with their eternal yelping. I took a solemn oath during that journey that if I ever lived to get free, I would thereafter shoot every dog I could find, and I pretty near kept that oath, too." Every plantation had several farm curs whose job was to stop anyone moving across the land after dark. J. Madison Drake, a New Jersey firefighter who escaped from Columbia, spent much of his journey back to Union military lines fighting dogs with a club he had fashioned for that very purpose. "We had all we could handle between beating them back with clubs and running before them," he noted in his diary. "They sprang at us whenever the opportunity offered." Property owners in Charleston depended upon their guard dogs during the Federal bombardment, when bands of thieves roamed an increasingly lawless city. "The dogs are invaluable," Augustine Thomas Smythe said. "I would not take $500 for them."[4]

Although slaveholders and slaves kept dogs, white South Carolinians classed them according to the social status and race of their human keepers. "Nigger dogs" were the ubiquitous mongrels living in the slave quarters. "Every negro in the country has a dog following him," a state senator commented. Slaves kept these animals for companionship and for hunting small game, particularly squirrels, coons, and possums, to supplement their diets. Poor whites had "curs" that provided companionship, guarded property, and hunted to provide necessary protein. "Hounds" were the dogs of the elite slaveholding class that provided companionship, hunting for sport, and policing of slaves. The hound was not a specific breed, although the term in South Carolina usually indicated an English or Irish foxhound, deerhound, or mastiff. White men of the planter class conducted ritualized fox, deer, and bear hunts that mimicked the pageantry of the European aristocracy. Slaves served as the "drivers," who beat thickets and tracked the game with the hounds. Planters often gifted the spoils of their hunt "to signal their authority to perceived social inferiors and reinforce dependence."[5]

Agricultural reformers in upcountry South Carolina in the late 1850s and early 1860s believed there were too many dogs in the state. They advocated sheep raising as a method of diversifying the state's economy, making profitable abandoned cotton land and ending dependence on the northern textile industry. They claimed that dogs threatened the scheme. One rural newspaper reported that canines killed ninety-four of the sheep in a flock of one hundred in a matter of weeks. At a meeting of the Union District Agricultural Society, the speaker recommended a tax on dogs to reduce the population and a law that required hunters to pay damages for any sheep killed "within the range of their fox-hunting excursions." He concluded, "We are determined to vote for no man who is not in favor of some law for the protection of stock from the depradations of the thousands of *worse* than useless dogs in our State." The depiction of them as "worthless" and "marauders" pervaded the rhetoric of the sheep-industry advocates. Dogs were "the destructive animals which infest every negro quarter in the State."[6]

Although the pressure from the upcountry districts was enough for the state legislature to pass an act to protect sheep, dogs were too important to the functioning of planation security and to the hunting activities of white men for the politicians to act against curs and hounds. They refused to tax the dogs of white landowners. Instead, the legislation discriminated against "Nigger dogs." The Senate Committee on Agriculture created a bill to "make owners of dogs liable for sheep killed by them." The first section required the owner, or the master of a slave who kept a dog, to pay double the value of any sheep killed by the animal. The second section required slaveholders to report the number of dogs kept by slaves and to pay an annual tax of one dollar for each. The third section imposed a tax of two dollars for every dog kept by a "free negro."[7]

Debate over canine control in the state senate focused on the issue of Black people keeping dogs. When the committee reported the bill for debate, Senator Mazyek moved to strike the second section that taxed those kept by slaves. "I think [it] the best of the whole," another retorted. "I cannot think of a greater grievance than the allowance of negroes to keep dogs." An upcountry senator remarked: "It is very important the bill should be passed; we find it impossible to keep or raise sheep. It does not propose to tax dogs in possession of white men, but only those in possession of negroes. Had we these trifling curs out of the country sheep raising would be profitable." Mazyek held his ground. "As a matter of feeling, he did not like to see this, as it would deprive the negro of his best friend," a newspaper reporter summarized. "It also interferes between the master and his negro. Besides, the management of the negro should be left entirely to his master. There are some dogs better than some men." Senator Moses wanted to delete the third section that taxed dogs of free Black people. "It is rather a dangerous mode of procedure," he said. It was doubtful "whether it was allowable for the free negro to own slaves, horses, and other property, and forbid him the right of owning dogs." A vote of 26 to 13 sent the bill forward without amendment, and it ultimately became law.[8]

In Civil War South Carolina, then, only whites had the untaxed privilege of keeping an unlimited number of dogs. Upcountry reformers were disappointed. "This is a good law, and had it been carried a little further and a reasonable tax laid upon all dogs, the benefit to the country would have been proportionally greater," the *Lancaster Ledger* editorialized. "It would rid it of the large number of worthless curs that now infest it and the places vacated by them would be filled with more profitable stock." The *Camden Weekly Journal* did not like the discrimination in the act. "The law should have been so framed as to impose a uniform tax on all dogs, no matter to whom belonging," its editorial (a reprint of one from a Columbia paper) stated. The majority of white men in South Carolina, however, viewed their dogs as essential to their sport, to their patriarchal authority, and to their mastery of slaves. "The possession of a dog has been one of the privileges claimed by the head of each family of laborers on a Southern plantation," The *Daily Phoenix* of Columbia noted. A northern scholar who worked on the Sea Islands during the war teaching Black children recognized the distinction that dogs marked: "Just as school was nearly through—they were standing at the map and pointing out states—when my attention was attracted by an elegant little dog running into the yard, the sure sign of a white man."[9]

Most slaveholders relied on ordinary farm dogs (curs or hounds) to manage slaves, but every South Carolina neighborhood boasted a specialist who owned and managed a pack of "bloodhounds" that tracked and recaptured runaways. Local officials called for these trained dogs when the need arose. During the Civil War, the Confederate army enlisted trainers and their animals to guard prisoners, track deserters, and hunt runaway slaves. A handler named Baker controlled the dogs stationed with the 2nd South Carolina Cavalry near Adams Run Station. Baker received a private's pay and a graduated reward for the captures his dogs made. The pack drew army rations, too. Although the uneducated referred to all dogs trained to hunt fugitives as "bloodhounds," in actuality a variety of breeds served the role. Baker used English foxhounds bred in his family for generations to hunt human quarry and bring them to bay. He trained two "catch dogs," part mastiff and part Irish deerhound, to attack the quarry at the end of the chase. Baker gave a demonstration of his pack's abilities to a captured Union naval officer. A slave selected for the purpose mingled with other slaves and 250 white men in the 2nd South Carolina's camp, waded up a stream, moved along a well-traveled road, mixed with soldiers and slaves at an artillery encampment two miles away, and meandered through dense woods to a hiding place. The pack followed his route exactly and found him. "Baker had not exaggerated when he told us that he could hunt a man through the mazes and traffic of New York City if he kept to his feet," the astounded witness acknowledged.[10]

Such bloodhound packs increased in importance when Confederate conscription drained South Carolina of white men between the ages of eighteen and forty-five. In 1860 there were 60,000 men in that age group living in the state, and by January 1864, South Carolina achieved nearly full enlistment. In coastal Horry District, 925 of the 1,000 military-aged white men were Confederate soldiers; in upcountry Lancaster, 88 percent of white males were in uniform. The Confederate government sent the majority of South Carolina's soldiers to Virginia or Tennessee. In February 1864 the Confederate Congress drafted seventeen-year-olds and men between the ages of forty-five and fifty for the Confederate Reserves. Conscription decimated the mounted patrols, drawn from the state militia, that slaveholders had used in the antebellum period to control the movement of slaves. Patrols in South Carolina operated only sporadically thereafter and relied upon teenagers, the elderly, and men injured in the war. The state passed laws to exempt men from military duty to oversee slave labor, as did the Confederate Congress, but with a majority Black population (57 percent), the number of white men remaining in the state was not enough to police slavery without the use of dogs.[11]

Faced with this manpower crisis, South Carolinians claimed that dogs were essential to the maintenance of white supremacy. Citizens who petitioned the Confederate government for exemptions prioritized the men who managed packs. Twenty-two residents of Darlington District asked Secretary of War James A. Seddon to release John B. Rhodes, drafted into Company H, 21st South Carolina. "We and the soldiers' families are continually annoyed by the depredations committed on us by the black population such as breaking open dwelling houses undermining meat houses, robbing hen houses, killing cattle, hogs, etc. and stealing everything they can lay their hands on knowing we are not able to help ourselves," the petition read. Rhodes had "an excellent pack of dogs . . . which no person with any success manage but himself. Have him discharged or detailed or otherwise as you think best so he can assist us. He will do more real good to us and soldiers families as ten other men."[12]

When the War Department planned to transfer the 4th South Carolina Cavalry to Virginia in March 1864, and with it the men in charge of the dog pack, overseers in charge of the rice plantations along the Combahee River protested. B. T. Sellers of the Hobonny plantation told his employer, Williams Middleton, that the dogs maintained control of slaves. "You are in great danger of losing the negroes at night, as from the very small force here it is impossible to picket the country so as to prevent a series of successful raids, by the Yankees & Negroes, who know every path in this section," he reported. "It will never do to allow the dogs to be sent off from here." Without the handlers and their hounds, he claimed, "We will not only be left defenseless but will not even have the means of moving our negroes." He asked Middleton to intervene with the secretary of war. Planters along the Combahee submitted a petition to Gen. P. G. T. Beauregard, commander of the Department of South Carolina, Georgia, and Florida, asking him to "preserve the detachment in charge of the dogs."[13]

Because Confederates in South Carolina associated dogs with slave control, the military used dogs to repel Union raids conducted by Black soldiers that attempted to liberate slaves, recruit Black men for the Union army, or commit sabotage. On September 13, 1863, eleven men from the 1st South Carolina (US), including Corporal Andrew Murray, an escaped slave and machinist from Saint Augustine, Florida, snuck behind Confederate lines and attached a wire to the telegraph cable running between Charleston and Savannah located one mile south of Green Pond station. They planned to intercept dispatches and then sever the line. The road master spotted them and reported to Lieutenant Colonel William Stokes of the 4th South Carolina Cavalry. Stokes dispatched men from two companies to track down the Federals and wired for the pack of dogs, which arrived by train. The raiders separated and hid in dense swamps, lagoons, and rice fields. The dogs found the Federal telegraph operator in a marsh near Lowndes' Mill on the Combahee. The next day they caught a lieutenant, two soldiers, and the regimental chaplain. The pack hunted the rest of the Federal sabotage party for five more days in the Combahee marshes, but a dense growth of briars blocked them from further pursuit. Corporal Murray and Private John Layern, a yeoman from Wells, Georgia, eluded the dogs "without food or nourishment" for seven days and rejoined their regiment.[14]

Confederate cavalry deployed dogs in attack formations against Black soldiers, a tactical choice they did not make when fighting white Union soldiers. On November 24, 1863, sixty men from the 1st South Carolina (US) raided the area around Pocotaligo, liberated twenty-seven slaves from the Daniel Heyward plantation, and captured two Confederate pickets posted opposite Barnwell Island. While the party waited for Federal boats to pick them up, a dismounted company of the 4th South Carolina Cavalry attacked the Black soldiers guarding the road leading to the landing. Five bloodhounds led the charge, and the Confederates followed in skirmish lines. The guard of the 1st South Carolina charged the dogs with bayonets, killed three of them, and fired a volley at the humans. The Confederate skirmishers scattered but attacked another Federal guard post, with the two remaining hounds in front. Volleys killed the last two dogs and a Confederate captain. The rebels retreated. The Federals took the body of one of the dogs back to camp as a trophy. "The men were delighted at this confirmation of their tales of dog-companies, which some of the officers had always disbelieved," Col. Thomas Wentworth Higginson, in command of the 1st South Carolina, noted. He ordered the carcass skinned, sent to New York, and stuffed for display at the US Sanitary Commission Fair in Boston. The skin spoiled on the passage north, however, and had to be discarded.[15]

Black people resisting slavery on the plantations, instigating rebellion in their home districts, or fighting as Union soldiers targeted the dogs whose skills slaveholders employed to support their oppressive regime. "A Negro soldier came in my backyard this morning and took deliberate aim at my house dog," Mary Jane Chadick, a slaveholder who lived in Huntsville, Alabama, recorded in her diary. "The ball missed the head of the dog, going between his legs." Slaves killed dogs as an act of defiance and as a strategy to facilitate escape. "Some of the negroes gave uncles favorite dog A bait," Mary E. Pendry wrote her parents from Georgia. "After they poisoned the dog their was 4 men runaway." Any slave planning to flee prepared for pursuit by hounds and, before starting out, rubbed turpentine or green onions on feet or shoes. These scents supposedly distracted the animals long enough for the fugitive to get well off the plantation. Route planning accounted for dog packs; escaped slaves traveled through water

FIG. 10.1. Dogs in Combat. *Terrible Fight with Bloodhounds.* This depiction of the fight between the 1st South Carolina (US) and the 4th South Carolina Cavalry (CS), and the charge of the bloodhounds appeared in the Grand Army of the Republic's official history of Black troops in the Civil War. It exaggerates the number of dogs involved. Author Joseph T. Wilson, a veteran of the 54th Massachusetts, wrote in the illustration's caption, "the hounds rushed fiercely upon the troops, who quickly shot or bayoneted them and exultingly held aloft the beasts that had been so long a terror to the negro race." Joseph T. Wilson, *The Black Phalanx: A History of the Negro Soldiers of the United States in the Wars of 1775–1812, 1861–'65* (Hartford, CT: American Publishing, 1888), 322.

as much as possible, entered rather than avoided swamps, and, if they heard the baying of hounds, poured pepper on the ground to disable the dogs' noses. Baker, the handler for the pack that assisted the 2nd South Carolina Cavalry, scoffed at these methods. The only hope for a fugitive slave pursued by dogs handled by a man who "knew his business," Baker claimed, was for a heavy rain to wash out the trail. Even then, the fugitive would have to stay still in the downpour and not move until the handler gave up pursuit.[16]

Federal soldiers who invaded the Deep South in the winter of 1864–65 recognized that dogs were soldiers for the Confederacy through their role in policing Blacks and tracking escaped prisoners of war and fugitive slaves. Dogs "were of more real service to the Confederacy, in this direction, than many regiments of soldiers would have been," Indiana private Lessel Long wrote. During Sherman's march through Georgia to Savannah and then north through South Carolina, Union soldiers killed thousands of canines. "We were determined that no dog should escape, be it cur, rat dog, or blood hound," a corporal in the 63rd Ohio recalled. "We exterminated them all. The dogs were easily killed. All we had to do was bayonet them." John Henry Otto, a cabinetmaker from Westphalia and a veteran of the 1848 German revolutions, was a captain in command of the foragers for the 21st Wisconsin. His men burned a slave market in Sandersville, Georgia, and killed dogs in multiple locations after that. They shot ten hounds at a plantation while Otto lectured its mistress. "The boys are only executing your police, your nigger catchers. You see that is a custom with the men to dispose of all the bloodhounds that come in their way," he told her. "They have the foolish notion that it is barbarous and brutal to hunt a human being with voracious wild beasts." At a farm in South Carolina in February 1865, a man opened his kennel and set a large pack of dogs on Otto's foragers. "But the fellow had made a mistake in playing this trump. That was just the sort of sport the boys liked to indulge in, and ere a minute had passed every hound laid low stretching his trembling limbs as a last farewell to slavery and rebellion," Otto said.[17]

After Confederate defeat and US Army occupation of South Carolina in April and May 1865, Federal soldiers continued their attack on dogs as the political symbols of slavery. A notorious incident occurred outside of Hamburg. Robert Butler owned the Star of Edgefield, a plantation with a beautiful peach orchard and a bloodhound pack worth $23,000 ($361,775 in 2020). Butler's pack was renowned for its effectiveness during the war in tracking fugitive slaves and escaped Federal prisoners. On May 22 a band of soldiers from the three Iowa regiments occupying Hamburg went to Butler's plantation, opened his kennels, and bayonetted or shot all the dogs to death. Butler complained to the brigade commander, who brought him to the army camp to identify the perpetrators. The 22nd Iowa, the 24th Iowa, and the 28th Iowa assembled on the parade ground. As Butler walked along the line of men, the soldiers "began to bawl like dogs," and some threatened to hang him. Butler fled without identifying the culprits but received a guard at his house to prevent further attacks. "The act of killing Butler's bloodhounds was a bloody repudiation of slaveholder power in a reunited nation," the historian of the incident argues. The Iowa soldiers were Republicans who had often expressed their belief that the brutal "Southern chivalry" was the enemy of republican free laborers. Butler was unable to replace his pack and owned only one dog in 1867.[18]

Emancipation and the political process of Reconstruction changed the role of dogs in South Carolina and gave agricultural reformers the opportunity to act against the canine population. In the summer of 1865, political and social chaos pervaded the state. Civil governments and courts were effectively defunct in many districts. Freedpeople were temporarily mobile, leaving plantations to search for better opportunities, and thousands of freedmen were in the US Army regiments occupying the coastal islands and Charleston. Freed men and women in the low country formed guerrilla bands that fought against white terrorists. With the assistance of the Freedmen's Bureau, thousands of freedpeople negotiated labor contracts with landowners and moved their living quarters out of the view of white people. Angry and bitter ex-Confederate soldiers returned home determined to salvage white supremacy from the ruins of their quest for an independent slaveholding nation. In Edgefield District they formed armed patrols. Freedman John Picksley reported to the Freedmen's Bureau, "It is almost a daily occurrence for black men to be hunted down with dogs and shot like wild beasts."[19]

Although the number of dogs had decreased in some locations because of killings by Federal armies, in other places it seemed like there were even more than before. Stray and wild dogs had followed Sherman's army, eating off of its refuse, and had spread over the land in its wake. Freedpeople kept thousands of dogs, too, none of them liable to the antebellum tax because that law was defunct. A planter in the Tidewater region of Virginia described similar conditions in his state. The dogs "have become wild in some neighbourhoods, & are killing hogs & sheep in every direction," wrote Hill Carter. "The negroes too over whom we have no control now, all keep dogs, though they have not bread for their families, and we are overrun with dogs." Carter advocated a tax on canines and a reward for killing every animal found off his master's property. "The dogs ought to be exterminated," he concluded.[20]

When President Andrew Johnson created a provisional government in South Carolina to hold elections for a convention to write a new constitution so the state could return to the Union, he named upcountry politician Benjamin F. Perry as governor. Perry had built his political career upon opposition to the disproportionate political power that low-country slaveholders had enjoyed under the state's 1808 Constitution, which allocated representation in the legislature based on a combination of population and taxation. This formula meant that white low-country elites, who lived among a slave majority in their districts, were overrepresented, while upcountry planters, who lived in regions with white majorities, did not have adequate representation. Perry supervised elections by an all-white electorate for delegates to the constitutional convention. Upcountry delegates pushed through reforms that began to shift the balance of political power in the state away from the low-country elites who had opposed previous dog-tax schemes. The convention abolished the tiny parishes in the coastal areas that had as many representatives as the large upcountry districts; the new constitution apportioned representation based on taxes and the white population rather than the total population. It also provided for the popular election of the governor and eliminated property qualifications for holding state office. An upcountry delegate gave a rousing speech attacking the planters of the low country, who "sought office with the pertinacity of the blood-hound and the cunning of the fox."[21]

The legislature that met in December 1865 reflected the shift in power toward the upcountry and its interests. Upcountry members secured control over the dog population along the lines that agricultural reformers had advocated in the late 1850s. For the first time in its history, South Carolina laid a tax on every dog in the state. On December 21 lawmakers passed an act that placed a $1 tax "per head on each and every dog, of every kind and description," that was in the state on January 1, 1866, or brought into the state between that date and the payment of taxes. There were many motivations for this. The war had largely destroyed the state's infrastructure and ruined its economy. A levy on the high number of dogs in South Carolina provided an immediate source of revenue. A substantial dog tax would discourage or even eliminate ownership among the freedpeople and give property-owning whites the exclusive privilege of using canines for security and hunting. This tax satisfied the upcountry agricultural reformers who believed that sheep raising was the path that would restore the state's economy. Assessors collected the dog tax throughout the state. Elias Montgomery, a planter with 325 acres in Greenville District, paid $4 for his four dogs. The district collected tax on 1,305 dogs that year, a number similar to that for other upcountry South Carolina districts. In total, the levy brought $43,050 into the state treasury.[22]

The dog tax was extremely unpopular. "There immediately arose a cry of direct taxation, which sent up a howl all over the land," the *Daily Phoenix* of Columbia reported. "This taxpayer swore he would resist it; that one asserted it to be unconstitutional; and we heard one farmer say to one of his Representatives, 'Well, when you legislators get down so low that you have to tax as mean a thing as a dog, you had better stay at home.'" The *Keowee Courier* wrote: "Aside from its littleness, it is manifestly unjust and oppressive. It is also unconstitutional." The tax hurt middle-class and poor white farmers who relied on dogs to secure their property in a time when thievery was perceived to be widespread and to hunt for the small game that kept hunger at bay for struggling families. Advocates for the freedpeople linked the Black codes the legislature also passed and the dog tax. Simeon Corley denigrated those who put "the odious features of the black code on the colored people of South Carolina, and, at the same time, taxed their heads and dogs $4.50 per annum to pay for such eminent services in the cause of oppression."[23]

Agricultural reformers believed that dog owners evaded the law and hid the true number of their animals from the tax collectors. They did not believe that Greenville District really had only 1,305 dogs. "The return made throughout the state was notoriously small," continued the *Daily Phoenix*, "and many thousands were returned, upon which no tax was paid." The paper estimated that there were 200,000 canines in South Carolina, so the dog tax should "yield a revenue equal to the whole amount of state taxes for the past year." Instead of enforcing the levy, however, in January 1867 the legislature passed a new act that exempted one dog from taxation for each plantation and each inhabited lot in a town or village. Dog-tax advocates were angry. "If dogs are property, they can be assessed and taxed; if they are not property, they can be shot with impunity, as the birds of the field or wild game of the forests, wherever met," one editorial warned.[24]

The legislators who passed the dog taxes lost office when Congress took over the process of Reconstruction in 1867. The defiance of the former Confederates who maintained power in the aftermath of the war, the passage of Black codes, and pervasive race riots and violence against freedpeople prompted Republicans to divide the defeated Confederate states into military districts, to grant the franchise to Black males, and to require states to hold constitutional conventions. Maj. Gen. Edward Canby commanded the Second Military District, comprising South Carolina and North Carolina. On December 3, 1867, he issued General Order No. 139, which provided for taxes to support the provisional government of South Carolina until its constitutional convention met. Among them was a tax of $1 on every dog in the state. Canine opponents rejoiced. "These animals are a public nuisance," the *Charleston Daily News* proclaimed. "If they protect house and property, the owner can afford to pay one dollar upon each of them; if they are kept for amusement, their owner must pay for the privilege; if they are of no value but for their howling, yelping, and fighting, a tax may consign them to the pound, or make them some direct benefit to the State itself." Editorials openly voiced the hope that people would kill their dogs rather than pay Canby's tax. "Curs will fall like leaves of the forest on a wintry day," one happily forecasted. Another gleefully wrote, "Farewell old *Trowser!*"[25]

The Black and white delegates who met in the January 1868 constitutional convention protected dogs from this fate, however. Seventy-three of the 124 delegates were Black, a percentage almost equal to the percentage of Blacks in the statewide electorate; thirty-six of the delegates were southern whites. These politicians wanted to change the state and wrote a constitution that did so. It ensured Black men the vote, created a tax structure designed to redistribute land from planters to freed people, eliminated imprisonment for debt, provided the tools for subsequent legislatures to establish free public schools for all children, and gave more autonomy to local courts and county governments.[26] Unlike the politicians in the legislatures of 1865 and 1866, delegates wanted Black and white poor people to be able to keep dogs for hunting and defense. When some members of the convention made a proposal to continue the dog tax, the delegates ultimately decided against it.

This debate over the dog tax reflected some delegates' concern for the fate of poor people and their animals. The Committee on Finance recommended a dog tax as part of the financing to cover the cost of the convention and to pay a per diem and mileage for the first state legislature held under the new constitution. The proposed rate was fifty cents on each person "keeping a dog or dogs," half that of the previous tax. The committee estimated that the new levy would produce $20,000 for the state. On the twelfth day of the convention, a delegate moved to strike the tax on dogs. In the ensuing debate upcountry delegates suggested a tax on every additional dog a person owned beyond one. "I do not propose to put a tax upon the guardian of a house, but upon all unnecessary dogs," one of them remarked. Mr. J. M. Rutland of Fairfield District said: "This tax is to be levied upon property. I submit that dogs, in a general sense, are not property." Delegate B. O. Duncan responded: "I think a dog quite as much property as a cow, horse, or any other property. There is no tax more proper than a dog tax. In the country we have too many dogs, and levying a high tax may rid us of some very worthless animals." Delegate Alexander Bryce of Pickens quickly retorted, "Will my friend take the dogs for the taxes?" Jonathan J. Wright, a northern-born Black teacher and lawyer who was the delegate from low-country Beaufort, said that if the tax was as high as fifty cents, it "will not be collected, because the people will kill their dogs." He suggested reducing it to twenty-five cents. In the end, the delegates decided to strike the dog tax altogether.[27]

Because Canby's tax order remained in place during the meeting of the constitutional convention and the subsequent elections for the state legislature in 1868, the ability to pay a dog tax became part of the political rhetoric that Democrats in South Carolina used to discredit the majority-Black constitutional convention, its delegates, and the Republican Party. White conservatives conducted a propaganda campaign emphasizing that the state's Black "rulers" levied taxes that they did not have to pay because they were not property holders (a false accusation). South Carolina's former Confederates sent a "remonstrance" to the US House of Representatives that James B. Beck of Kentucky read to his colleagues. Because the Black delegates lacked property, it claimed: "They have no interests in the affairs of the State, no interest in its property, no interest in its taxation, and compose no part of its intelligence, wealth or respectability. While they are spending millions of the property of other people, they do not themselves bear one dollar of the burden." South Carolina's Democrats claimed that fifty-nine Black members of the constitutional convention paid no taxes at all; its seventy-three overall Black members paid a combined total of $117.93. The Black delegates, "with three or four exceptions," only paid a poll tax "and in a few instances [the] tax on a dog—very likely a sheep killer—and the white delegates are in the same condition."[28]

White Democrats used dogs as a rhetorical weapon in political battles, and they continued to use their actual animals as physical weapons against the freedpeople during Reconstruction. When Democrats mobilized paramilitary forces and employed terrorist tactics in 1868 to disrupt the election process and undermine Republican control of the state, canines handled by humans perpetrated some of the violence. Terrorists whipped white Republican Mack Martin and "put the dog on him, and the dog attacked him (naked as he was) and tore large pieces from his side and limbs," a witness reported to Federal investigators. Employers who wanted to impose control over the bodies of their freed Black laborers used dogs to intimidate and punish. In Augusta, Georgia, for example, Mary Ann Walker told Federal authorities that her employer, Calvin Ward, "hit her twice with an axe and set his dogs on her because she 'refused to allow him . . . to have elicit intercourse with her.'"[29]

Although dogs at the instigation of humans took part in some of the violence against white and Black Republicans, the canine violence that pervaded the public print in South Carolina during the late 1860s and 1870s was attacks on sheep. The number of articles about sheep-killing dogs increased as the state experienced a deep economic depression in the 1870s. The war left 1.5 million acres of land in South Carolina fallow, and 60 percent of the value of livestock was gone. Cotton prices plummeted, interest rates soared, and one hundred firms in Charleston shut down.[30] With no dog taxes in place under the state's Republican regime (except municipal ordinances), the dog population remained high and continued its vital role of hunting to supplement the diet of the poorest residents. Southern agricultural reformers, especially the members of the Granger movement, used newspapers to make their case that dogs held back the economic progress of the South and that reducing their population was a vital necessity in order for southern states to develop the healthy sheep industry that would revive their economies.

Agricultural reformers used two main rhetorical tactics to win converts to their program. The first was to associate dogs with Black people and with poverty. The *Newberry Herald* printed a joke about "Old Si," who explained why Black people preferred their dogs to the vote. "When de mussels ob a niggar's hart git twined roun' a dog, he fines mor' comfort in dat property dan in all de votes dat yer could cram into a fo-bushel ballot box." The *Abbeville Press and Banner* claimed, "no colored family is without one of these pests." The *Anderson Intelligencer* reprinted the report of a traveling correspondent who visited Tennessee: "Curse the worthless dogs! Wherever you find them in the greatest numbers, you find the people correspondingly poor and the country wretched." The writer summarized, "ignorance, idleness and dogs (they all go together)."[31]

The second tactic was to offer mathematical calculations designed to persuade people that dogs hurt the economy. A letter to the editor of South Carolina's *Edgefield Advertiser* on January 29, 1868, used dark humor to make the point after General Canby implemented the $1 tax on each dog in the state. "This is a short chapter on dogs, and was suggested by a big fat, sleek, worthless cur in my own yard," the author began. He estimated that there were 3,000 dogs in Edgefield District, at least one per farm. "It may be safely assumed that what will keep a dog in good condition for a year, will raise a pig that will weigh 200 pounds gross," he noted. "These 3000 dogs if killed would save to the District $3000 of taxes (see Gen. Canby's tax order) while the 3000 hogs substituted for them, with proper care, in the course of the year, will make at least 3000 loads of good manure, worth $3,000. Then it may be assumed also, that each dog will destroy and injure stock to the value of one sheep, worth in the aggregate $3000." The writer provided a precise calculation of the value of killing dogs and replacing them with hogs:

| | |
|---|---|
| 600,000 lbs gross pork at 10 cents | $60,000 |
| Taxes on 3000 dogs at $1 | 3,000 |
| Value of 3000 sheep saved which would be destroyed by dogs | 3,000 |
| Value of 3000 loads manure at $1 | 3,000 |
| Value of 3000 dog skins at 33 1/3 c. | 1,000 |
| Making in the aggregate | $70,000 |

"Is it true that $70,000 may be saved to the people of Edgefield District so easily? And will we, in light of such facts, continue to give our children's bread to the dogs," he asked.[32]

Throughout the 1870s, South Carolina's newspapers used similar statistics and startling comparisons to support the contention that dogs cost the state too much of its potential revenue. Because they were "worthless," feeding them took resources away from "productive" and "useful" animals, and their sheep-killing activities lost the agricultural industry hundreds of thousands of dollars every year. Sheep-industry advocates proclaimed that counties paid a "tax" to support dogs. The paper for Abbeville calculated that dogs cost the county $78,000 a year: $48,000 in the amount used to feed dogs ("three times the amount it takes to run the county government"), $5,000 to replace the animals they killed, and $25,000 in lost revenue from the sheep industry. The *Yorkville Enquirer* noted: "It costs South Carolina more to feed her dogs than it does to support her clergy. There is scarcely a man in the State who does not spend more on dogs than he gives for the gospel."[33]

What agricultural reformers neglected in these calculations was the contribution that dogs made to the subsistence living of rural families. Agricultural reformers obsessed with the potential profits of the sheep industry could not overcome the simple fact that the majority of people in South Carolina, white and Black, kept dogs and found them useful animals. The advocates of hunting and those who relied on dogs for security outnumbered and outweighed the influence of their opponents through the end of Reconstruction.

With the debate in the public print focused on dogs as "sheep-killers," white Democrats deployed "bloodhounds" in the violence that brought down the

Republican government and reestablished white supremacy in South Carolina. US soldiers had killed Robert Butler's pack in 1865, but the former slaveholder still knew how to manage dogs. On July 4, 1876, Butler's son and son-in-law had a run-in with the Black militia that drilled in Hamburg. On July 8 a gun battle erupted between hundreds of armed white men and Black members of the militia. The whites stormed the building where the militiamen had taken shelter, took prisoners, and shot six of them. A mob then spent the night terrorizing the town's Black residents. The next day Butler used a pack of hounds to hunt the militiamen hiding in the swamps surrounding Hamburg.[34] When it came to keeping Black people in their place, dogs remained a weapon of choice.

## NOTES

1. Thomas Jordan to Ripley, June 2, 1863; W. S. Walker to Thomas Jordan, June 17, 1863; and John F. Lay to Thomas Jordan, June 24, 1863, *The War of the Rebellion: A Compilation of the Official Records of the Union and Confederate Armies,* 70 vols. in 128 parts (Washington, DC: Government Printing Office, 1880–1901), ser. 1, 14:290–91, 301, 963 (hereafter *OR,* all citations to series 1 unless otherwise stated); James Montgomery to David Hunter, June 3, 1863, 34th USCT Regimental Letter, Order, and Endorsement Book, vol. 3, Record Group (RG) 94, National Archives and Records Administration, Washington, DC (hereafter NARA); Alfred Marple Diary, June 3, 1863, Alfred Marple Diary and Letters, South Caroliniana Library, Columbia; William Lee Apthorp, "Montgomery's Raids in Florida, Georgia, and South Carolina," ed. Dan Shafer, Florida History Online, https://www.unf.edu/floridahistoryonline/montgomery/index.html.

2. Thomas Wentworth Higginson, *Army Life in a Black Regiment and Other Writings* (New York: Penguin Books, 1997), 55.

3. This essay does not consider the agency of dogs, how their choices may have affected events, or whether their relationship with humans was that of a "cobelligerent species." It does not fully develop the relationship between dogs and people or consider the question of human domination. These are important considerations when writing about dogs in war but would have required more space than available here. For scholarly discussion of these issues, see Gervase Phillips, "Technology, 'Machine Age' Warfare, and the Military Use of Dogs, 1880–1918," *Journal of Military History* 82, no. 1 (January 2018): 67–94; Phillips, "Animals in and at War," in *The Routledge Companion to Animal-Human History,* ed. Hilda Kean and Philip Howell (New York: Routledge, 2018); Ryan Hediger, ed., *Animals and War: Studies of Europe and North America* (Boston: Brill, 2013); Margo DeMello, *Animals and Society: An Introduction to Human-Animal Studies* (New York: Columbia University Press, 2012); and Kimberly Brice O'Donnell, *Doing Their Bit: The British Employment of Military and Civil Defence Dogs in the Second World War* (Warwick, UK: Helion, 2018).

4. Alonzo Cooper, *In and out of Rebel Prisons* (Oswego, NY: R. J. Oliphant, 1888), 139, 147, 150; J. Madison Drake, *Narrative of the Capture, Imprisonment, and Escape of J. Madison Drake, Captain Ninth New Jersey Volunteers* (N.p., 1866), 23, Huntington Library, San Marino, CA; Eric W. Emerson, and Karen Stokes, ed., *Days of Destruction: Augustine Thomas Smythe and the Civil War Siege of Charleston* (Columbia: University of South Carolina Press, 2017), 101; "An Account of Captain Conley's Escape from Prison," 11, Rare Books and Manuscripts Division, Library of Congress (LOC); Luther Guiteau Billings Memoir, 91, ibid.

5. "Columbia, December 13, 1859," *Keowee Courier* (Pickens Court House, SC), December 17, 1859, 2; "A Chance for Sausage Makers," *Charleston Daily News,* December 5, 1867, 3, James J. Broomall, *Private Confederacies: The Emotional Worlds of Southern Men as Citizens and Soldiers* (Chapel Hill: University of North Carolina Press, 2019), 26–28; Rod Andrew Jr., *Wade Hampton: Confederate Warrior and Southern Redeemer* (Chapel Hill: University of North Carolina Press, 2008), 25–27. For other discussion of the role of dogs in marking racial and class divides in society, see Brian Patrick Duggan, *General Custer, Libbie Custer, and Their Dogs: A Passion for Hounds, from the Civil War to Little Bighorn* (Jefferson, NC: McFarland, 2019), 75; Janet M. Davis, *The Gospel of Kindness: Animal Welfare and the Making of Modern America* (New York: Oxford University Press, 2016), 92–94; and Harriet Ritvo, *The Animal Estate: The English and Other Creatures in the Victorian Age* (Cambridge, MA: Harvard University Press, 1987), 4–5, 88–115.

6. "The Woolen Manufacture," *Independent Press* (Abbeville Court-House, SC), September 30, 1859, 2; "Sheep and Dogs," *Yorkville (SC) Enquirer,* June 3, 1858, 4; "Sheep-Killing Dogs—Tax Them," *Edgefield (SC) Advertiser,* August 3, 1859, 2.

7. "Columbia, Dec. 13, 1859," *Keowee Courier* (Pickens Court House, SC), December 17, 1859, 2; "Acts Passed by the Legislature of 1859," *Lancaster (SC) Ledger,* January 18, 1860, 2; *Yorkville (SC) Enquirer,* December 22, 1859, 2.

8. "Columbia, Dec. 13, 1859," *Keowee Courier* (Pickens Court House, SC), December 17, 1859, 2; "Acts Passed by the Legislature of 1859," *Lancaster (SC) Ledger,* January 18, 1860, 2; *Yorkville (SC) Enquirer,* December 22, 1859, 2.

9. "Recent Acts," *Lancaster (SC) Ledger,* January 18, 1860, 2; "The Dog Law," *Camden (SC) Weekly Journal,* January 24, 1860, 1; James Robert Hester, ed., *A Yankee Scholar in Coastal South Carolina: William Francis Allen's Civil War Journals* (Columbia: University of South Carolina Press, 2015), 118. South Carolina taxmen collected the levy on dogs kept by slaves and free Blacks at least through 1862. Notices about collecting this tax are common in state newspapers in 1860 and 1861. The latest notice in a digital search through Chronicling America was "Notice to Tax Payers," *Yorkville (SC) Enquirer,* April 3, 1862, 2.

10. Billings Memoir, 96–97, 101–2; "Statement of James Morgan," Record Book of the Provost Marshal General, Hilton Head, South Carolina, RG 393, NARA. Escaped prisoner Willard Glazier thought there were two categories of hounds in a pack. "The baying or yelping hounds take the lead, and are followed by the bloodhounds, which make little noise. These yelping curs will not come nearer to a person than four or five rods, but will cut circles, and thus mark their locality until the bloodhounds or planters come up." See Willard W. Glazier, *The Capture, the Prison Pen, and the Escape* (Albany, NY: J. Munsell, 1866), 301–2.

11. Sally E. Hadden, *Slave Patrols: Law and Violence in Virginia and the Carolinas* (Cambridge, MA: Harvard University Press, 2001), 42–43, 168–83; Lorien Foote, *The Yankee Plague: Escaped Union Prisoners and the Collapse of the Confederacy* (Chapel Hill: University of North Carolina Press, 2016), 50–51.

12. Ira Berlin et al., *Freedom: A Documentary History of Emancipation, 1861–1867*, ser. 1, vol. 1, *The Destruction of Slavery* (Cambridge: Cambridge University Press, 1985), 806–7.

13. B. T. Sellers to Williams Middleton, December 5, 1863, March 29, 1864; and Theodore Hanckel to Williams Middleton, March 28, April 4, 1864, Williams Middleton Papers, South Caroliniana Library, Columbia.

14. Andrew Murray and John Layern Entries, Descriptive Book, vol. 1, 33rd USCI Regimental Books, RG 94, NARA; Report of William Stokes on Capture of Union Telegraph Party, September 13–14, 1863; and Extract from Journal of Operations in Charleston Harbor, September 13, 16, 1863, *OR*, 28(1):128–29, 729–30.

15. Rufus Saxton to Quincy A. Gillmore, November 30, 1863; and C. S. Walker to Thomas Jordan, November 26, 1863, *OR*, 28(1):745–46; Higginson, *Army Life in a Black Regiment*, 179; Christopher Looby, ed., *The Complete Civil War Journal and Selected Letters of Thomas Wentworth Higginson* (Chicago: University of Chicago Press, 2000), 329–32, 338; John Appleton to Mary Appleton, January 6, 1864, Box 2, Appleton Papers, West Virginia University Library, Morgantown. Hunting fugitives with dogs in attack formations, according to David Karunanithy, was a "surviving vestige" of Spanish, English, and Scots-Irish use of canines brought to the New World. The conquistadors used war dogs to conquer and pacify Indigenous peoples. "This appears to have been hybridized with the Anglo-Saxon tradition of tracker dogs," he notes, "and perhaps one other hypothetical source—the Scotch-Irish, who . . . came from regions where dogs were used in pursuit capacities from as early as the medieval period." *Dogs of War: Canine Use in Warfare from Ancient Egypt to the 19th Century Seminole Wars* (London: Yarak, 2008), 203. The US Army brought Cuban bloodhounds to Florida for use in the Second Seminole War (1835–42), and after the war slaveholders more widely incorporated them into slave control. See John Campbell, "The Seminoles, the 'Bloodhound War,' and Abolitionism, 1796–1865," *Journal of Southern History* 72, no. 2 (May 2006): 284–88. Officers in the US Army during the US–Mexican War utilized dogs on the march, on hunts, in camp, and in battle. Dogs may have run alongside individual officers into battle, but the army did not formally deploy them as part of battle tactics. See Douglas A. Murphy, "Dogs of Destiny, Hounds from Hell: American Soldiers and Canines in the Mexican War," *Military History of the West* 26, no. 1 (Spring 1996): 35–48.

16. Nancy Rohr, ed., *Incidents of the War: The Civil War Journal of Mary Jane Chadick* (Huntsville, AL: SilverThreads, 2005), 212; Mary E. Pendrey to Richard F. Pendrey and Mary A. Pendrey, May 15, 1861, Private Voices, https://altchive.org/private-voices/; Billings Memoir, 99; Glazier, *Capture, Prison Pen, Escape*, 301–2; Daniel Avery Langworthy, *Reminiscences of a Prisoner of War and His Escape* (Minneapolis: Byron Printing, 1915), 40.

17. Lessel Long, *Twelve Months in Andersonville: On the March—in the Battle—in the Rebel Prison Pens, and at Last in God's Country* (Huntington, IN: Thad and Mark Butler, 1886), 175; Oscar L. Jackson, *The Colonel's Diary: Journals Kept before and during the Civil*

*War by the Late Colonel Oscar L. Jackson* (N.p.: privately printed, 1922), 191–92; David Gould and James B. Kennedy, eds., *Memoirs of a Dutch Mudsill: The "War Memories" of John Henry Otto, Captain, Company D, 21st Regiment Wisconsin Volunteer Infantry* (Kent, OH: Kent State University Press, 2004), 299, 304, 329–30.

18. Cormac Broeg, "Killing Butler's Bloodhounds: An Act of Political Violence by Iowa Soldiers in Reconstruction South Carolina," *Annals of Iowa* 78 (Spring 2019): 131–57.

19. Richard Zuczek, *State of Rebellion: Reconstruction in South Carolina* (Columbia: University of South Carolina Press, 1996), 18; Walter Edgar, *South Carolina: A History* (Columbia: University of South Carolina Press, 1998), 377–83; Thavolia Glymph, "Rose's War and the Gendered Politics of a Slave Insurgency in the Civil War," *Journal of the Civil War Era* 3, no. 4 (December 2013): 501–32; Foote, *Yankee Plague*, 138–40.

20. Stephen V. Ash, *When the Yankees Came: Conflict and Chaos in the Occupied South, 1861–1865* (Chapel Hill: University of North Carolina Press, 1995), 229.

21. "Columbia Correspondence," *Charleston Daily News*, September 25, 1865, 1; *Journal of the Convention of the People of South Carolina, Held in Columbia, S.C. September 1865* (Columbia: J. A. Selby, 1865); Hyman Rubin, *South Carolina Scalawags* (Columbia: University of South Carolina Press, 2006), 4–8, 16; Andrew, *Wade Hampton*, 310.

22. "An Act to Raise Supplies for the Year Commencing in October, 1865, December 21, 1865," no. 4728, Published Laws of South Carolina, South Carolina Department of Archives and History, Columbia; Greenville District, Tax Record Book, 1865, ibid. In Newberry District 1,710 dogs were taxed; 1,915 in Abbeville District; 2,087 in Spartanburg District; 1,366 in Darlington District; and 1,337 in Lexington District. I am grateful to Michael Emett for conducting research for me in South Carolina's dog-tax records. For a discussion of the role dog taxes and licensing has played in social control of working classes in the United States, see Katherine C. Grier, *Pets in America: A History* (Chapel Hill: University of North Carolina Press, 2006), 214.

23. "Taxes, Direct and Indirect—Tax on Dogs," *Daily Phoenix* (Columbia), March 21, 1867, 2; *Keowee Courier* (Pickens Court House, SC), December 22, 1866, 2; Letter to editor from Simeon Corley, *Daily Phoenix* (Columbia), February 3, 1871, 1.

24. "Taxes, Direct and Indirect—Tax on Dogs," *Daily Phoenix* (Columbia), March 21, 1867, 2; "The Tax Act," *Newberry (SC) Herald*, January 16, 1867, 1; "Taxes," *Carolina Spartan* (Spartanburg, SC), May 31, 1866, 3; "State Taxes," *Orangeburg (SC) News*, April 6, 1867, 4; *Edgefield (SC) Advertiser*, January 2, 1867.

25. "Taxation in the State," *Lancaster (SC) Ledger*, December 12, 1867, 2; "A New Tax Bill," *Charleston Daily News*, November 18, 1867, 3; "A Chance for Sausage Makers," ibid., December 5, 1867, 3; "Cruel! Cruel!" *Lancaster (SC) Ledger*, December 12, 1867, 2.

26. Edgar, *South Carolina*, 386; Thomas Holt, *Black over White: Negro Political Leadership in South Carolina during Reconstruction* (Urbana: University of Illinois Press, 1977), 37; Rubin, *South Carolina Scalawags*, 26, 30–32; Andrew, *Wade Hampton*, 341.

27. *Proceedings of the Constitutional Convention of South Carolina, Held at Charleston, S.C., beginning January 14th and ending March 17, 1868*, vol. 1 (Charleston: Denny & Perry, 1868), 149–56, 166–70; "The Convention," *Charleston Daily News*, January 29, 1868, 1; "Proceedings of the Ring Streaked and Striped Convention," *Fairfield Herald* (Winnsboro,

SC), February 5, 1868, 1; Holt, *Black over White*, 241. South Carolinians paid a tax of $1 per dog in 1868 based on Canby's tax order. It was widely advertised in local newspapers. See, for example, *Southern Enterprise* (Greenville, SC), March 4, 1868, 4; "Attention! Tax-payers," *Keowee Courier* (Pickens Court House, SC), March 6, 1868, 3; "Rate of State Taxation," *Charleston Daily News*, January 3, 1868, 3; and "Tax Paying," *Fairfield Herald* (Winnsboro, SC), February 26, 1868, 3. Charleston residents paid an additional town tax of $2 per dog, and people who lived in Abbeville paid a town tax on their dogs. "Ways and Means," *Charleston Daily News*, January 4, 1869, 2 and "Town Taxes," *Abbeville (SC) Press*, May 8, 1868, 2.

28. "Admission of Southern States," *Daily Phoenix* (Columbia), May 19, 1868, 2; "The South Carolina Reconstruction Scandal," ibid., May 23, 1868, 2; "The State Taxation: An Appeal to Governor Scott," *Charleston Daily News*, August 11, 1869, 1; Andrew, *Wade Hampton*, 353–54; Holt, *Black over White*, 37.

29. Rubin, *South Carolina Scalawags*, 42; Stephanie McCurry, *Women's War: Fighting and Surviving the American Civil War* (Cambridge, MA: Belknap Press of Harvard University Press, 2019), 166.

30. Edgar, *South Carolina*, 396.

31. "Old Si on the Negro Franchise," *Newberry (SC) Herald*, January 24, 1877, 1; untitled reprint, ibid., September 19, 1877, 3; "Granger Sam on the Dog," *Abbeville (SC) Press and Banner*, July 11, 1877, 2; "A Tennessee Picture That Will Answer for South Carolina," *Anderson Intelligencer* (Anderson Court House, SC), May 6, 1875, 1; "Protecting Sheep from Dogs," ibid., September 5, 1872, 4; "A Dog Tax," *Abbeville (SC) Press and Banner*, December 8, 1875, 2.

32. "Practical Economy," *Edgefield (SC) Advertiser*, January 29, 1868, 6.

33. "Granger Sam on the Dog," *Abbeville (SC) Press and Banner*, July 11, 1877, 2; "Those Dorgs," *Newberry (SC) Herald*, August 2, 1876, 1; "Sheep," *Yorkville (SC) Enquirer*, November 19, 1874, 4; "A Dog Tax," *Abbeville (SC) Press and Banner*, December 8, 1875, 2; "Are We All to Be Bitten to Death?" *Weekly Union Times* (Union Court House, SC), May 4, 1877, 2; "Sheep, Goats, Turnips," *Newberry (SC) Herald*, August 29, 1877, 3. There were unsuccessful attempts to pass a dog tax in the South Carolina legislature in January 1873 and December 1875. See *Daily Phoenix* (Columbia), January 18, 1873, 2; "Senator Cochran's Reform," *Anderson Intelligencer* (Anderson Court House, SC), November 25, 1875, 1; and "Columbia Correspondence," ibid., December 23, 1875, 2. Much of the debate was over whether dogs were property and if it was constitutional to tax them.

34. Broeg, "Killing Butler's Bloodhounds," 131–57; Zuczek, *State of Rebellion*, 163–64. For the lasting legacy of dogs enforcing white supremacy into the present, see Tyler D. Parry, "Man's Best Friend," *History Today* 66 (December 2016): 50–53; and Charlton Yingling and Parry, "The Canine Terror," *Jacobin* (May 19, 2016), https://www.jacobinmag.com/2016/05/dogs-bloodhounds-slavery-police-brutalityracism/.

# VI

# Animals after THE Civil War

# "Has He Not Been in the Service of His Country?"

## *Union Regimental Mascots in War and Peace*

**BRIAN MATTHEW JORDAN**

ON MAY 23 AND 24, 1865, thousands of civilian spectators in Washington, DC, looked on as veterans of the eastern and western Union armies strutted triumphantly down Pennsylvania Avenue. With glinting bayonets poised atop their shouldered muskets, the bronzed survivors of Antietam and Atlanta filed beyond a flag-festooned reviewing stand, "exemplars of disinterested patriotic sacrifice."[1] But the Grand Review involved much more than rows of marching men. The *New York Times* noted that, on the parade's second afternoon, "a display of pack-horses and mules" supplied "much amusement." Atop the mules were mounted "the pets of soldiers," including "a coon, a dog and a goat." A US Patent Office examiner, Horatio Nelson Taft—ever the keen observer of wartime Washington—similarly remarked upon the colorful menagerie of "cats and dogs, Coons, opposums, fighting Cocks and other fowls" that brought up the rear. Deeming the animals "living specimens of the country [through] which the Army had passed," Taft tellingly included them among his careful inventory of the baggage trains—the "frying pans, the kettles, the buckets, and tin dishes"—that trundled behind Sherman's legions. Like the delighted crowds lining the nation's avenue, the diarist regarded such animals as passive objects rather than historical actors. For the rank and file, however, these regimental pets were battle-tested veterans who, through long service and great sacrifice, had earned a rightful place in any celebration of Union victory.[2]

Indeed, the participation of animals in the Grand Review offers a striking illustration of the relationship between human and nonhuman actors during the Civil War—and the deep significance that many soldiers attached to their beastly companions. Just as men developed a "fictive kinship" in camp, on the march, and under fire, so too did soldiers develop meaningful and affective ties with animals—especially those they adopted as pets. Union troops regarded their animal companions as full members of what the historian Barbara A. Gannon has called the regimental community. "The community of the regiment, as understood by its members," Gannon writes, "was not always the same as the official military organization defined by the army." In her formulation, membership in the regimental community extended to anyone who had shared in the war's physical hardships, material deprivations, and unhygienic environments—regardless of their participation in combat. While Gannon and other scholars have identified nurses, cooks, and camp servants as members of the regimental community, historians have not fully appreciated that the world of the regiment also included furry and four-legged, winged and plumed creatures. Displaying physical bravery, reinforcing unit pride, and powerfully evoking their cause, animals were Civil War veterans, too.[3]

Much like the bonds of comradeship forged between regimental comrades, the ties that connected animal veterans and their human companions survived the conflict. The Civil War poses no challenge to the scholar who concludes, "the terrible conditions of [military] conflict have intensified human bonds with other animals." Celebrated in the popular press, paraded at veterans' reunions, and placed on public display, regimental mascots became esteemed, "living relics" of the war. When not physically present, their framed likenesses adorned soldiers' homes and Grand Army of the Republic (GAR) meeting spaces. Although virtually unacknowledged in scholarship on Civil War memory, regimental mascots were—together with bullet-riddled flags, pinned-up trousers, and empty coat sleeves—among the conflict's most eloquent and evocative *lieux de mémoire*. As participants in and witnesses to the war's violence, animal veterans supplied a ready connection to the past. Regimental pets embodied the fidelity, selflessness, and persistence that the war for the Union demanded of ordinary enlisted men. As powerful emblems of the troops' persistence and resolve, animal veterans lent ready support to a heroic narrative of Civil War soldiering—one that left no room for either southern treason or northern treachery. Animal mascots thus sustained their human companions after the war just as they had during the conflict itself. Yet by the late nineteenth century, these creatures faced mounting public scrutiny. As policymakers sought to expose pension fraud and purge the swelling rolls of illegitimate claims, questions about the authenticity and identity of the war's animal heroes multiplied.[4]

A distinct though as yet understudied category of war animals, Union regimental mascots represented a broad array of creatures. Perhaps the most "famous" of these was Old Abe, the eagle mascot adopted by the men of the 8th Wisconsin Volunteer Infantry. Old Abe's wartime service and postbellum pursuits demonstrates the intimate and enduring nature of the human-animal relationship during the Civil War. Furthermore, it supplies a compelling example of how animal history can yield fresh insights into the culture of a Civil War regiment and the character of Civil War memory.[5]

## UNION REGIMENTAL MASCOTS

A remarkable number of Union regiments relied on animals for companionship during the Civil War. "No well-regulated command was considered 'fully up to date' that did not possess a 'mascot,'" claimed the historian of one Illinois light artillery battery. Some units actually marched to the front with a regimental pet. A "bright-eyed spaniel" named Curly, a parting gift from a young Columbus gal, accompanied the 11th Ohio when it embarked for western Virginia in 1861. The dog quickly "won his way to the hearts of all in the regiment." A citizen of Eau Claire purchased the young eagle that hovered above the 8th Wisconsin, deeming the national bird an exemplary talisman for the Badger State volunteers to hold aloft in the struggle for liberty and Union. Animals presented to regiments upon their departure supplied the rank and file with living reminders of their support back home. Not unlike homespun uniforms or crates brimming with medical supplies and provisions, these mascots expressed the enduring bonds between battlefield and home front.

More frequently, however, mascots were acquired by soldiers in the field. A drummer boy in the 6th Iowa acquired a puppy on the regiment's trek to winter quarters, concealing his new companion (soon dubbed Jeff Davis) in his haversack. The 18th New York adopted a dog during the First Battle of Bull Run, while a canine embedded himself in the ranks of the 13th Illinois as the Federals retreated from Wilson's Creek. (One mascot was apparently inadequate for that regiment, for the following May, they took in a "small pup" while camped near Salem, Arkansas.) Jack, a small hound, wandered into the 35th Ohio's camp at Paris, Kentucky, and remained with the unit for the balance of the war, seeing action at Mill Springs, Shiloh, Perryville, Chickamauga, and atop Missionary Ridge. On the Peninsula the 104th Pennsylvania "collected about them a fine array of pets to cheer the solitude of their tents."[6]

In their memoirs, regimental histories, and contributions to veterans' newspapers, soldiers affirmed the psychological benefits of regimental pets, revealing in the process their utter "dependence" on them. "It mattered not whether the object of their affection was a dog, cat, possum, cow, or horse, of whatever name or species," one veteran claimed, "the brute was loved by all, and woe be to the outsider who dared to insult or injure one of these pets." As constant companions, mascots supplied both familiarity and an aura of domesticity that allayed the anxieties of soldiers' untamed, peripatetic lives. "It is natural for soldiers, leading the roving life of gipsies, isolated a large portion of their time from all society but themselves," one Wisconsin soldier held, "to form strong and lasting attachments" with their animals. Mascots became a source of unit pride, such that "companies and regiments soon became known by the peculiarity of their dogs."[7]

Evidence suggests that animals identified with their human companions, too. Numerous veterans marveled that mascots could distinguish "every man" belonging to their regiments. The historians of the 11th Ohio, for example, insisted that Curly "was never mistaken in identifying an Eleventh man." Nor, in still another suggestion of the powerful bonds of comradeship shared by humans and animals, did these powers of recognition dim after the war. In 1870 J. J. Stevens of the 18th New York visited his old canine comrade, who lived with the regiment's colonel in Albany. "He recognized me at once by every demonstration a dog could give of joy at meeting an old comrade," Stevens alleged. "The Colonel said he never failed to recognize any member of the regiment who came where he was." Old Doc, the dog mascot of an Iowa regiment, "seemed also to remember his old friends" at postwar reunions, where he was "caressed and petted by thousands of old veterans who had not forgotten the many pleasant and unpleasant times they had passed together in field, camp, and battle."[8]

As Old Doc's companions would attest, regimental pets helped relieve the dull tedium of soldier life in the intervals between battle. For enlisted men who were physically spent or emotionally exhausted from the demands of camp and campaign, mascots supplied both a welcome release and a predictable source of amusement. The raccoon belonging to the 12th Wisconsin Battery helped "while away the dull hours of camp life." Dogs were especially "plentiful" in the western armies, and, in the estimate of one veteran, their presence "tended to enliven the soldiers." With his clever repertoire of tricks, Old Harvey invited "convulsions of laughter" from his human companions in the 104th Ohio. The canine mascot may help explain the report, inked on the final day of August 1864, that the "discipline and spirits of the regiment" remained strong despite a taxing summer of marching, maneuvering, and fighting in Georgia. Roosters were likewise abundant within the regimental camps of western armies, prompting many soldiers to place bets on cock fights. Training, taming, and otherwise making sport of animals afforded the men the pretense of mastery amid the war's great uncertainties.[9]

Mascots likewise encouraged human companions with their conspicuous displays of loyalty and selfless acts of daring under fire. Observing the remarkable fortitude of their animals persuaded soldiers that they, too, could persevere—and even distinguish themselves—in combat. Old Bull, a canine attached to Capt. Joseph Foust's Battery E, 1st Missouri Light Artillery, "ran himself ragged chasing Confederate projectiles" during a hot artillery duel at Prairie Grove. It was perhaps no coincidence that Foust's six guns delivered a "particularly effective" enfilading fire that swept the field that afternoon. Wounded at Port Gibson by a shell that incapacitated him for three weeks, Old Doc "bore his sufferings with all the heroism of a veteran soldier." Jeff Davis, the dog belonging to the 6th Iowa, not only "chased grapeshot" but also inspired his companions with his faithfulness. "Jeff would follow any man of the regiment," recalled Private Julius Nott. "Through his fidelity each and every man of the regiment became greatly attached to him." When the pooch was killed atop Missionary Ridge, the enlisted men attended to his body with the "individuation . . . reserved for one's comrades," planting a wooden marker bearing "a suitable inscription" at the foot of his freshly made grave.[10]

Animals doubtless supplied many genuine examples of courage and devotion, but their human companions also engaged in much anthropomorphism. Soldiers readily attributed political opinions, support for the war, ideas about military strategy, and attitudes about race to their animals, a curious practice that at once revealed and reinforced the integral role of regimental pets. The historian of the 13th Illinois concluded that Salem overcame his "antipathy to the negro race"—an artifact of his "bloodhound" pedigree and nativity in a slaveholding border state—through "careful training in Union camps." The dog soon exhibited "a loyalty that could not be shaken." The men left little doubt about Salem's status as a full-fledged member of the regimental community; the dog's metamorphosis, after all, paralleled that of the many Yankees who eventually embraced emancipation as a pragmatic war measure. The men of the 35th Ohio, meanwhile, delighted in contrasting Jack's "good sense" and "judgment" with that of his fellow Kentuckians Simon Buckner, John Breckenridge, and Beriah Magoffin, all of whom had forsaken the Union. Jack, they reminded, "stood firmly by the flag, not only until the last rebel was whipped, but until the confederacy was reconstructed and back in the union of states." Spiting treason, the mongrel embraced "hard war" policies as a liberal forager, raiding "hen-roosts" and acquiring a taste for "secesh ham." "His conscience never smote him, or prevented him from taking what he wanted," the regimental historian insisted. Jack "damaged the confederacy as much as lay in his power by doing his best to eat the rebels out of house and home, which was an approved way to put down the rebellion."[11]

## "A LIVING REBUKE TO INGRATITUDE AND TREASON"

Soldiers and veterans thus turned mascots into paragons of persistence and emblems of their cause. Old Abe, the eagle attached to the 8th Wisconsin, embodied the "hopes that hung upon the coming contest." The majestic bird, mounted on a shield-shaped perch and bedecked with red, white, and blue ribbons, accompanied the fresh recruits of Company C as they embarked from Eau Claire, bound for Madison and their camp of instruction. Admired by spectators and saluted in editorials, Old Abe became the pride of his regiment. Perhaps nothing illustrates this so well as a tale the Wisconsin men told after the war about the Second Battle of Corinth, fought in October 1862. According to the Badger State veterans, Confederate major general Sterling Price identified the eagle's capture or killing as among his foremost aims, advising his troops that he would rather them bag the bird "than the whole brigade." Old Abe's companions effortlessly interpreted the three desperate assaults Price made on their fortified position as evidence of the rebel Missourian's intent.[12]

Although a Confederate bullet grazed his wing and Company C lost half its strength, Old Abe eluded capture at Corinth. The following spring, tethered to his perch by a "strong cord about twenty feet long," he saw action at Jackson, Big Black River Bridge, and Champions Hill—three battles in the grueling campaign that delivered the Army of the Tennessee to the defenses of Vicksburg. Flapping above the siege lines, Old Abe was struck by a spent ball. Yet this proved a minor injury, for the following year, he participated in no fewer than five engagements during the Federals' disastrous Red River Campaign in Louisiana. After spending a well-earned, month-long furlough in Wisconsin, the living emblem of the Union returned to the front and contributed to one final effort—driving Major General Nathan Bedford Forrest's troops from a sturdy defensive line behind Mississippi's Hurricane Creek. In September 1864, with his three-year term of enlistment expired, Old Abe mustered out of army service. Governor James Taylor Lewis received the "hero-bird" in Madison on September 22, 1864, pledging to give him a "permanent roost" in the state capitol. Alongside "the old flags of the regiments," Old Abe would be cared for as "an honored and inspiring memento" of the war. Not unlike the regimental colors, "sadly torn and soiled," riddled with "the affection of our misguided Southern 'brethren' in every fold," Old Abe "look[ed] a little rough," having "seen over two years of hard service."[13]

An evocative site of memory, the eagle's home became a postwar tourist attraction, enthralling "thousands of people from all parts of the country." On warm summer days Old Abe would take leave of his "large room" in the basement of the state capitol and greet curiosity seekers in a shady, nearby park. With a veteran companion, the bird also traveled to fairs and expositions, commanding handsome admission fees. "Everybody," one newspaper insisted, "wanted to see the famous war eagle that had gone through so many actions." There was "something grand in his presence, and, as you look upon him, you cannot but feel that you are looking upon an important personage," marveled one visitor. Predictably, quills and feathers became coveted relics. To satisfy the popular demand while preserving something of the eagle's plumage, Old Abe's custodian would "surreptitiously hand out 'just one more'" from his "supply of chicken and turkey feathers." Still, this clever stratagem notwithstanding, more than a few visitors managed to pluck their own souvenirs. These they would preserve alongside a host of prints, postcards, stereographs, and biographies that, adorned with martial imagery and the Stars and Stripes, esteemed sacrifice and reinforced a heroic narrative of the war.[14]

The postwar public commoditized Old Abe, but the survivors of the 8th Wisconsin embraced him as a "full-fledged, laurel-crowned veteran." The bird had played an integral role in the 8th Wisconsin's survival as a regiment, inspiring the men amid their long, foot-blistering marches and many trying battles with disease, hunger, and thirst. "Sharing alike the dangers of march and battle," declared John Melvin Williams, who compiled one of the unit's regimental histories, "the Eagle was companion and warrior, sign and seal of victory." The affinity that the men shared with their mascot was "mystical" by any estimation. "I believe the eagle knew our regiment as well as we knew it ourselves," recalled one veteran who, when asked to account for the phenomenon in an interview after the war, referred his interrogator to a "philosopher."

This old soldier was hardly alone. For instance, many veterans believed that Old Abe had joined in the "composite consciousness" achieved by the regiment on the firing line. Williams insisted that the eagle knew how to interpret aural and visual information in battle. "At the sound of the regimental bugle, which [the eagle] had learned to recognize, however engaged he might be," Williams wrote, "he would start suddenly, dart up his head, and then bend it gracefully, anticipating the coming shock."

> Then, with a silent, excited, animation, he would survey the moving squadrons, and, as they rushed into line, his breast would tremble like the human heart, intensified to warring action between hope and fear—an undaunted suspense—a blending of caution and courage—a precipitancy of will, inspiring and sublime. Click would go a thousand locks, and he would turn again, curving that majestic neck, scrutinizing the ranks, and dipping his brow forward to await the crash; and when it came, rolling fiery thunder over the plain, he would spring up and spread his pinions, uttering his startling scream, heard, felt, and gloried in by the desperate soldiers.

Colonel J. W. Jefferson agreed, remarking that the bird "was well informed in regard to army movements, dress parade and preparations for the march and battle." He was, as one postwar commentator put it, "every inch a soldier."[15]

The eagle's soldier-comrades recommended that sturdy political convictions had contributed to his exemplary battlefield performance. "That he was in full sympathy with his comrades and the cause in which they were engaged," purported one postwar account, "was evident from the beginning." To evidence their claim, veterans cited Old Abe's physical comportment and vocal expressions, betraying not only their careful scrutiny of his movements and mannerisms but also their rather remarkable presumption that animals could develop and display political convictions. Soldiers described how the bird "screeched a wild defiance" at the sound of the rebel yell, "lustily flapped his wings" whenever the regiment "cheered," and "jump[ed] up and down on his perch" amid the din of battle. "Soldierly in his instincts," Williams remarked, Old Abe "seemed to understand that the war was to be carried to the bitter end—to the last dying gasp of an enslaving rebellion."[16]

Having attributed courage, loyalty, and ideological conviction to the eagle, veterans enlisted him in the pitched political battles over the Civil War's meaning and legacy during Reconstruction. Keenly aware of Old Abe's "eloquent," emotional power—something amplified by the seemingly deliberate decision to assign maimed and one-armed veterans as his chaperones—the old soldiers deployed the eagle as a "living rebuke to ingratitude and treason." Reunion committees forwarded requests "for the use of the eagle" to Madison with great regularity. He was, in the telling estimate of one editorial, "ever the vigilant sentinel, regarding only the end to be gained and the earnest realities of his great mission." Old Abe became a fixture at Republican rallies, Fourth of July parades, GAR meetings, soldiers' reunions, and monument dedications—doing almost "constant duty," one editor remarked, "as a 'relic.'" He was embraced as a true comrade; the GAR post in Eau Claire, Wisconsin, even took the unusual step of naming him an "honorary member," a move all the more remarkable when one considers the organization's notorious exclusivity and its refusal to admit as members lineal descendants.[17]

In September 1866 Old Abe assumed the "post of honor" at the Pittsburgh Soldiers' and Sailors' Convention, a massive gathering that welded Union veterans from across the nation "into an effective political force." Warning that they "still had another round" in their cartridge boxes, convention-goers determined to sustain the military occupation of the South and resist President Johnson's too-lenient program of Reconstruction. Freely contrasting their loyalty with the treason of the rebels, delegates deemed themselves the true arbiters of the war; they endorsed the proposed Fourteenth Amendment as "wise, patriotic, and just" and pledged "sympathy and cordial cooperation" to "all peoples struggling for freedom." A host of prominent Union veterans crowded the dais—among them John Burns, the Gettysburg civilian who had rushed into the battle, and Robert Hendershott, the "Drummer Boy of the Rappahannock"—but perhaps the heartiest ovation was reserved for Old Abe, whom the *New York Herald* deemed the assembly's "most distinguished delegate." Assuming his familiar perch alongside the national colors, the eagle "stretched up and flapped his pinions" each time the audience of 25,000 applauded. Observers, of course, were quick to interpret these displays as signals of the eagle's endorsement of a thorough and broad-minded Reconstruction, supplying reassuring evidence that Old Abe had let up nothing of his wartime zeal. Later, conveyed in an "open carriage drawn by four white horses," the eagle was paraded through streets "thronged" with admiring veterans eager to catch a glimpse of the soldier-bird.[18]

As the "enraptured multitude" that greeted him in Pittsburgh made evident, Old Abe continued to cheer his old companions after the war, sustaining Union veterans in their efforts to "recover the passion of the conflict" and resolve its unfinished work. "He has not forgotten the sound of the drum or the significance of marching," one observer explained. "The war cry, with which he was wont to inspire the soldiers, again rings out with all its shrill intensity." In May 1868 the bird journeyed to Chicago, where Union veterans from twenty-two states vowed to reenlist "for three years or the war" should the battles over Reconstruction occasion another rebellion. "The Wisconsin Eagle, 'Old Abe,'" one newspaper remarked, "seemed to imagine himself once more amid the exciting scenes of war, and flapped his wings while he looked proudly around upon the scene, as though saying to the multitude: 'Boys, the graves of your comrades are scattered all over the South; you won't forget them, nor the cause for which they died.'"[19]

By maintaining such a demanding schedule on what the historian James Marten has called the "old soldier circuit," it did not take the eagle long to gain a reputation as an unapologetic apostle of the Union cause. Old Abe flapping his wings became the beastly equivalent of "waving the bloody shirt." In a measure of his effectiveness as a reminder of the war, the eagle not only earned the ire of Democratic newspaper editors but also became a proxy in disputes over the war's legacy and the care, treatment, and character of Union veterans. In 1872, against the backdrop of the presidential campaign during which Democratic nominee Horace Greeley urged his fellow Americans to forgive, forget, and "clasp hands across the bloody chasm," the *New York Herald* recalled Old Abe's 1866 appearance in Pittsburgh—and his alleged endorsement of Jeff Davis's execution—with disgust. "The platform was none the cleaner for the presence of the noble bird," the editors opined. "It may interest his friends to know further that he is now in extremely comfortable circumstances, and that the State of which he is an honored citizen has appropriated fund[s] for his support and appointed a special keeper to attend to him."[20]

FIG. 11.1. The Most Famous Mascot. Old Abe, the eagle mascot of the 8th Wisconsin, appears in this carte-de-visite of 1876. The most famous animal mascot of the Civil War poses proudly eleven years after the conflict. Abe endured many battles, surviving the conflict to become not only a long-lived veteran of Union military service but also an icon of the animal-human experience of war. Liljenquist Family Collection of Civil War Photographs, Library of Congress, LC-DIG-ppmsca-34513.

Predictably, criticism of state expenditures on Old Abe's care and maintenance only multiplied as the fight over pensions swelled in intensity. Indeed, as opponents of Civil War pension legislation purported widespread fraud, one Kansas newspaper maintained that the eagle's heroic war record had been invented of whole cloth. "'Old Abe' was considered a sort of nuisance about camp," the biting editorial began. "He was filthy and ugly, and used to sicken the soldiers by feeding on carrion like a buzzard. During engagements he used to hide away in sutlers' wagons, and could not be induced to come out until the cannonading and rattling of musketry had ceased. . . . He was a living example of what hero-worship will do for an individual or thing. He was a base fraud, and no doubt he would have blushed scarlet if he could at the fuss that was made about him. He was a hero by compulsion." Nor was this the only imputation of deceit related to the eagle. In 1878 a "spirited discussion" erupted over Old Abe's identity. The press propagated rumors that the soldier-bird had died four years before, and that the winged mascot exhibited at Philadelphia's Centennial Exposition was an "impostor." The controversy invited a state-senate resolution and subsequent investigation, which concluded that the eagle then in Wisconsin's care was the genuine war veteran.[21]

The controversy was all but forgotten when Old Abe succumbed to smoke inhalation, the unfortunate consequence of a fire at the state capitol in 1881. From Bangor, Maine, to Santa Cruz, California, hundreds of newspapers lamented his demise. The "hero of thirty battles" even scored a short obituary in the *New York Times*. Yet even in death, the eagle invited the odd blend of veneration and disdain known to many veterans. A brouhaha erupted when an allegation was made—eleven years after his death—that Old Abe was, in fact, a hen. "He was pointed out to the youth of the land as the emblem of liberty," one detractor announced. "The truth is, after Old Abe was taken to Madison, Wis., he got tired of doing nothing and went to laying eggs." By the late nineteenth century, readjustment problems, physical disabilities, chronic diseases, and public lobbying for pension benefits contributed to an emerging perception that the men who saved the Union were somehow less than manly. With pension benefits for Civil War veterans annexing more and more of the federal budget, a growing number of Americans regarded Union soldiers as "pension beggars." Perhaps it was no surprise, then, that the war eagle, once celebrated as the paragon of martial daring, would find his gender identity questioned.[22]

## CONCLUSION

It was appropriate that Old Abe shared in the trials and tribulations of Union veteranhood. Just as the bird shared in the experiences of war, so too did he share in the experiences of the peace. Nor, it appears, was he alone. After making his own rounds on the veterans' reunion circuit, Curly lived out his final days at the Central Branch of the National Home for Disabled Volunteer Soldiers in Dayton, Ohio, where his old companions eventually buried him. Jack's companions in the 35th Ohio, meanwhile, "voted" him a "silver collar" at a reunion "soon after the war." When the dog passed, he was "buried with appropriate ceremonies." Such acts of sincere devotion suggest that Civil War soldiers never forgot the important work—real and symbolic—undertaken by nonhuman actors during the war and its long aftermath. Though animals have, until relatively recently, eluded the gaze of most Civil War historians, they remained esteemed members of regimental communities to the very end.[23]

## NOTES

*Note to essay title: The Home Fair Journal* (Milwaukee), as quoted in John Melvin Williams, *"The Eagle Regiment," 8th Wis. Inf'ty Vols.* (Belleville, WI: Recorder Print, 1890), 79.

1.Gary W. Gallagher, *The Union War* (Cambridge, MA: Harvard University Press, 2011), 7–8; "The Grand Review," *Muscatine (IA) Evening Journal,* June 1, 1865. For fuller treatments of the Grand Review, see Brian Matthew Jordan, *Marching Home: Union Veterans and Their Unending Civil War* (New York: Liveright, 2014), chap. 1; and Cecily Zander, "Victory's Long Review: The Grand Review of Union Armies and the Meaning of the Civil War," *Civil War History* 66, no. 1 (March 2020): 45–77.

2.*New York Times,* May 25, 1865; Diary of Horatio Nelson Taft, May 24, 1865, vol. 3, Library of Congress, Washington, DC.

3.Barbara A. Gannon, "'She Is a Member of the 23rd': Lucy Nichols and the Community of the Civil War Regiment," in, *This Distracted and Anarchical People: New Answers for Old Questions about the Civil War–Era North,* ed. Andrew L. Slap and Michael Thomas Smith (New York: Fordham University Press, 2013), 185.

4. On "fictive kinship," see Jay Winter, "Forms of Kinship and Remembrance in the Aftermath of the Great War," in *War and Remembrance in the Twentieth Century,* ed. Jay Winter and Emmanuel Sivan (Cambridge: Cambridge University Press, 1999), 40–60; and Ryan Hediger, "Animals and War: Introduction," in *Animals and War: Studies of Europe and North America,* ed. Ryan Hediger (Leiden: Brill, 2013), 2–3. For "sites of memory," see Pierre Nora, "Between Memory and History: *Les Lieux de Mémoire,*" *Representations* 26 (Spring 1989): 7–24. On flags as sites of memory, see Robert E. Bonner, *Colors of Blood: Flag Passions of the Confederate South* (Princeton, NJ: Princeton University Press, 2002), 158–59. Presented by a local GAR post, a portrait of Old Abe adorned the state soldier's home in Pennsylvania. See *Report of the Trustees of the Pennsylvania State Soldier's and Sailor's Home, 1889–90* (Philadelphia: J. B. Lippincott, 1891), 44. On battles over the care and treatment of Union veterans, see especially James Marten, "'Not a Veteran in the Poorhouse: Civil War Pensions and Soldiers' Homes," in *Wars within a War: Controversy and Conflict over the American Civil War,* ed. Joan Waugh and Gary W. Gallagher (Chapel Hill: University of North Carolina Press, 2009), 202–22.

5. Scholars of other conflicts have cast a critical eye on the relationship between soldiers and animals. See especially Andrew McEwen, "'He Took Care of Me': The Human-Animal Bond in Canada's Great War," in *The Historical Animal,* ed. Susan Nance (Syracuse, NY: Syracuse University Press, 2015), 272–88. See also Helena Pycior, "The Public and Private Lives of 'First Dogs': Warren G. Harding's Laddie Boy and Franklin D. Roosevelt's Fala," in *Beastly Natures: Animals, Humans, and the Study of History,* ed. Dorothee Brantz

(Charlottesville: University of Virginia Press, 2010), 176–203; Jon T. Coleman, *Vicious: Wolves and Men in America* (New Haven, CT: Yale University Press, 2004); and Etienne Benson, "The Urbanization of the Eastern Gray Squirrel in the United States," *Journal of American History* 100, no. 3 (December 2013): 691–710. All of these sources inform this essay.

6. Charles B. Kimbell, *History of Battery 'A' First Illinois Light Artillery Volunteers* (Chicago: Cushing Printing, 1899), 80; "Company Dog Jeff," *Our Dumb Animals* 46, no. 1 (June 1913): 6; "The Hero of the Regiment—A Faithful Dog," *Evansville (IN) Daily Journal*, July 18, 1864; *Daily Ohio Statesman* (Columbus), July 21, 1864; "Curly," *National Tribune* (Washington, DC), February 23, 1888; William W. H. Davis, *History of the 104th Pennsylvania Regiment, from August 22nd, 1861 to September 30th, 1864* (Philadelphia: J. B. Rogers, Printer, 1866), 15; "Pet of the Regiment," *National Tribune* (Washington, DC), July 27, 1893; *Military History and Reminiscences of the Thirteenth Regiment of Illinois Volunteer Infantry* (Chicago: Woman's Temperance Publishing, 1892), 189; Frederick Keil, *Thirty-Fifth Ohio: A Narrative of Service from August, 1861 to 1864* (Fort Wayne, IN: Archer, Housh, 1894), 222–25; David McLain, "The Story of Old Abe," *Wisconsin Magazine of History* 8, no. 4 (June 1925): 407. On the emotional power of homespun, see James Broomall, *Private Confederacies: The Emotional Worlds of Southern Men as Citizens and Soldiers* (Chapel Hill: University of North Carolina Press, 2019), 36–37.

7. Hediger, "Animals and War," 2–3; Frazar Kirkland, *The Pictorial Book of Anecdotes and Incidents of the War of the Rebellion* (Hartford, CT: Hartford Publishing, 1867), 504; George W. Griggs, *Opening of the Mississippi; Or Two Years Campaigning in the South-West* (Madison, WI: Wm. J. Park, 1864), 38. George W. Quimby quoted in *The Perfect Scout: A Soldier's Memoir of the Great March to the Sea and the Campaign of the Carolinas*, ed. Anne Sarah Rubin and Stephen Murphy (Tuscaloosa: University of Alabama Press, 2018), 108–9. On Union soldiers and the persistence of home front mores and domesticity, see Reid Mitchell, *The Vacant Chair: The Northern Soldier Leaves Home* (New York: Oxford University Press, 1993).

8. J. H. Horton and Solomon Teverbaugh, *A History of the Eleventh Regiment, Ohio Volunteer Infantry* (Dayton, OH: W. J. Shuey, 1866), 246; "Pet of the Regiment," *National Tribune* (Washington, DC), July 27, 1893. Curly, Jack, and Old Bull allegedly recognized every man in their regiments. *Dodgeville (WI) Chronicle*, December 30, 1920; "Old 'Doc,' A War Veteran, Dead," *Daily Inter-Ocean* (Chicago), December 27, 1875.

9. J. O. Barrett, *The Soldier Bird "Old Abe": The Live War-Eagle of Wisconsin* (Madison, WI: Atwood & Culver, 1876), 17; Nelson A. Pinney, *History of the 104th Regiment Ohio Volunteer Infantry* (Akron, OH: Werner & Lohmann, 1886), 129; Janet B. Hewett, ed., *Supplement to the Official Records of the Union and Confederate Armies*, 100 vols. (Wilmington, NC: Broadfoot, 1993–2000), pt. 2, 559; George W. Quimby quoted in Rubin and Murphy, *Perfect Scout*, 109.

10. William L. Shea, *Fields of Blood: The Prairie Grove Campaign* (Chapel Hill: University of North Carolina Press, 2009), 161–62; *Daily Inter-Ocean* (Chicago), December 27, 1875; Julius Nott, "That Dog Jeff," *National Tribune* (Washington, DC), March 17, 1898; Drew Gilpin Faust, *This Republic of Suffering: Death and the American Civil War* (New York: Alfred A. Knopf, 2008), 71.

11. *Military History and Reminiscences of the Thirteenth Regiment,* 190; Keil, *Thirty-Fifth Ohio,* 222–24. On the embrace of emancipation among western-theater officers, see Kristopher A. Teters, *Practical Liberators: Union Officers in the Western Theater during the Civil War* (Chapel Hill: University of North Carolina Press, 2018).

12. Barrett, *Soldier Bird,* 18–20, 24, 34; *Eau Claire* (WI) *Telegram,* June 9, 1930; *Dodgeville* (WI) *Chronicle,* December 30, 1920; Williams, *"Eagle Regiment,"* 51; Charles D. Miller, *Report of the Great Re-union of the Veteran Soldiers and Sailors of Ohio Held at Newark, July 22, 1878* (Newark, OH: Clark & Underwood, 1879), 114; Timothy B. Smith, *Corinth 1862: Siege, Battle, Occupation* (Lawrence: University Press of Kansas, 2012), 196; Albert E. Smith, "A Few Days with the Eighth Regiment, Wisconsin Volunteers at Iuka and Corinth," in *War Papers: Being Papers Read before the Commandery of the State of Wisconsin, Military Order of the Loyal Legion of the United States,* vol. 4 (reprint, Wilmington, NC: Broadfoot, 1993), 61–68.

13. *National Tribune* (Washington, DC), March 29, 1883; Williams, *"Eagle Regiment,"* 52, 61, 72–76; McLain, "Story of Old Abe," 407–14; Barrett, *Soldier Bird,* 89; *Fox Lake (IL) Gazette,* June 29, 1864; Brian Steel Wills, *A Battle from the Start: The Life of Nathan Bedford Forrest* (New York: Harper Collins, 1992), 238; "Note from the Eagle Regiment," newspaper clipping, n.d., Edwin Bentley Quiner Scrapbook, vol. 9, Wisconsin Historical Society, Madison.

14. Barrett, *Soldier Bird,* 101–4; Williams, *"Eagle Regiment,"* 80; "Old Days," *Capital Times* (Madison, WI), June 15, 1936; *Eau Claire* (WI) *Ledger-Telegram,* April 15, 1926; "The Tail Feathers of Old Abe," *Wausau* (WI) *Daily Herald,* June 30, 1931; Edwin Bentley Quiner Scrapbook, vol. 10. The competition for Old Abe's feathers and quills began during the war itself, part of the "traffic" in relics identified in Joan E. Cashin, "Trophies of War: Material Culture in the Civil War Era," *Journal of the Civil War Era* 1, no. 3 (September 2011): 339–67.

15. Frederick Francis Cook, *Bygone Days in Chicago* (Chicago: A. C. McClurg, 1910), 36; Williams, *"Eagle Regiment,"* 55, 60, 63–64, 79 (*Home Fair Journal* quote); *Eau Claire* (WI) *Telegram,* June 9, 1930; *Dodgeville* (WI) *Chronicle,* December 30, 1920; McLain, "Story of Old Abe," 412; *Lindsborg (KS) Localist,* April 21, 1881; Earl J. Hess, *The Union Soldier in Battle: Enduring the Ordeal of Combat* (Lawrence: University Press of Kansas, 1997), 113; *Memphis Daily Post,* October 2, 1866. The survivors of the 8th Wisconsin were not alone in alleging that their mascot joined in human thought, action, and emotion during battle. Veterans of the 11th Ohio, for instance, alleged that Curly "knew . . . when a march or movement was in contemplation as if he understood every word of the order issued, and made his preparations accordingly." See Horton and Teverbaugh, *History of the Eleventh Regiment,* 246.

16. Williams, *"Eagle Regiment,"* 66–67; Cook, *Bygone Days in Chicago,* 35–36; McLain, "Story of Old Abe," 412; *Memphis Daily Post,* October 2, 1866; "The Eagle of the Eighth Wisconsin," in *The Rebellion Record: A Diary of American Events,* ed. Frank Moore, vol. 4 (New York: D. Van Nostrand, 1866), 59.

17. *Vancouver (WA) Independent,* May 12, 1881; *Wisconsin State Journal* (Madison), October 25, 1866; *Daily Inter-Ocean* (Chicago), May 13, 1875, April 19, 1881; "The First Grand

Army Post at Eau Claire," *Abbotsford Clarion* (Eau Claire, WI), April 13, 1933; "A Comrade of the G.A.R.," *Christian Science Monitor,* July 9, 1926. Old Abe's caretakers included four one-armed veterans: William J. Jones, Hugh Lewis, Eugene Brown, and George Baker. Still another custodian, Harry W. Lovejoy, was described as a "scarred veteran." See Barrett, *Soldier Bird,* 92. See also Mary Ashton Livermore, *My Story of the War* (Hartford, CT: A. D. Worthington, 1889), 628.

18. *Baltimore Sun,* September 26, 1866; Williams, *"Eagle Regiment,"* 80–81; Sam Ross, *The Empty Sleeve: A Biography of Lucius Fairchild* (Madison: State Historical Society of Wisconsin, 1964), 82–83; *Salt Lake Daily Telegraph,* September 28, 1866; *New York Herald,* October 5, 1866, July 20, 1872; *San Francisco Bulletin,* October 26, 1866; *Milwaukee Sentinel,* October 5, 1866; Barrett, *Soldier Bird,* 105–8; Charles D. Cashdollar, "The Pittsburgh Soldiers' and Sailors' Convention, September 25–26, 1866," *Western Pennsylvania Historical Magazine* 48 (1965): 331–43.

19. *Daily Inter-Ocean* (Chicago), May 13, 1875; *Daily Iowa State Register* (Des Moines), May 20, 1868; *Weekly Champion and Press* (Atchison, KS), June 4, 1868; Zachery A. Fry, "'Let Us Everywhere Charge the Enemy Home': Army of the Potomac Veterans and Public Partisanship, 1864–1880," in *The War Went On: Reconsidering the Lives of Civil War Veterans,* ed. Brian Matthew Jordan and Evan C. Rothera (Baton Rouge: Louisiana State University Press, 2020), 22; Brian Matthew Jordan, "'Our Work Is Not Yet Finished': Union Veterans and Their Unending Civil War, 1865–1872," *Journal of the Civil War Era* 5, no. 4 (December 2015): 484–503.

20. *Girard (KS) Press,* April 14, 1881; *New York Herald,* July 20, 1872.

21. *Little Globe* (Atchison, KS), April 14, 1881; *Weekly Marysville (OH) Tribune,* September 18, 1878; *Journal of Proceedings of the Thirtieth Annual Session of the Wisconsin Legislature* (Madison: Carpenter & Tenney, 1877), 175–76.

22. Williams, *"Eagle Regiment,"* 89; "Wisconsin's Famous War Eagle," *New York Times,* March 29, 1881; *Bangor (ME) Daily Whig and Courier,* April 7, 1881; *Santa Cruz (CA) Weekly Sentinel,* May 7, 1881; James Marten, *Sing Not War: The Lives of Union and Confederate Veterans in Gilded Age America* (Chapel Hill: University of North Carolina Press, 2011); "The Gender of the Eagle," *Austin (TX) Daily Statesman,* May 27, 1892. The issue was definitively settled in 2016, when the University of Wisconsin–Madison's Molecular Archaeology Group conducted genetic testing on three of Old Abe's feathers. See Haley Hansen, "Tests Confirm Wisconsin Civil War Mascot Old Abe Was Indeed a Male Bald Eagle," *Wisconsin State Journal* (Madison), July 15, 2016.

23. *Ohio Soldier* (Chillicothe), May 5, 1888; Horton and Teverbaugh, *History of the Eleventh Regiment,* 246–47; Keil, *Thirty-Fifth Ohio,* 225. Animals—especially regimental mascots—have long been the province of amateur historians and purveyors of human-interest stories. See, for example, Charles G. Worman, *Civil War Animal Heroes: Mascots, Pets, and War Horses* (Lynchburg, VA: Schroeder, 2011); and Michael Zucchero, *Loyal Hearts: Histories of American Civil War Canines* (Lynchburg, VA: Schroeder, 2011). When professional historians have written about animals, they have trained much of their attention on Civil War mounts. See, for example, James I. Robertson Jr., "A Dead Horse," in *Lens of War: Exploring Iconic Photographs of the Civil War,* ed. J. Matthew Gallman and

Gary W. Gallagher (Athens: University of Georgia Press, 2015), 195–202; Dane DiFebo, "Old Baldy: A Horse's Tale," *Pennsylvania Magazine of History and Biography* 135, no. 4 (October 2011): 549–52; Drew Gilpin Faust, "Equine Relics of the Civil War," *Southern Cultures* 6, no. 1 (Spring 2000): 23–49; Ann Norton Greene, "Civil War Horses," in *Horses at Work: Harnessing Power in Industrial America* (Cambridge, MA: Harvard University Press, 2008); and David J. Gerleman, "Unchronicled Heroes: A Study of the Union Cavalry Horses in the Eastern Theater: Care, Treatment, and Use, 1861–1865" (PhD diss., Southern Illinois University, 1999). Judkin Browning and Timothy Silver make a preliminary attempt to write a broader assortment of animals into Civil War history in *An Environmental History of the Civil War* (Chapel Hill: University of North Carolina Press, 2020).

# The Sectionalism OF THE National Zoo, 1888–1891

*Animals, Language, Politics, and Laughter*

DANIEL VANDERSOMMERS

WILLIAM FORNEY took to the floor of the House of Representatives on September 12, 1888, as a well-respected Democrat from Alabama. He stood before his peers in the Capitol chamber as a veteran politician. He also stood before them as a former brigadier general of the Confederate States of America, wounded at Dranesville, Williamsburg, Salem Church, and Gettysburg. Though he was captured twice, he was paroled and then exchanged. He returned to combat both times and eventually surrendered alongside Robert E. Lee at Appomattox. Over the course of his US House career, Forney had been witness to controversial legislation centered on postwar nation-building projects like the Desert Land, Chinese Exclusion, Edmund-Tucker, Dawes, and Interstate Commerce Acts as well as the formation of the District of Alaska. On this day, though, he confronted legislation of a new kind. Bestowed upon the House by the Senate was an amendment that sought to establish a federally subsidized zoo.[1]

Forney did not rant against the proposition. Instead, he stated simply that the government had no business creating a zoo until it was out of debt. Though the appropriation was for $200,000 (the equivalent of $5.43 million in 2020), Forney believed that future costs would be inevitable. "Next year we will buy buffaloes, tigers, lions, monkeys, and other animals. After that, reptiles, snakes, and things of that kind." Laughter filled the chamber. Forney exaggerated, yet he was not completely wrong. Maintaining a zoo was expensive, and many southern Democrats found the "zoo bill" to be a laughing matter. Yet very seriously, the notion of a national zoo sat at the center of longstanding disagreements about the purpose of government.[2]

Zoogoers themselves found little controversy in zoos. Such places offered everything a middle-class urbanite could ask for—education, amusement, and scientific advancement. Though this trinity was inscribed upon the banners of zoo boosters everywhere, from Berlin to Tokyo, progress was its true godhead. By going to the zoo, one could not only escape the quagmire of the city but also become a part of a teleology that was rushing onward toward a new century. The zoo offered a transfiguration. One who entered, who gazed into the eyes of Nature on display, could become something more. The zoo was indeed peculiar. It transformed millions of animals into capital, mere life, for the escapism of the masses, offering withdrawal from the very thing it embodied. Such a deception requires a discourse.[3]

While zoogoers rarely encountered politics along the footpaths between paddocks, in the halls of Congress, the ties that bound the zoo and its animals to politics proved more visible. The National Zoological Park (or National Zoo), the only zoo in American history whose governance fell under the purview of the federal legislature, offers a unique window into a semiology that fused animals to debates about government that divided a nation through and after the Civil War. Animals were used by congressmen to conjure sectional ideologies that could not be wielded aggressively in an era of reconciliation. Using methods derived from animal studies, this essay calls attention to the sectionalism of the National Zoo.

The idea of a national zoo was not an entirely new one. Congress had already heard appeals for such a place in the District of Columbia in 1873 and 1876. Both times the idea went nowhere. This time, in 1888, things were different. First, the National Museum's Department of Living Animals, established by taxidermist William Hornaday, had already acquired the "nucleus of a zoo." Originally, the department included a cinnamon bear, white-tailed deer, Columbian black-tailed deer, cross fox, mule deer, golden eagle, spotted lynx, two badgers, two foxes, and five prairie dogs. Acquired to serve as living models for his displays, Hornaday housed them in a temporary structure alongside the Smithsonian Castle. The department opened its doors to the public on New Year's Eve, 1887. Afterward, its population and popularity expanded rapidly. By June 1889, it was teeming with 341 animals. Floods of citizens came to see them, especially the representatives of species on the verge of extinction. Particularly popular were the carrier pigeons Liberty and Minstrel; the jaguar, cinnamon bear, and prairie dogs; First Lady Frances Cleveland's spotted fawn; the black bears named after Stonewall Jackson, Lee, and Dabney Maury; and the six bison that muddied their corral behind the castle.[4]

The zoo bill emerged from this reality—there was already a de facto zoo in Washington—and it gained strong bipartisan support in the Senate. On April 23, 1888, Senator James Beck, Democrat from Kentucky, proposed Senate Bill 2752 to establish a zoo in the capital. Science, education, recreation, and the passionate support of Justin Morrill (Republican from Vermont) pushed the bill through the Senate. Yet, through debate, the zoo inherited additional purposes. First, it would protect American species by preserving them in enclosures and spearheading breeding projects. Second, it would bolster nationalist ambitions by being the grandest of its kind in the world (rhetoric, to be sure, but powerful nonetheless). What could be controversial about a national zoo?[5]

The opposition in the House (galvanized around the zoo bill and its first funding bill) answered simply that the government had no right to create an institution of this kind. The way in which representatives made this claim is illuminating. Missouri Democrat Richard Bland pointed out, as many others did, that other cities established parks and zoos to beautify their landscapes. Why should Washington not have the same responsibility? He argued that it was not right to tax citizens for an institution that would just benefit local real-estate markets. To strengthen this position, Bland addressed the science mission that boosters extolled, since this purpose (more than education and recreation) was a goal infused with *national* interest. He asserted sarcastically that it was not in the interest of science to bring monkeys, bears, and elephants to Washington. Then he joked: "Hundreds of the people of my State would prefer, if this circus is to be inaugurated, that it be put on wheels. Let us appoint the clown." Bland concluded, fittingly for a politician who backed silver miners, "I am opposed to the amendment and to all appropriations of public money that go simply to the benefit of the aristocratic classes."[6]

Others echoed these arguments, often with a sarcasm appropriate for what they saw to be a joke. Like Forney and Bland, Tennessee Democrat Benton McMillin (who, though prevented by his father from serving in the army, was still jailed by Union troops for refusing to take an oath of allegiance) believed that a zoo was a local matter. He considered it a crime for the national government, through eminent domain, to "sell the homes of the people in order to make them the habitations of monkeys"—a claim that led to laughter. McMillin further asseverated that the federal government had done plenty to beautify the capital, offering Judiciary Square, Lafayette Square, and the Capitol and White House grounds as evidence. "If the people of Washington," he declared, "want a display of rabbits, snakes, and all kinds of animals, let them have it; but let them pay for it themselves." Congress had no right to force Americans who would never even visit Washington to "pay the fiddler for others' dancing." He, like Bland, invoked a proletarian critique, referencing both Cicero and Edward Gibbon (like a good southern statesman), as he stated that "the display of wild beasts" had led to the "degeneracy" of the Roman Empire.[7]

Mississippi Democrat (and former Confederate lieutenant colonel) Thomas Stockdale was antizoo from the beginning. Not only did he, with Bland and McMillin, believe the zoo to be a scheme for the district's wealthy class but he also declared eminent domain unconstitutional. Only despots "condemn private property for the pleasure of citizens." Stockdale described the zoo as a stupendous folly and as a never-ending expense. In 1891, when addressing the House about an additional appropriations request for the zoo, Stockdale asked rhetorically, "Who will determine the price of a buffalo or a monkey or a rhinoceros? Why, the man who has it to sell; and these fellows that the Government sends out, how are they going to know the price of a rhinoceros or an elephant or a monkey?" Again, laughter filled the chamber. "Why, what does one know about the price of a rhinoceros?" Then modest laughter turned into a "great laughter." Amid the din, Marcus Smith, Democrat from the Arizona Territory, interjected, "Or sea lions." Stockdale, turning to his "friend," acknowledged the additional species tossed into the fray, "Yes, or of sea lions, or, as my friend from New Jersey said the other day, of coyotes?" He concluded his diatribe with a guilt trip: "Congress ought to be ashamed." Commotion consumed the House, and the Speaker's "hammer fell" to bring the menagerie to order before other Democrats started shouting out more unnamed species—"Or polar bears," "Or alligators," "Or, maybe, coatimundi!"[8]

The idea of a national zoo ignited an ire in those opposed, but not because politicians really cared about the animals themselves. The zoo as a symbol, though, reached into beliefs about government. This allowed it to be read, in part, through a North-South lens. Usually, these sectional differences inscribed into the zoo lay dormant; most representatives did not consciously view the zoo and its animals as overt sectional symbols. Occasionally, though, sectional meanings projected into the zoo cracked through the surface, for example, when James Blount, Georgia Democrat and former Confederate lieutenant colonel, stated: "The great agricultural sections of this country are agitated by straitened financial conditions. The cloud of despondency hangs over them." How could these poor Americans support a zoo hundreds of miles away?[9]

Nothing explicit in this statement referenced the Civil War, and nothing explicit cast the regionalism (the city-country rhetoric) of it in terms of North-South sectionalism. The subtext—the Civil War—was, however, palpable to every statesman in the room. This burst onto the page when Massachusetts Republican (and former Union corporal) Elijah Morse, in response to Blount, gave it voice. "Prior to the war," he bellowed, "the doctrine of State rights prevailed. In 1861 with the election of Abraham Lincoln a change came. We began immediately to emphasize the fact that we were a nation by macadamizing the streets, by laying out parks, and by the erection of statuary . . . until this city has come to be the finest Capital city in the world." Morse placed the zoo into this national postwar narrative. In his rehearsal of what would have been heard by southern statesmen as northern revisionism, especially through his invoking of Lincoln, Morse acknowledged what he saw as the *real* issues surrounding the zoo. Georgia Democrat (and former Confederate first lieutenant) Judson Clements responded to Morse's "reading" with humor, refusing to take the sectionalist bait: "I do not propose to be drawn by the gentleman from Massachusetts into the question as to whether this is a nation or a union of States, or both, nor will I now discuss the former tendency of Massachusetts toward secession."[10]

Missouri Democrat Alexander Dockery recoiled at Morse's rhetoric, though for different reasons. "This Government," Dockery reasoned, "has been maintained (passing meanwhile through a great civil war) without the aid of any zoological park." How could a zoo be likened to macadamizing the streets? He continued that he knew "of no functions connected with a monkey, tiger, or lion which are . . . essential to the public defense or necessary to discharge the functions of government." Again, the chamber resounded with laughter. Yet in this case, the laughter heightened (instead of punctuating) tension, prompting Dockery to launch a diatribe of his own. The topic concerned the question of whether the city of Washington itself should have financial responsibility for the zoo being bestowed upon it since other cities like New York, Philadelphia, and

Cincinnati capably supported their own zoos. After quoting the Sermon on the Mount, he explained that, though he was staunchly against the zoo, he was also (if there must be one) staunchly against forcing the capital city to pay for it. Since the District of Columbia was under taxation without representation, Dockery (who had been a southern sympathizer in a border state) believed that "we may have right here under the very shadow of the Capitol an exemplification of the type of government which some gentlemen in this country are so anxious to impose upon the people of the South." He then spiraled into an anecdote about "colored troops," an attack on the Republican Party, and a mocking of Morse's conjured Lincoln, "a Republican gentleman in the White House who was acting as President." Laughter consumed any further discussion, and the Speaker dropped the hammer.[11]

Sometimes anger over the National Zoo spiraled deeper into sectional territory, directing attention to the discourses of animality, upon which race was constructed. On April 18, 1890, Democrat and former Confederate lieutenant colonel James McCreary, representing the border state Kentucky, stated: "I am one of those not in favor of that Zoological Park. I do not think we came here to legislate for the purpose of furnishing homes for monkeys, zebras, and lions, but rather to legislate for *white* people and the people at large [emphasis added]." Maryland Republican Louis McComas, whose support during the war from a different border state lay with the Union, interjected, "And for the colored people." Though McCreary respoke—"I said for the people at large. I say we came here to legislate for the people: white people, colored people, and all the people"—the gallery filled with hisses and an anonymous representative shouted, "And saddle-colored." Then McCreary drove home his antizoo rhetoric: "But we did not come here to legislate for monkeys. Let it [the zoo] be strangled." The chamber filled with hisses, prompting the Speaker to again bring the melee to order, "Unless demonstration ceases in the gallery, the Chair will order the gallery cleared." North Carolinian Henry Cheatham, a former slave and the only Black representative in the House, surely reacted to this language that bound race and animality to both each other and an institution often viewed as progressive. But at least on record, Cheatham never spoke a word about the zoo.[12]

It would be reductionist to claim that the Civil War determined whether a representative supported or opposed the zoo. It was never that simple. On February 28, 1889, the House voted in favor of the zoo, 131 to 98. Eighteen of the yeas were indeed southern votes, and one-third of these (6 votes) were South

Carolinian since Democrats Samuel Dibble and John Hemphill broke ranks with their party and region to outspokenly support the zoo. With their support (as a public educator and a chairman of the Committee on the District of Columbia, respectively), they rallied their fellow South Carolinians to the zoo cause. These 18 votes, though, were outliers when compared with the other 40 southern nay votes. More telling, only 2 of 32 Deep-South votes (other than the South Carolinia block) voted in support of the zoo. Of course, party also correlated to voting outcomes; only 17 of 112 Republican votes were cast against the zoo. It was clear, though, that no matter why representatives voted against the zoo, sectionalist rhetoric did indeed undergird or overlay antizoo rhetoric.[13]

All of this explains why, on June 1, 1890, the *Dallas Morning News* published a column-long parody about the "monkey park bill." In an imagined dialogue among representatives, the parody depicts a $10,000 "buffalo wallow," a "big hole filled with water." It describes the spending of "$50,000 for housing and feeding the monkeys," "$40,000 for a tank of seals and sea lions," and "$15,000 for an aviary for sea gulls." The story continues in hyperbolic fashion, imagining objections like "Sea lions, sea lions! My goodness, this is downright robbery!" It also depicts zoo supporter and Speaker of the House Tom Reed of Maine as speaking in a "broad *yankee* tone." After the "monkey bill passed," the caricature concludes with the House moving to the next item of business, a bill for constructing a fictional government building in the fictional town of Whapwallopy, Pennsylvania. Clearly, this sketch drew both its political stance and comedy from sectionalist objections to the federal government. The citizens of Dallas, though, could not have been too opposed to zoos in general. Just a few months later, the same newspaper announced in excitement that Dallas's own zoo in Marsalis Park (which, established in 1888, was one of the first of the public-park animal displays to evolve into a zoo) acquired new black bears.[14]

Laughter, which riddled these congressional zoo debates, serves many purposes. A deep history of laughter would surely find its origins in primate social behavior, if not mammalian behavior generally, since studies have suggested that rats and dolphins laugh alongside chimpanzees, bonobos, orangutans, and humans. The latest evolutionary studies suggest that laughter gained utility (reproductive advantage) when primates began to live in cohesive groups of twenty or more individuals. So when laughter interrupted congressional proceedings, these outbursts were everything but noise. It was saturated with meaning, which is why the *Congressional Record* notes laughter in the first place. Laughter signaled unease. Laughter marked contention. Laughter gave voice to the unspeakable. Laughter served as borders between ideologies, as signposts that signaled "stop" or "don't go any further." And it certainly serves as windows into humans' semiconscious, yet embodied, reactions to ideological discord. When the House debated the zoo, members laughed for two reasons; one was when debate turned to the war; the other was when animals were named.[15]

What lessons can we glean from this zoo opposition? First, though they were instrumental to every aspect of American society throughout the Civil War era, and though they were taken seriously within their prescribed roles, animals themselves were not considered subjects worthy of discussion. They did not belong in the public sphere; they surely did not belong in a legislature. Animals did not deserve subjectivity. This particular fact should come as no surprise, though, since the perception of animals as automata—lacking emotion, personality, volition, and spirit—had been established, intellectually, in the West since Descartes. It makes sense, then, that the literal act of naming the animals of the proposed zoo, that acknowledging the unacknowledgeable—"monkey," "seal," "rhinoceros"—always incited laughter. Philosopher Tom Tyler, in *CIFERAE: A Bestiary in Five Fingers*, interrogates the rhetorical animals of Western philosophy and demonstrates that they—whether Buridan's ass or Derrida's cat—are almost always used as ciphers, "chosen placeholders, unwittingly serving some higher pedagogic purpose." Laughter was the vehicle through which "the animal" entered politics. And laughter continually erupted in the House, not because antizoo representatives were using animals rhetorically and not because legislators (actually, in reality) found the named-animals comical. Rather, laughter filled the House because the named animals were objects-turned-subjects, background-turned-foreground, tools-turned-persons. The act of naming felt new, felt blasphemous even, so laughter, to representatives, felt like the appropriate response. Furthermore, these animals were named unconsciously—below consciousness—to delegitimize their *named* purpose in a national zoo. Detractors, for example, named monkeys, foregrounded them in their rhetoric, for the purpose of undercutting their foregroundedness in a zoo just a few miles from the White House. Representatives felt (even if surely they did not recognize) the dissonance, the disjuncture, between the monkey-signifiers, both of which circumvented the living monkeys themselves. Even more, they felt the gap between the animal sensibilities of old, established since the Enlightenment, and the new ones emerging within the ethos of conservation as well as alongside nineteenth-century Romanticism. Their physical reactions to change, embedded in the historical shift from timeless menagerie to zoological park, were simply knotted into and expressed through the ejaculations of laughter.[16]

The second lesson is more historical, drawn from the conscious purposes of antizoo representatives. As Kenneth Greenberg argues in *Honor and Slavery*, the language of the Old South functioned as a system of heterogeneous signs—duels, noses, masks, and cross-dressing, to name a few—bound together for a common purpose. After the Civil War, southern representatives enlisted zoo animals into their language for a clear purpose: they symbolized the ever-expanding state. Not only did monkeys, seals, and rhinoceroses embody the "expansion of federal power" that Drew Gilpin Faust claims "characterized the transformed postwar nation," but the language of zoo animals also allowed representatives to disguise sectionalism when, in an age of reconciliation, straightforward North-South talk upon the House floor would not have been tolerated. The nature of federalism was the quintessential American question of the nineteenth century, a question that led to civil war. Zoo animals gave representatives a voice to talk about what could not be spoken about. As David Blight has demonstrated in *Race and Reunion*, memories of the war had always "clashed or intermingled in public memory." Whereas Blight emphasizes that much of postwar remembering was actually about forgetting, Caroline Janney, in *Remembering the Civil War*, has argued the opposite. In the decades after the Civil War, remembering was indeed about remembering—"forgetting was what they all feared most." The metonymic animals of a national zoo allowed representatives to both remember *and* forget a national trauma that was still relevant to interpreting the purpose of government.[17]

The final lesson is methodological. Scholars need to continue to think about animals across scales and disciplines. We need to examine them as proxies for ecological change and as windows into the history of environmental ideas. We must think about them as parts of larger systems while we simultaneously consider them as individual beings. Scholars also must excavate the layers of meaning we bestow upon them, consciously or not, while we interrogate the labor—physical and symbolic—that humans have required of them. Animals have much to say, and we have only begun to listen. Concerning the House of Representatives and the controversy of the National Zoo, looking at traditional primary sources through the lens of animal studies can help the historian discover both new meanings surrounding zoo animals and new languages surrounding legislating humans. Yet "real" animals can still elude us as well as they did the representatives mentioned above.

For congressmen, zoo animals were merely discursive. Opposition had nothing to do with *real* rhinoceroses or *real* sea lions, but it had everything to do with how the zoo, and thus its animals, opened sectional wounds. If these legislators were to look at real, living, and breathing zoo animals, they would not have seen symbols of the state imposing its will onto the nation. Instead, they might have seen objects that offered potential business to those living on the margins across American regions. Indeed, more often than not, the animals that would arrive at the zoo, especially in its early years, originated from citizens who had captured them around their homes and then decided to either sell them for profit or donate them in patriotic duty. A large proportion of these citizens (and animals) came from the American South or West. Cultural-environmental histories of the animal trades of the South still need to be written. Nonetheless, the story of the National Zoo became one of copperhead snakes from Hillsboro, Virginia; pocket gophers from Stovall, Texas; bobcats from Saint Augustine; Sand Hill cranes from Orlando; chipmunks from Sewanee, Tennessee; and pet kinkajous from New Orleans. And if these representatives were looking at *real* zoo animals, they would have acknowledged that not only was a zoological park underway in Dallas, but there was also one underway in Atlanta, formed when a bankrupt circus donated its animals to the city.

By the first decade of the twentieth century, southern cities would be swept up in the American zoo movement, from Mobile to Chattanooga to San Antonio. While the National Zoo could be seen in terms of *national* reconciliation, the broader zoo movement transcended regions and nation. The hundreds of zoos that emerged across the world between 1840 and 1920 should be seen as a response to the divorce from Nature that had been felt by many people since at least the eighteenth century. This larger reconciliation project was a *human* one more than a *national* one. In Congress, National Zoo boosters extolled both projects, though this human project usually remained disguised within the nationalist purposes of conservationism. National Zoo detractors, though, simply attacked the national-reconciliation project, decrying the federal government.[18]

In Congress zoo animals were not animals. Zoo animals represented a language through which the unacknowledgeable could be given a voice. As Congress debated the National Zoo, the United States still remained divided over the purpose of federal government. Yet animals would be held captive in zoos regardless.

## NOTES

1. John H. Eicher and David J. Eicher, *Civil War High Commands* (Redwood City, CA: Stanford University Press, 2001), 239–40. I would like to acknowledge the Consortium for History of Science, Technology, and Medicine for the NEH postdoctoral fellowship that provided time and resources for writing this work. A version of this essay also appears in Vandersommers, *Entangled Encounters at the National Zoo: Stories of Science, Culture, and Conservation* (Lawrence: University Press of Kansas, forthcoming).

2. Forney, September 12, 1888, 50th Cong., 1st sess., *Congressional Record,* 19(9):8545 (hereafter *CR*); Helen L. Horowitz, "The National Zoological Park: 'City of Refuge' or Zoo?," *Records of the Columbia Historical Society* 49 (1973–74): 412–15.

3. Both zoo history and a broader interdisciplinary zoo studies has been on the rise over the last few years. For an overview, see Tracy McDonald and Daniel Vandersommers, *Zoo Studies: A New Humanities* (Montreal: McGill-Queen's University Press, 2019).

4. S. 1531, February 5, 1873, 42nd Cong., 3rd sess.; and H.R. 1529, January 24, 1876, 44th Cong., 1st sess., via *ProQuest Congressional* (subscription service); Hornaday to Goode, December 2, 1887, Folder 10, Box 17, Record Unit 201, Smithsonian Institution Archives, Washington, DC, (hereafter SIU); Hornaday, "Report . . . ," 2–3, Box 5, RU 158, ibid.; Langley, "Report . . . ," "The Department of Living Animals," Scrapbook, 1887–1902; clippings, "An Embryo Zoo," *Evening Star,* June 2, 1888, and "The National Zoo," *Evening Lamp,* July 14, 1888, Scrapbook, vol. 2, 1888–1891, Folder 1, Box 285/286, RU 74, ibid. See also Diane Smith, *Yellowstone and the Smithsonian: Centers of Wildlife Conservation* (Lawrence: University Press of Kansas, 2017).

5. S. 2752, April 23, 1888, 50th Cong., 1st sess., via *ProQuest Congressional* (subscription service); Langley, "Zoological Park in the District of Columbia," February 2, 1889, report to accompany H.R. 11810, Scrapbook, 1887–1902, Box 285, Record Unit 74, SIA.

6. Bland, September 12, 1888, 50th Cong., 1st sess., *CR,* 19(9):8547.

7. McMillin, February 27, 1889, 50th Cong., 2nd sess., *CR,* 20(3):2422; Leonard Schlup, "Benton McMillin," October 8, 2017, Tennessee Encyclopedia, last updated march 1, 2018, https://tennesseeencyclopedia.net/entries/benton-mcmillin/.

8. Stockdale, August 13, 1888, 50th Cong., 1st sess., *CR,* 19(8):7498; Stockdale, February 5, 1891, 51st Cong., 2nd sess., *CR,* 22(3):2211–12.

9. Blount, April 9, 1890, 51st Cong., 1st sess., *CR,* 21(4):3208.

10. Morse, ibid., 3210; Clements, ibid., 3213.

11. Dockery, ibid., 3214–15.

12. McCreary, April 18, 1890, ibid., 3489.

13. February 28, 1889, 50th Cong., 2nd sess., *CR,* 20(3):2456.

14. "Fooled the Watch-Dog," *Dallas Morning News,* June 1, 1890; "The Park Zoo," ibid., October 30, 1890.

15. Gregory A. Bryant and C. Athena Aktipis, "The Animal Nature of Spontaneous Human Laughter," *Evolution and Human Behavior* 35, no. 4 (July 1, 2014): 327–35.

16. Matthew Senior, "The Souls of Men and Beasts, 1637–1764," in *A Cultural History of Animals in the Age of Enlightenment,* ed. Matthew Senior (New York: Bloomsbury, 2009),

23–46; Tom Tyler, *CIFERAE: A Bestiary in Five Fingers* (Minneapolis: University of Minnesota Press, 2012), 29.

17. Kenneth S. Greenberg, *Honor & Slavery: Lies, Duels, Noses, Masks, Dressing as a Woman, Gifts, Strangers, Humanitarianism, Death, Slave Rebellions, the Proslavery Argument, Baseball, Hunting, and Gambling in the Old South* (Princeton, NJ: Princeton University Press, 1996); Drew Gilpin Faust, *This Republic of Suffering: Death and the American Civil War* (New York: Vintage, 2008), xiv; David W. Blight, *Race and Reunion: The Civil War in American Memory* (Cambridge, MA: Harvard University Press, 2001), 1, 5; Caroline E. Janney, *Remembering the Civil War: Reunion and the Limits of Reconciliation* (Chapel Hill: University of North Carolina Press, 2013), 5. I would also like to thank Joan Cashin for her insights into memory and the Civil War.

18. Goode to Purcell, September 13, 1890; Baker to Adair, September 15, 1890; Baker to Langley, January 12, 1891; Baker to Rerdell, October 2, 1891; Baker to Palmer, May 18, 1891; and Baker to Tracy, July 21, 1891, Folders 1, 2, 4, Box 7, Record Unit 74, SIA.

# Jim Key AND Jim Crow

## *African American Animal Advocacy, Equine Performance, and Civil War Memory*

PAULA TARANKOW

*I cannot refrain from expressing my admiration for the marvelous intelligence of Beautiful Jim Key. I consider him the most accomplished specimen of his kind I have ever seen.*

— JOHN PHILIP SOUSA

*It is impossible to describe the feeling that comes over one as he sees such human intelligence displayed by a dumb animal.*

—FRANCIS J. TORRANCE, president of the Pittsburgh Exposition

BEAUTIFUL JIM KEY, an Arabian-Hambletonian mahogany bay standing at sixteen hands high, was one of the most recognized and beloved celebrity horses at the turn of the twentieth century. His highly interactive and largely unscripted performance repertoire required simple props, such as a clock, a chalkboard, a postal cabinet with lettered and numbered slots holding mail, a letter file, a custom-built register from National Cash Register, a shelving rack displaying large cards with the complete alphabet and numbers one through thirty, and a display stand with a thin nickel rail onto which the horse could slide cards that he selected with his incisors. Jim's spontaneous, nonverbal responses to unscripted audience queries required complex mental processes. Billed as a "horse with the human brain," Beautiful Jim could pick out any lettered or numbered card asked of him and use the cards to add, multiply, divide, and subtract any numbers below thirty, to spell any common name, to tell time, and to offer quotations from the Bible where a horse is mentioned by displaying chapter and verse. He could write his name using a stick of chalk held between his incisors. He retrieved letters from the onstage post office and filed them according to their corresponding number or letter. Jim distinguished colors and flags as well as pieces of money. He could ring up any amount on the cash register and make change. Jim also routinely performed "one of the greatest feats ever accomplished by an animal," holding his breath in order to retrieve a silver dollar from the bottom of a water-filled glass jar without drinking a single drop.[1] He convinced many who witnessed his performances, such as Union veteran Evan Russell, who in 1898 caught his act in Pennsylvania at the York County Fair, to sign testimonials affirming that the equine prodigy proved worthy of his title, "King of All Educated Horses," and was "without a doubt the best attraction" at the fair.[2]

Jim Key's subversive and highly collaborative performances furnished proof to the Civil War generation of equine reason; his actions were nonimitative and dependent upon the cultivation of intelligent choice, communication, and comprehension of the human language. Mediating across the language barrier between audience and Beautiful Jim was his coperformer, owner, and trainer, William Key, a formerly enslaved man born in Shelbyville, Tennessee, in 1833. While he married four times, William Key had no children but treated Beautiful Jim, a reportedly sickly, rehabilitated former circus horse born in 1889, as his only child.[3] A conspicuous presence in promotional materials, William Key was billed as a real-life Uncle Tom, a personification of the avuncular loyal slave of Lost Cause mythology, who lent the performance southern flair and imparted a regional lesson in humane sentiment to a national audience. Each was part of the allure of the other. Each reinforced the cultural work of the other.

Between 1898 and 1906, the duo performed for hundreds of thousands of Americans as far north as Minneapolis; as far south as New Orleans; as far west as Omaha; along the East Coast in cities such as Boston, Providence, and Charleston; and in dozens of places in between.[4] They enchanted visitors to the Saint Louis World's Fair, including the president's daughter Alice Roosevelt in the Silver Horseshoe Building along the pike. At the Convention Hall in Kansas City, the animal celebrity outsold famed French actress Sarah Bernhardt's previous

FIG. 13.1. Beautiful Jim Key. Between 1898 and 1906, Beautiful Jim Key and his formerly enslaved owner and trainer from Tennessee, William Key, performed in partnership to bring the message of equine intelligence and kindness to animals to tens of thousands of Americans. This photograph from around 1900 depicts William Key, then aged sixty-seven, alongside the handsome fourteen-year-old mahogany bay standing sixteen hands high. Courtesy Beautiful Jim Key Collection, Tennessee State Library & Archives.

engagement in *Camille* by a margin of 15,000 tickets. Three-day admissions totaling nearly 53,000 broke the attendance record set by bandleader and composer of patriotic standards John Philip Sousa.[5] During their six-week engagement at the Twenty-First Massachusetts Charitable Mechanic Association Fair, Jim Key often performed eighteen shows a day to accommodate fairgoers who were consistently unable to make it into the theater.[6]

Analyzing William and Jim Key's performances excavates forgotten cultural borrowings among animal welfare, the public-amusements industry, African American reform ethics, and Civil War memory. The war was a turning point in human-animal relationships to the extent that Confederate defeat and emancipation set an emotional standard for sympathetic identification with animals, albeit in unexpected ways; the highly sentimentalized mythology of the faithful slave not only helped southerners manage the devastation of sectional defeat but also channeled humane affect in ways that were palatable to white audiences. William Key's animal ethics were part of a larger tradition of African-descended reform that occurred outside the white-dominated realm of anticruelty reform vis-à-vis state and national societies for the prevention of cruelty to animals (SPCAs). William Key's stage persona did not merely repackage a humane message within the cultural trappings of Confederate memory; rather, he refashioned a white fantasy of the loyal slave, which white Americans deployed to justify white supremacy, to encourage these audiences to transgress multiple categories of constructed difference. By staging the relationship between a slave and his horse, Jim and William mutually reinforced racial knowledge about Black and animal belonging. Together, they invited audiences to pass through the world of illusion into a realm of emancipation from bounded beliefs about the humanity of people and other sentient beings.

## SLAVERY AND THE ROOTS OF ANIMAL WELFARE

The context of locating animals in the consciousness of the Civil War generation is important. Hitherto, there has been a dearth of scholarly labor that writes animals into Civil War histories. Scholarship that informs the study of animal welfare in the United States tends toward arguments for cultural continuity across the antebellum and postbellum eras. Studies of American humanitarianism chronicle how prevailing understandings of dependency, community, and citizenship from the early republic through the eve of the Civil War produced a multivalent humane toolkit. The postbellum advent of institutionalized animal welfare appear, therefore, as simply the latest in an ongoing sentimental project since the Age of Revolutions to solve problems left unresolved by politics and strengthen the moral bonds necessary to sustain a fledgling, egalitarian democracy.

During the American Revolution, proponents of a culture of sensibility, or human sensitivity of perception—especially the belief that citizens bore at least some responsibility for the pain of others—advocated for finely attuned emotional responses to suffering that would help maintain social cohesion and purify society through mutual obligation.[7] Other radical thinkers in late-eighteenth-century England considered animal rights to be an important component of revolutionary political change that aimed to level hierarchies in and between humans and animals.[8]

Theologians of the Second Great Awakening, novelists, abolitionists, and temperance advocates incorporated themes of humanity's moral duty of stewardship over "fellow creatures," linking a progressive view of humanity with an ethic of kindness "toward the least among us." This "gospel of kindness" was a salient feature of American exceptionalism that transformed animal welfare into a moral benchmark for national belonging, assimilation at home and in the nascent US empire abroad, and readiness for citizenship.[9] Antebellum middle-class values that informed the rise of pet-keeping guided a host of postbellum reform campaigns such as animal and child protection, railroad regulation, conservation, and public health.[10] Animal welfare often attracted individuals who were also drawn to human-centered reforms such as abolition and women's, labor, and civil rights.[11]

A range of scholars who reveal cultural precedents nonetheless suggest ways in which the Civil War's political revolution marked a dividing line; for example, how the shifting political terrain of liberalism and the expansion of state power drove the public-private reform alliances and legislative benchmarks that paved the way for an animal-welfare movement.[12] On the heels of recklessly violent campaigns in the West, further expropriations of Native lands by cattle ranchers received direct and sustained support from the newly strengthened federal government. The unchecked forces of colonialism, capitalism, and consumption conspired to draw the attention of anticruelty reformers to the unequivocal modern dependency on equine "living machines" and the flesh of cattle newcomers raised on invasive Great Plains grasses that were negligently transported by rail to the terminus of the abattoir.[13] Unlike the spectacle of the killing floor that remained, for a time at the turn of the century, open to the public gaze before it became sequestered and concealed, the spectacle of equine suffering on municipal thoroughfares was ubiquitous.[14]

After Appomattox, many of the same factors that brought tremendous suffering to the three million war horses—half of whom perished—such as poor road conditions; heavy loads; poor and insufficient fresh water, feed, and forage; and a lack of shelter and horseshoeing, made postbellum equines similarly vulnerable to lameness, disease, and subsequent verbal abuse, heavy application of the whip, and even death.[15] Just as horses were left on the battlefield where they fell, so often was this the case on the roadways of postwar cities. This resonance was not lost on animal anticruelty reformers, some of whom were veterans, who witnessed the obliteration of the Confederate dream.

The central outcomes of the war—emancipation and Confederate defeat—especially social and cultural remembrance of slavery, imbued the discourse of animal advocacy with new and oftentimes oppositional lessons from the war. Furthermore, proslavery ideology infused humane sentiment. Unlike northern anticruelty reformers who argued that animals had rights based on their slave-like commodification, southern welfarists favored analogies between loyal animals and faithful slaves that showcased both benevolent antebellum and postemancipation master-animal bonds. They fabricated cultural and ethical continuities with the paternalism of antebellum slavery through Lost Cause remembrance. If anything, it was the longstanding white American ideology of paternalism, which reinforced hierarchical dependencies among and between humans and animals, that provided a similar structure of feeling for northern and southern reformers. In these ways the debate over US slavery played a defining role in shaping competing sectional visions about humaneness and cruelty.[16]

The bifurcation of postwar anticruelty ideologies and tactics along antislavery and proslavery lines reveals the extent to which humane sentiment in the United States begins on the Atlantic shores that witnessed the arrival of the first enslaved Africans in 1619 at Point Comfort, Virginia. As historian Thomas Andrews has asked, "Why have scholars and activists alike assumed that the roots of contemporary animal-rights philosophies and politics must have originated with white abolitionists, but not with their enslaved counterparts?"[17] By grounding the history of animal welfare in Black voices and perspectives, the indelible markings of slavery and emancipation are laid bare.

## BLACK ANIMAL ETHICS AND NEW NEGRO PERFORMANCE

According to promotional materials, William Key had an astounding life. Readers were introduced to "the fascinating and thrilling story of Dr. Key," a "mulatto" and "typical Uncle Tom," who took the name of his Tennessee master, John W. Key. Young Bill "was a defender on the plantation" of "many a dog or worried cat" and had trained a rooster and a yellow dog by the time he was six. "Fortunately he had a kind master, and when the war clouds began to hover over the Southland, and his master's sons left home to defend their cause, Uncle Bill went with them 'to look after his young masters,' as he says." Key was allegedly a groom, cook, scout, and guide for the Confederate general and later first grand wizard of the Ku Klux Klan Nathan Bedford Forrest, who led the massacre of Black soldiers at Fort Pillow. At Fort Donelson, Tennessee, where the Union army captured the post and its garrison, Key reportedly "stole them [his masters] out of prison, and took them into the rebel lines." The tale highlights his other adventures during the war, such as when he was twice captured by Union forces and sentenced to be hanged as a Confederate spy but each time escaped. In a section titled "In a Slave Driver's Grasp," Key recounts a fateful encounter with a ruthless man who tried to buy him years ago from his master and from whom he made a daring, Hollywoodesque escape. The biography also alleged that "Bill" was active in the Underground Railroad.[18] By its twelfth edition, a condensed version of "The Story of 'Beautiful Jim Key'" reportedly sold over 200,000 copies, a portion of which the Massachusetts SPCA distributed by mail order for fifteen cents.[19]

This web of fantasies glistened with verisimilitude between William Key and Uncle Tom. Postbellum theatrical portrayals of the titular abolitionist icon in Harriet Beecher Stowe's novel perpetuated anti-Black prejudice; this distorted version staged Uncle Tom as a race traitor and model of Black deference and servility to whites.[20] During the 1890s, when the Keys were on tour, "Tom shows" were so popular that, according to one estimate, no fewer than five hundred US theater companies staged productions.[21] Many elements of Key's biography reflected a budding American romance with a plantation landscape where harmonious human-animal relationships mirrored peaceful master-slave relationships. It retold a thrilling Civil War story that incorporated a chief tenet of Lost Cause interpretation—that enslaved peoples were faithful to their masters as well as the Confederate cause and were unprepared for freedom.[22] And yet, the inclusion of William's participation in the Underground Railroad might have elicited elements of reunionist sentiment by casting Bill as both a Confederate loyalist and a traitor to the cause. Perhaps this contradiction heightened his appeal across the political spectrum and marked kindness to animals as nonpartisan and nonsectional—in other words, as thoroughly American.

Upon first glance, William Key could appear merely accommodationist for the ways in which his onstage persona safely recycled racist stereotypes. The postbellum invention of the loyal slave steadily reassured the white Civil War generation that they had done nothing for which to be hated and offered a white fantasy of willing and peaceful racial reconciliation. As historian Adam Domby explains, "stories about the benevolence of slavery were used to argue that whites should be in charge, races were unequal, and that even many slaves had agreed with the principles of white supremacy."[23] Lost Cause myths reclaimed regional and national pride in a fictive "golden age" and preserved white supremacy through a model of mastery, social control, and Black deference embodied in the "faithful" slave.[24]

William Key's third wife, Dr. Lucinda Key, a graduate of Howard University's medical school, had first suggested that Beautiful Jim's gifts could be put to a higher calling. This encouragement brought her husband, then aged sixty-four, to the Negro Building at the 1895 Tennessee Centennial and International Exposition after he had already retired with a small fortune amassed from his mail-order patent-medicine business, Keystone Liniment, an analgesic for horse and mule afflictions such as joint spasms, cuts, splints, swelling, cholera, saddle sore, lameness, and colic.[25] The Negro Building at these events showcased African Americans' industrial, material, and educational accomplishments since emancipation and promoted a "New Negro" project of forging modernity through Black achievement in education and the arts. Exhibitions provided countervailing evidence to white belief in Black racial inferiority, retrogression, and degeneration. The organizers' belief in the inevitability of progress from bondage to freedom encouraged racial pride and favored accommodationist approaches to inequality while opening the door to critiques of Jim Crow society.[26] At the Negro Building, William and Beautiful Jim Key provided a cross-species analogy for racial uplift though patience, dedication, and education. They also participated in broader debates about the progress of freedmen since emancipation.

The performance drew the attention of Albert Reynolds Rogers, a white Cincinnati native and amusements promoter with whom William Key forged a business partnership that spanned nine years until the Keys' retirements. The exposition offered many scenes of sectional accord, such as the wildly popular Union and Confederate reunions and battle reenactments that provided symbols of patriotism designed to promote reconciliation. In the Vanity Fair amusements area, Rogers served as the booking agent for an exhibition of the birthplace cabins of Abraham Lincoln and Jefferson Davis. A rumor steeped in reunion sentiment, probably started by Rogers, that the disassembled logs had been mixed up during shipment, fanned its popularity. He oversaw other amusements, including Shoot the Chutes, a hybrid roller coaster and slide, and a sprawling, interactive display called The Old Plantation in the Agricultural Building. On this rural vista—replete with rows of movable cotton plants, full-scale Colonial plantation homes, and slave cabins—visitors could study "that interesting phase of slave life before the war, which is illustrated by a party of Georgia negroes, with songs, dances and the manners and customs of those days."[27] The "Plant show" genre typified how Americans came to see the South through a "magnolia-shaped lens"; performances of reconciliation on white terms allayed anxieties about modernity, with its rise in mass consumerism and the emergence of mass culture.[28]

What might have flashed before Rogers's eyes was a vision of how to redirect commercialized sentiments associated with the so-called Old South by intimately tying the staging of slavery to humane education. Through their partnership, Key and Rogers pledged to donate a portion of their proceeds to animal-welfare organizations. At each of Beautiful Jim Key's shows, they made available free Jim Key Pledge cards and application forms for establishing a Beautiful Jim Key Band of Mercy ("sign up ten other friends and have your names listed on the great Jim Key banner roll.")[29] In their thirty-minute repertoire titled "The Scholar and Model Office Boy," the Keys urged teachers to persuade their "scholars" to "become a part of the great army of boys and girls who are to gain victory over cruelty in all its forms" under the banner of Boston lawyer and Massachusetts SPCA founder George Thorndike Angell's American Humane Education Society (AHES): "Glory to God, Peace on Earth, Kindness, Justice, and Mercy to Every Living Creature."[30] In shifting from a primarily African American to a primarily white audience, from a message of racial uplift to racial deference, William Key nevertheless performed radical labor.

By the time he partnered with Rogers, William Key was a practiced storyteller who had used itinerant minstrel troupes to sell Keystone Liniment.[31] As a less-threatening mode of self-representation, Key's self-presentation as a formerly enslaved animal interlocutor heightened his and Beautiful Jim's authority while enticing, entertaining, and mystifying white audiences. Key and Rogers placed the story of animal kindness within the history of slavery that saturated public amusement at the turn of the century. What they showed on stage was more than a personal relationship: it was a reconstructed relationship between a freedman and a horse that bridged the Old and New South. The Keys modeled a radical ideal of human-animal relations that was sustained through neither violence nor paternalism. Together, Rogers and Key reclaimed a figure that emboldened white supremacy to amplify a message of kindness across constructed differences.

William Key's life should be viewed as a part of a lineage of African-descended reformers, such as abolitionists Olaudah Equiano, Ignatius Sancho, and Frederick Douglass, who, to borrow literary scholar Lindgren Johnson's phrasing, made room "for the question of the animal within the Black fight for racial justice." Johnson's research counters "a generalized historical narrative of black detachment from animal politics" by demonstrating how Douglass and other activists identified "shared vulnerabilities (or animalities), both biological and socially constructed." Johnson exposes "the ways that such a black recuperation of animality—and often animals themselves—made radical use of dehumanization." Johnson goes on to assert that "African Americans were animal agents long before animal rights or even animal welfare movements existed in the United States, and their perspectives are essential to understanding the full scope of thinking on both human and animal liberation."[32] Literary scholar Cristin Ellis likewise argues that antislavery discourse was "not simply a debate over the borders of the human." Douglass and other abolitionists provided complex contestations of "the meaning of 'the human' as such." His writings drew slave-animal comparisons to erode "the moral distinction between human and nonhuman life."[33]

For some African American leaders at the turn of the century, such as Booker T. Washington, who neither directly agitated for social equality nor challenged racial injustice but instead advocated for self-reliant separatism, humane reform afforded an opportunity to address racial politics. Washington and William Key were personal acquaintances who might have first met when the educator addressed fairgoers at the Tennessee Exposition's Negro Building.[34] Both men allied with George Angell's humane-education initiatives. In 1883 Washington established a chapter of the Bands of Mercy—a nationwide movement under the aegis of Angell's AHES, which organized bands of two or more children to pledge kindness to animals—at his alma mater, the Hampton Institute.[35] In 1896 his Tuskegee Normal and Agricultural School had 150 members enrolled in Bands of Mercy, with a corps of fifteen officers who had "the power to arrest any one on the school grounds found cruelly treating animals." Washington might have embraced anticruelty reform as a further way of emphasizing, as he did elsewhere, that Blacks were law-abiding, self-controlled, and moral citizens. In his attempts to persuade the African American community to aspire to "industry, thrift, intelligence, and property," his humane ethics could have also aligned with respectability politics.[36] Other African American reformers in the South employed by the AHES believed that the philosophy of the ethical consideration of animals was essentially antiracist. As historian Janet Davis argues, the AHES's Black animal protectionists "espoused a synthetic social justice project of animal kindness, self-help, and racial uplift," believing that kindness was "a universal expression of American ideals of mercy and self-determination."[37]

Performances of contented enslavement contributed to the mythologizing of slavery as benevolent and beneficial for both enslavers and those they enslaved. Yet many Black entertainers used the modern commercial exploitation of racial undercurrents to regain control over white performative interpretations of African American culture.[38] As historian Christopher Dingwall shows, Black performers in "Plant shows" laboring in an industry shaped by blackface minstrelsy reclaimed ownership over plantation themes and refashioned Black subjectivity. They did so by staging emancipation as an historical event and showcasing scenes of African American progress through racial uplift, thereby capitalizing on the symbolic value of slavery for antiracist ends.[39]

It is within this context that we can begin to understand why Rogers and Key promoted "Uncle Bill," at once steadfastly loyal to his former master and who inspired the loyalty of Beautiful Jim through his kindness. William Key asserted his personhood and staked his claim to humanity on the deeply personal relationships he nurtured with animals.[40] He offered the radical lesson that within humaneness lies true humanity.

## CIVIL WAR MEMORY AND BEAUTIFUL JIM KEY'S PERFORMANCE

While the Uncle Tom trope was endlessly reproduced, Beautiful Jim Key's singular performance was the lynchpin that secured fame, fortune, and influence. He challenged the notion that the animal is defined by its body and cannot rise above its corporeal existence. His display of higher-order reasoning countered the narrative that animal sentience comprised merely species-specific interests, such as the horse's flight response from predators. The "categorical leaps" in Beautiful Jim's performance, in the words of theater historian Kim Marra, eschewed or "queered" cultural norms and interlocking "normative hierarchies and categories."[41]

But rather than evaluate the ethics of animal acts in human-made performances, the focus here falls on Beautiful Jim's embodied labor. Nevertheless, an ethical argument could be made based on the value that nineteenth-century animal advocates placed on him. According to performance-studies scholar Michael Peterson's criteria for assessing acts that promote "the fantasy of touching animals and being touched by them," the Keys' act surpassed entertainment through its "philosophical depth, aesthetic complexity" and authenticity, and by demanding a complex emotional response to both the human and the animal performers.[42] "In the many cities in which he has been exhibited," Rogers maintained, Beautiful Jim "has been the means of not only creating a new interest in humane work, but has been indeed a missionary to his fellow horses."[43]

Beautiful Jim Key was a real-life Black Beauty who could "speak" for himself and to children directly. George Angell had, in fact, rediscovered and rebranded Anna Sewell's English novel for Americans in 1890 by subtitling the first US edition he sponsored "the *'Uncle Tom's Cabin'* of the Horse."[44] Beautiful Jim appealed to many SPCAs because laboring equines were the original objects and beneficiaries of anticruelty legislation. Caroline Earle White, president of the Women's Pennsylvania SPCA, publicly endorsed the "southern horse," as he was frequently billed, "as an object lesson, showing what patience and kindness will accomplish in the teaching of animals, and how much more effective they prove than severity and cruelty."[45] The Keys provide a compelling case study for Peterson's overarching evaluative question: "Do we use the animal to become more human, or less so?"[46] By staging nonviolent, mutually communicative, cooperative, and fundamentally humane relations, Jim's labor troubled the identity of the spectator and moved them beyond mere mystification.

According to Angell, who formally endorsed the Keys in 1898, one million children had taken the Jim Key Pledge by 1909, vowing lifelong kind and protective care toward animals.[47] Beautiful Jim also served as the honorary equine member of the American Humane Association, the parent organization of all humane organizations in the United States, as well as the Bands of Mercy of the World, which comprised three million US members.[48] Rogers, who handled all correspondence for the National Jim Key Band of Mercy, instructed its 700,000 members, "If you see anyone ill-treating an animal, do not hesitate to ask them to stop, show them your Star, and tell them you belong to the Band of Mercy." He implored his little humanitarians: "I want you to remember that animals feel just as keenly as human beings do, that the flesh and bones of a dog or a cat are as tender as your own. It hurts them to be struck or handled roughly as much as it would you yourself."[49] While the act's sectional elements may have mattered less to humanitarian reformers than its embedded message, the Civil War generation would have encountered other examples of postbellum themes that shaped equine subjectivity.

Many Americans encountered a range of animals through sentimental strands of the war and its remembrance. Antebellum blackface performance, which comforted white Americans with its boundary transgressions, originally took place between circus acts that blurred the species boundary.[50] Trained horses and other performing animals belonging to America's sprawling postbellum railroad circuses frequently participated in show-opening patriotic spectacles played to plantation music.[51] War themes suffused the so-called hippodrama, a genre of live equestrian drama that, in the 1890s, staged Union cavalry combat with actual horses.[52] "Immersed in a society that still depended on horses for power and transportation," as Marra explains, audiences "consumed hippodramas with a historically specific knowledge and special appreciation" for horses' "commanding presence and fiery spirit" as well as their responsiveness to human body signals that enabled them to overcome flight instincts during the chaos of battle.[53]

After the war, relationships with animals sustained veterans who turned to them for emotional and other collaborative labor. Lieutenant General Ulysses S. Grant had allowed Confederate soldiers to return home with their horses, and Union soldiers could purchase from the government the horses to whom they had become attached.[54] A menagerie containing an array of mammal and bird species provided moral and physical "uplift" for the Union veterans who were the resident "keepers" at a California soldiers' home.[55] Confederate veterans living at a soldiers' home in Virginia cared for Old Sorrel, Lieutenant General Thomas "Stonewall" Jackson's horse, until the animal perished in 1886. War horses were seen as extensions of their masters and venerated as such. According to historian Drew Faust, the exhibition of Robert E. Lee's equine companion, Traveller, "provided a valuable connection to the Lost Cause," and he was often described in ways that "sounded not unlike the ideal slave"; his loyal service reflected his master's hallowed character.[56] Beautiful Jim's performance as the loyal servant to his kind master contained kernels of insight about citizenship and belonging in the United States.

In the late nineteenth century, animal cruelty was often associated with racialized others.[57] Beautiful Jim told a story of kindness that could perform race work in the age of Jim Crow. Observers took notice that Jim performed without visible forms of coercion, such as the whip and the riding equipment that visibly demarcated domestication and dominion. In an interview with the *Newark Evening News,* William Key attested: "No, sir, I never use a whip in training Jim. The whip makes 'em stubborn and fearful." He implied that fear destroyed trust, which served as the basis for education.[58] Jim's ability and seeming choice to interact with audience-participants obscured the training that had taken place over many years. The fact that he had never felt the sting of a whip demonstrated what was possible in the evolution of human-animal relationships. It suggested the extent of animals' innate ability to reveal their true humanity when in trust-based partnerships with humans—perhaps with a little help from apples and sugar, which were the keystone in Beautiful Jim Key's education.

Further aspects of Jim's performance communicated knowledge about slavery. That Beautiful Jim shared the surname of his master's master signified a cross-species inheritance of kindness and benevolence borne of enslavement. Elements of a romance of reunion played out in a notable comedic sketch where William played a Republican and Jim played a Democrat. At the Nashville Exposition in 1897, the last president to have seen service in the Civil War, William McKinley, "conversed" with Beautiful Jim Key and discovered the horse's "political preferences." When McKinley asked him "if he would not turn Republican," Jim "shook his head vigorously."[59]

That Jim was a Democrat was one way in which the Keys used charm and humor to appeal to audiences across the political spectrum. That he possessed a political identity was part of the act's subversive topsy-turvy. At the end of every performance, in "one of his most amusing and laughable feats," William Key would offer Beautiful Jim for sale, at which point Jim, not wanting to leave, feigned lameness by lying down and rolling on his back until William assured him that the sale was off, and Jim would make a full and speedy upright recovery.[60] That Jim emphatically desired to remain owned, combined with his fear and his willingness to throw a sale by simulating illness, provided proof of William's character. Such stagings of slavery reinforced their humane message that kind masters were the antidote to the problem of cruelty in the age of emancipation.

## CONCLUSION

"In multispecies relationships," as labor-studies scholar Kendra Coulter observes, "we can see the best in people, how much and how many humans benefit from animals, and examples of how people could act more ethically."[61] Writing on interspecies performance, Una Chaudhuri observes: "Animal acts bring us face to face with our assumptions about what we know and how we know it. . . . The great gift that the other animals have always offered to the human species is the gift of their radical otherness, their ultimate unknowability."[62] Was Beautiful Jim Key a trained performer, or was he simply "being himself"? The disbelief, and belief, that he inspired invited Americans at the turn of the century to experience themselves in the same space as animals in a completely different way.

The story of the Keys reveals the ways in which the antebellum plantation was a petri dish for cultivating new bonds for humane ethics in a postemancipation world. It sheds light on how the powerful cultural symbol of the loyal slave helped white Americans develop sentimental and ethical attachments to animals. William Key and Albert Rogers retooled the Lost Cause to accommodate humanitarianism by reconfiguring the ideology of humanity on the imagined plantation-scape onstage. The Keys' collaborative cultural work ushered animal welfare into conversation, with contemporary debates surrounding the limits of personhood for African Americans and animals. In an era of a growing proslavery consensus on the memory of slavery in the United States, it is likely that many white audiences, like many anticruelty reformers (particularly in the South), did not feel conflicted about embracing both animal ethics and white supremacy. While humane sentiment holds the potential to generate broad concern for multispecies injustice, such connections, even today, often need to be made explicit to be recognized. The Keys suggest that white interest in disavowing multispecies oppression is limited to how comfortable they feel in the process.

Important questions therefore remain: Did William and Jim's relationship confirm or deny white perceptions of Black inhumanity? Both inhabited liminal space within the framework of humanism and its exclusions. In all likelihood, Beautiful Jim enjoyed more latitude to move into the category of human. Working within a culture of whiteness to complete race and animal work undoubtedly placed limitations on William Key's personhood. While the degree of separation between humans and animals drastically diminished onstage, a gulf remained between Black and white men in the age of Jim Crow. The story of the Keys nevertheless speaks to the challenges and possibilities of fostering connectivity across race and species lines. That it is practically impossible to measure how animal ethics translates into human ethics does not make their example any less radical. Is it possible to bridge racial divides through humane ethics? The Keys provide one answer: an expansive Black model of humane ethics challenges us to recognize the humanity in our fellow humans and expand our sympathies with the nonhuman world through the animal partnerships that are closest to us.

## NOTES

*Note to Sousa epigraph: How He Was Taught: The Story of Beautiful Jim Key*, 12th ed., Beautiful Jim Key Collection, 1885-[1897–1907]-1933, acc. no. 2005-015, Tennessee State Library and Archives, Nashville (hereafter TSLA), microfilm, 17.

*Note to Torrance epigraph:* "Four pages of a photocopied program/brochure regarding Jim Key, c. 1897–1900," Beautiful Jim Key Collection, TSLA.

1."Small souvenir brochure from Jim Key appearance in Atlantic City, New Jersey," n.d., Beautiful Jim Key Collection, TSLA.

2."Signature sheets for guests of Jim Key appearances at (5) York County Fair, October 1898 (Pennsylvania)," scrapbook #1, ibid.

3."Biographical Sketches," 3, ibid.

4.*How He Was Taught*, 15, 17, 30.

5.Mim Eichler Rivas, *Beautiful Jim Key: The Lost History of the World's Smartest Horse* (New York: HarperCollins, 2005), 243–44.

6. *How He Was Taught*, 25.

7. Sarah Knott, *Sensibility and the American Revolution* (Chapel Hill: University of North Carolina Press, 2009).

8. Jane Spencer, *Writing about Animals in the Age of Revolution* (Oxford: Oxford University Press, 2020).

9. Janet M. Davis, *The Gospel of Kindness: Animal Welfare and the Making of Modern America* (New York: Oxford University Press, 2016).

10. Diane L. Beers, *For the Prevention of Cruelty: The History and Legacy of Animal Rights Activism in the United States* (Athens: Ohio University Press, 2006); Bernard Unti, "The Quality of Mercy: Organized Animal Protection in the United States, 1866–1930" (PhD diss., American University, 2002); Etienne Benson, "The Urbanization of the Eastern Grey Squirrel in the United States," *Journal of American History* 100 (December 2013): 691–710; Katherine C. Grier, *Pets in America: A History* (Chapel Hill: University of North Carolina Press, 2006); Mary J. Henninger-Voss, "Childhood Socialization and Companion Animals: United States, 1820–1870," *Society and Animals* 7 (1999), 95–120; Mary J. Henninger-Voss, "Animal House: Pet Keeping in Urban and Suburban Households in the Northeast, 1850–1900," *Dublin Seminar for New England Folklife Annual Proceedings* 18 (1993): 109–29. On pet-keeping values among enslaving families, see Sarah Hand Meacham, "Pets, Status, and Slavery in the Late-Eighteenth-Century Chesapeake," *Journal of Southern History* 77 (August 2011): 521–54.

11. Beers, *For the Prevention of Cruelty*, 5, 7, 9.

12. Susan J. Pearson, *Rights of the Defenseless: Protecting Animals and Children in Gilded Age America* (Chicago: University of Chicago Press, 2011), 12, 101, 167.

13. Clay McShane and Joel A. Tarr, *The Horse in the City: Living Machines in the Nineteenth-Century City* (Baltimore: Johns Hopkins University Press, 2007); Christopher Ketcham, *This Land: How Cowboys, Capitalism, and Corruption Are Ruining the American West* (New York: Penguin Random House, 2019); Joshua Specht, *Red Meat Republic: A*

*Hoof-to-Table History of How Beef Changed America* (Princeton, NJ: Princeton University Press, 2019), esp. chap. 1.

14. Brett Mizelle, "Unthinkable Visibility: Pigs, Pork, and the Spectacle of Killing and Meat," in *Rendering Nature: Animals, Bodies, Places, and Politics*, ed. Marguerite S. Shaffer and Phoebe S. K. Young (Philadelphia: University of Pennsylvania Press, 2015); Timothy Pachirat, *Every Twelve Seconds: Industrialized Slaughter and the Politics of Sight* (New Haven, CT: Yale University Press, 2013).

15. Gene C. Armistead, *Horses and Mules in the Civil War: A Complete History with a Roster of More Than 700 War Horses* (Jefferson, NC: McFarland, 2013), esp. intro., chap. 5.

16. Paula Tarankow, "Loyal Animals, Faithful Slaves: Animal Advocacy, Race, and the Memory of Slavery" (PhD diss., Indiana University, 2019).

17. Thomas G. Andrews, "Beasts of the Southern Wild: Slaveholders, Slaves, and Other Animals in Charles Ball's Slavery in the United States," in Shaffer and Young, *Rendering Nature*, 47.

18. "How He Was Taught: The Story of Beautiful Jim Key, the Most Wonderful Horse in All the World," [ca. 1900], Beautiful Jim Key Collection, TSLA.

19. "The Story of 'Beautiful Jim Key,'" 12th ed., ibid.

20. Patricia Turner, *Ceramic Uncles and Celluloid Mammies: Black Images and Their Influence on Culture* (Charlottesville: University of Virginia Press, 2002).

21. Christopher Dingwall, "The Sale of Slavery: Memory, Culture, and the Renewal of America, 1877–1920" (PhD diss., University of Chicago, 2015), 67.

22. Caroline Janney, "The Lost Cause," *Encyclopedia Virginia*, Virginia Humanities, https://encyclopediavirginia.org/entries/lost-cause-the/ (accessed July 27, 2016).

23. Adam H. Domby, *The False Cause: Fraud, Fabrication, and White Supremacy in Confederate Memory* (Charlottesville: University of Virginia Press, 2020), 4–7.

24. Karen L. Cox, *Dixie's Daughters: The United Daughters of the Confederacy and the Preservation of Confederate Culture* (Gainesville: University Press of Florida, 2019).

25. Rivas, *Beautiful Jim Key*, 19, 97.

26. Nathan Cardon, "The South's 'New Negroes' and African American Visions of Progress at the Atlanta and Nashville International Expositions, 1895–1897," *Journal of Southern History* 80, no. 2 (May 2014): 290–91, 294, 303, 311; Robert W. Rydell, *All the World's a Fair: Visions of Empire at American International Expositions, 1876–1916* (Chicago: University of Chicago Press, 1984), 72–104.

27. "On the Gay Esplanade: Pictures of the Avenue of Amusements of the Exposition," *Clinch Valley (TN) News*, December 8, 1899, 3; Rivas, *Beautiful Jim Key*, 93.

28. Karen L. Cox, *Dreaming of Dixie: How the South Was Created in American Popular Culture* (Chapel Hill: University of North Carolina Press, 2011), 1–8, esp. 1.

29. Rivas, *Beautiful Jim Key*, 198–99.

30. *How He Was Taught*, 27.

31. Rivas, *Beautiful Jim Key*, 20; *How He Was Taught*, 14.

32. Lindgren Johnson, *Race Matters, Animal Matters: Fugitive Humanism in African America, 1840–1930* (London: Routledge, 2017), intro., 140. On Equiano and Sancho, see Spencer, *Writing about Animals in the Age of Revolution*, esp. chap. 5.

33. Cristin Ellis, *Antebellum Posthuman: Race and Materiality in the Mid-Nineteenth Century* (New York: Fordham University Press, 2018), 1, 12, 14, 15.

34. Rydell, *All the World's a Fair*, 89. A typed copy of one of Washington's speeches was possibly sent directly to Key from Washington. "Typed address of Booker T. Washington delivered before the National Educational Association in St. Louis on June 30, 1904," Beautiful Jim Key Collection, TSLA.

35. Beers, *For the Prevention of Cruelty*, 89; *The Booker T. Washington Papers*, vol. 2, *1886–1889*, ed. Louis Harlan (Chicago: University of Chicago Press, 1972), 242–43; "Tuskegee, Alabama, Normal School," *Our Dumb Animals*, 29, no. 1 (June 1896): 4.

36. Quoted in Rydell, *All the World's a Fair*, 83.

37. Davis, *Gospel of Kindness*, 85, 101, 103.

38. Cardon, "South's 'New Negroes' and African American Visions of Progress," 312–13.

39. Christopher Dingwall, *Selling Slavery: Race and the Industry of American Culture* (Cambridge: Cambridge University Press, forthcoming), esp. chap. 1.

40. Andrews, "Beasts of the Southern Wild," 46; Spencer, *Writing about Animals in the Age of Revolutions*, esp. chap. 5.

41. Kim Marra, "Horses Queer the Society and Stage of *Shenandoah*," in *Performing Animals: History, Agency, Theater*, ed. Karen Rader and Monica Mattfeld (University Park: Pennsylvania State University Press, 2017), 155.

42. Michael Peterson, "The Animal Apparatus: From a Theory of Animal Acting to an Ethics of Animal Acts," *Drama Review* 50, no. 1 (Spring 2007): 40, 44.

43. *How He Was Taught*, 31.

44. "The 'Uncle Tom's Cabin' of the Horse," *Our Dumb Animals* 22, no. 11 (April 1890): 125; Pearson, *Rights of the Defenseless*, 124, 127.

45. "Letter from Caroline Earle White of the Women's Pennsylvania Society for the Prevention of Cruelty to Animals from 1899 announcing an essay contest for children on the subject of 'What patience and kindness will accomplish with animals,'" 11 (front), TSLA.

46. Peterson, "Animal Apparatus," 45.

47. *How He Was Taught*, 28.

48. "Letterhead of the National Jim Key Band of Mercy," 11 (front), Beautiful Jim Key Collection, TSLA.

49. "Welcome letter to children from Uncle Bert RE: The National Jim Key Band of Mercy and new membership," 1906, 35 (back), Beautiful Jim Key Collection, TSLA.

50. Justyna Wlodarczyk, *Genealogy of Obedience: Reading North American Dog Training Literature, 1850s–2000s* (Leiden: Brill, 2018), 48.

51. Janet M. Davis, "The Circus Americanized," in *American Circus*, ed. Susan Weber, Kenneth L. Ames, and Matthew Whitman (New Haven, CT: Yale University Press, 2012), 45.

52. Marra, "Horses Queer the Society and Stage of *Shenandoah*," 154–56.

53. Kim Marra, "Massive Bodies in Mortal Performance: *War Horse* and the Staging of Anglo-American Equestrian Experience in Combat," in *Performing Animality: Animals in*

*Performance Practices,* ed. Lourdes Orozco and Jennifer Parker-Starbuck (London: Palgrave Macmillan, 2015), 117, 118, 120, 121.

54. Armistead, *Horses and Mules in the Civil War,* 95–97.

55. Teresa Lloro-Bidart, "The Entwined Socioecological Histories of the Sawtelle, California War Veterans and the Animal 'Menagerie' at the Pacific Branch Soldier's Home (1888–1918)," in *Historical Animal Geographies,* ed. Sharon Wilcox and Stephanie Rutherford (London: Routledge, 2018), esp. 25.

56. Drew Faust, "Equine Relics of the Civil War," *Southern Cultures* 6, no. 1 (Spring 2000): 38, 35.

57. Davis, *Gospel of Kindness,* esp. chap. 3; Justin Marceau, *Beyond Cages: Animal Law and Criminal Punishment* (New York: Cambridge University Press, 2019), 166–69.

58. Rivas, *Beautiful Jim Key,* 133.

59. "Jim Key a Clever Horse," *New York Times,* December 1, 1897, 10.

60. *Beautiful Jim Key,* 6.

61. Kendra Coulter, *Animals, Work, and the Promise of Interspecies Solidarity* (New York: Palgrave Macmillan, 2016), 2.

62. Una Chaudhuri, "Animal Acts for Changing Times, 2.0: A Field Guide to Interpsecies Performance," in *Animal Acts: Performing Species Today,* ed. Una Chaudhuri and Holly Hughes (Ann Arbor: University of Michigan Press, 2018), 7–8.

# Contributors

JOAN E. CASHIN, professor of history at Ohio State University, received her doctorate in American history from Harvard University. She is the author or editor of seven books, including *War Stuff: The Struggle for Human and Environmental Resources in the American Civil War.*

LORIEN FOOTE is the Patricia & Bookman Peters Professor in History at Texas A&M University. She is the author of four books and the editor of two books about the cultural, intellectual, and military history of the American Civil War.

DAVID J. GERLEMAN is a nineteenth-century historian at George Mason University, recipient of several distinguished fellowships, and a former assistant editor of *The Papers of Abraham Lincoln.* His current book project explores wartime equine care, treatment, and use.

ABRAHAM GIBSON teaches in the School of Life Sciences at Arizona State University. He has published extensively on a variety of topics in the history of science. His first book, *Feral Animals in the American South,* examines the social, cultural, and evolutionary consequences of animal domestication.

EARL J. HESS, emeritus professor of history, Lincoln Memorial University, is the author of twenty-four books on Civil War subjects, most recently *Civil War Supply and Strategy: Feeding Men and Moving Armies*. He also has coauthored three books on film history.

BRIAN MATTHEW JORDAN is associate professor and chair of the History Department at Sam Houston State University. He is the author or editor of several books, including *Marching Home: Union Veterans and Their Unending Civil War*, a finalist for the Pulitzer Prize in History.

JASON PHILLIPS is the Eberly Family Professor of Civil War Studies at West Virginia University. His most recent book is *Looming Civil War: How Nineteenth-Century Americans Imagined the Future* (Oxford University Press, 2018).

MARK SMITH is Carolina Distinguished Professor of History and director of the Institute for Southern Studies at the University of South Carolina. A Fellow of the Royal Historical Society and former book reviewer for the *Wall Street Journal*, he has authored over a dozen books on US and sensory history.

PAULA TARANKOW earned her doctoral degree in US history at Indiana University. Her research explores the relationships among white supremacy, humane sentiment, and Civil War memory. The recipient of grants from the Culture and Animals Foundation and the Animals and Society Institute, she has taught at Indiana University and Smith College.

DANIEL VANDERSOMMERS is an assistant professor of environmental history at the University of Dayton. He is author of the forthcoming *Entangled Encounters at the National Zoo: Stories of Science, Culture, and Environment* and coeditor (with Tracy McDonald) of *Zoo Studies: A New Humanities*.

MICHAEL E. WOODS is associate professor of history at the University of Tennessee, Knoxville, and director of the Papers of Andrew Jackson. Most recently, he is the author of *Arguing until Doomsday: Stephen Douglas, Jefferson Davis, and the Struggle for American Democracy*.

# Index